GENDERING MIGRATION

Studies in Migration and Diaspora

Series Editor:
Anne J. Kershen, Queen Mary College, University of London, UK

Studies in Migration and Diaspora is a series designed to showcase the interdisciplinary and multidisciplinary nature of research in this important field. Volumes in the series cover local, national and global issues and engage with both historical and contemporary events. The books will appeal to scholars, students and all those engaged in the study of migration and diaspora. Amongst the topics covered are minority ethnic relations, transnational movements and the cultural, social and political implications of moving from 'over there', to 'over here'.

Also in the series:

Contemporary British Identity: English Language, Migrants and Public Discourse
Christina Julios
ISBN 978-0-7546-7158-9

Migration and Domestic Work: A European Perspective on a Global Theme
Edited by Helma Lutz
ISBN 978-0-7546-4790-4

Negotiating Boundaries in the City: Migration, Ethnicity, and Gender in Britain
Joanna Herbert
ISBN 978-0-7546-4677-8

The Cultures of Economic Migration: International Perspectives
Edited by Suman Gupta and Tope Omoniyi
ISBN 978-0-7546-7070-4

Writing Diaspora: South Asian Women, Culture and Ethnicity
Yasmin Hussain
ISBN 978-0-7546-4113-1

Food in the Migrant Experience
Edited by Anne J. Kershen
ISBN 978-0-7546-1874-4

Gendering Migration

Masculinity, Femininity and Ethnicity in Post-War Britain

Edited by

LOUISE RYAN
Middlesex University, UK

WENDY WEBSTER
University of Central Lancashire, UK

ASHGATE

Published by
Ashgate Publishing Limited
Gower House
Croft Road
Aldershot
Hampshire GU11 3HR
England

Ashgate Publishing Company
Suite 420
101 Cherry Street
Burlington, VT 05401-4405
USA

www.ashgate.com

British Library Cataloguing in Publication Data
Gendering migration : masculinity, femininity and ethnicity
in post-war Britain. - (Studies in migration and diaspora)
1. Immigrants - Great Britain - History - 20th century
2. Sex distribution (Demography) - Great Britain 3. Great
Britain - Emigration and immigration - History - 20th
century 4. Great Britain - Emigration and immigration -
Social aspects
I. Ryan, Louise II. Webster, Wendy
304.8'41'009045

Library of Congress Cataloging-in-Publication Data
Gendering migration : masculinity, femininity and ethnicity in post-war Britain / edited by
Louise Ryan and Wendy Webster.
    p. cm.
Includes bibliographical references and index.
ISBN 978-0-7546-7178-7
  1. Great Britain--Emigration and immigration--20th century. 2. Women immigrants--Great
Britain--Social conditions--20th century. 3. Immigrants--Great Britain--Social conditions--
20th century. I. Ryan, Louise. II. Webster, Wendy.

JV7625.G46 2008
304.80941'09045--dc22   2008019106

ISBN 978-0-7546-7178-7

Mixed Sources
Product group from well-managed
forests and other controlled sources
www.fsc.org Cert no. SGS-COC-2482
© 1996 Forest Stewardship Council
FSC

Printed and bound in Great Britain by
TJ International Ltd, Padstow, Cornwall

Contents

List of Tables

Notes on Contributors

Ali Nobil Ahmad is a doctoral researcher in the Department of History at the European University Institute in Florence, Italy. He worked at University College London in 2004 as a Research Officer on the Leverhulme Project on Smuggling and Trafficking. His PhD is a comparative study of Pakistanis in Europe, focusing on gender and illegality.

Kathy Burrell is Senior Lecturer in Modern History, De Montfort University. She works on European migration to Britain and her publications include *Moving Lives: Narratives of Nation and Migration among Europeans in Post-War Britain* (Ashgate, 2006) and an edited collection with Panikos Panayi — *Histories and Memories: Migrants and their History in Britain* (I.B. Tauris, 2006).

Venetia Evergeti is a Senior Research Fellow at Middlesex University. She has published a number of articles on ethnicity and migration in journals such as *Ethnic and Racial Studies*, including work on minority communities in Greece and on Greek female migrants in Britain.

Joanna Herbert is a Leverhulme Early Career Fellow in the Department of Geography, Queen Mary, University of London. Her current research is on oral histories of Ugandan Asians in Britain. She is author of *Negotiating Boundaries in the City: Migration, Ethnicity and Gender in Britain* (Ashgate, 2008).

Sarah J. Keeler recently completed a PhD in the Department of Anthropology, University of Kent. Her research dealt with Kurdish diaspora in Britain, specifically on discourses of cosmopolitan identity amongst the second generation, and their role in the shaping of alternative political spaces. She has been a Marie Curie fellow at the Centre for Conflict Studies, Utrecht University, and is currently a lecturer in political sociology at the University of Kurdistan.

Tony Morgan is Deputy Head of the Department of Languages and Communication at Anglia Ruskin University and Director of the European Migration and Mobility Unit. His research interests are in Spanish culture and society, and he has published widely on Spanish employment. His most recent book is *The Spanish Migrant Community in the United Kingdom* (APU/Spanish Ministry of Employment and Social Affairs, 2004).

Louise Ryan is Deputy Director of the Social Policy Research Centre at Middlesex University. She has published numerous articles on migration in journals such as

Sociology, Sociological Review, Journal of Ethnic and Migration Studies, Immigrants and Minorities, and *Ethnic and Racial Studies*. She has published several books including *Re-presenting the Past: Women and History*, co-edited with Anne Marie Gallagher and Cathy Lubelska (Longman, 2001) and *Irish Women and the Vote: Becoming Citizens*, co-edited with Margaret Ward (Irish Academic Press, 2007). Her current research is on Polish migrants in London (funded by the ESRC).

Richard Smith works in the Department of Media and Communications, Goldsmiths College. His first book, *Jamaican Volunteers in the First World War*, was published by Manchester University Press in 2004. He continues to research the imperial dimensions of race and masculinity in the armed forces and the black presence in Britain during the early decades of the twentieth century.

Dolly Smith Wilson is Assistant Professor in British and Empire History at Texas Tech University. Her research interests focus on gender, race and labour in the twentieth century. She has published in *Twentieth Century British History* and *Gender and Education* and has a forthcoming book on gender and work in post-war Britain.

Inge Weber-Newth is Principal Lecturer in German and Applied Language Studies at London Metropolitan University. She works on twentieth century European migrants in Britain and her most recent book with Johannes-Dieter Steinert is *German Migrants in Post-war Britain: An Enemy Embrace* (Routledge, 2006).

Wendy Webster is Professor of Contemporary British History, University of Central Lancashire. She has published widely on questions of race, ethnicity, gender, immigration and imperialism in contemporary Britain, including *Imagining Home: Gender, Race and National Identity* (UCL Press, 1998) and *Englishness and Empire 1939-1965* (Oxford University Press, 2005), and is currently a Leverhulme Research Fellow researching Englishness and Europe, 1940-1973. She is a member of *Women's History Review* editorial board and of the Arts and Humanities Research Council Peer Review College.

Preface

Though people have been migrating since biblical times it was not until the late nineteenth century that migration, as a phenomenon to be studied and theorised in its own right, was recognised. It was the geographer, E.G. Ravenstein, in a lecture to the Statistical Society in March 1885, who first put forward a series of laws – later condensed by students of migration into the 'push and pull' theory – which sought to explain the dynamics of migration. Number seven on his list of Laws of Migration stated that, 'Females are more migratory than males', though he qualified this by explaining that though women were 'more migratory within the kingdom of their birth … more males leave the kingdom of their birth'.[1] There, for all intents and purposes, the place of women in the study of migration rested until the late 1980s when feminist researchers and writers ended the female migrants' century of invisibility and began revealing their experiences. However, even though acknowledged as actors on the stage of migration, female migrants were still cast in traditional feminine roles, as domestic workers, carers or as part of the family reunification flows that followed the male pioneers.

As Louise Ryan and Wendy Webster, editors of this volume, have sought to demonstrate, this is not even half of the picture. To be fully understood, gendered migration has to be located within an interdisciplinary context and incorporate a binary – female/male – methodology. As the chapters in this book illustrate the experiences of migration are not common to all men and all women and gender is only one part of the migrant experience; it intersects with ethnicity, identity, the labour market, household strategies, politics, social mores and personal ambition and ability, variances that the chapters in this book identify and record. Several chapters reveal the way in which the dynamics of the workplace and modes of employment can empower the previously disempowered migrant female and emasculate the once-dominant migrant male pioneer. Other chapters illustrate the way in which the processes of migration and settlement change both 'self', and other, perceptions of gendered migrant identity.

Gendered migration invariably incorporates issues of sexuality. As an early chapter records, in the First World War black migrant males were portrayed as representing threatening masculinity, whilst another highlights the way in which, following the Second World War, female refugees became symbols of suffering femininity. Additionally, as readers we are made aware of the instances in which receiving societies have used gender and sexuality as tools to promote the most favourable indigenous male images.

---

1   E.G. Ravenstein, 'The Laws of Migration', in *Journal of the Statistical Society of London* 48:2. (Jun., 1885), p 198.

The editors of this volume set out to demonstrate the diverse approaches to the use of gendered migration as a tool to enhance our understanding of migration at a time when the number of those 'on the move' is increasing at an almost immeasurable rate. By bringing together a range of disciplines, research methods and subject foci, readers are able both to hear the personal voice and confront the public face. In so doing Ryan and Webster have more than fulfilled the *raison d'être* of this series, which is to highlight the way in which migration impacts on every facet of life and thus on a multiplicity of disciplines. By focusing on gendered migration in the binary sense they have also taken gender studies forward from the singular to the dual and accentuated the complexity of the lives of the men and women who migrate.

Anne J. Kershen
Queen Mary, University of London
Spring 2008

Introduction

Louise Ryan and Wendy Webster

Gendering Migration demonstrates the significance of studying migration through the lens of gender and ethnicity and the contribution this perspective makes to migration histories. As an interdisciplinary work, it draws on a range of methodological approaches and brings together social science theories and approaches with historical perspectives that emphasise continuities and changes over time. As recently argued (Donato et al. 2006), migration studies need an interdisciplinary dialogue between history and social science which, on questions of gender and migration, helps to articulate the fluidity of gender, drawing attention not only to movement across space but also through time. However, there appears to be an historical myopia, even within gender-sensitive approaches to the study of migration (Kofman 2004). By focusing mainly on the post-1945 period, this volume provides an essential historical dimension to the study of gender and migration. Through its consideration of the impact of migration on men and masculine identities as well as women and feminine identities, it opens up a new area of research. The volume brings together a range of disciplines and research methods that draw on oral narratives, documentary and archival sources. It incorporates a wide range of migrant groups including European migrants (German, Greek, Irish, Polish and Spanish) as well as East African-Asian, Caribbean, Pakistani and Kurdish. The diversity as well as some of the commonalities of their experiences allows for an exploration of the ways in which gender and ethnicity have been negotiated over time by different migrants in Britain.

The Post-war Context

In 1997, Caryl Phillips observed: 'For many British people, to accept the idea that their country has a long and complex history of immigration would be to undermine their basic understanding of what it means to be British ... In the face of overwhelming evidence, the mythology of homogeneity not only exists but endures ... Britain has developed a vision of herself as a nation that is both culturally and ethnically homogenous' (Phillips 1997, xii). Reactions in October 2000 to the publication of *The Future of Multi-ethnic Britain* — the Report of a Commission set up by the Runnymede Trust — suggested that such a vision commanded considerable popular support in the new millennium. The Report stated that a genuinely multicultural Britain urgently needed to reimagine itself, and that this involved 'rethinking the national story and national identity' (Parekh 2000, 15, xiii). Much of the press strongly censured this view — the *Daily Telegraph* suggesting that the report attempted to 'destroy a thousand years of British history' ('Don't Diss Britannia', 12 October 2000). Much mainstream British historical writing has also taken for granted the idea of an ethnically homogenous nation. Unlike their counterparts writing about the United States, mainstream historians of Britain have rarely been concerned with questions of immigration (Kushner and Lunn 1990, vii; Panayi 1999). As Tony Kushner and Katharine Knox (1999, 1-5) have noted, the history of refugee movements to Britain in the twentieth century is another area that historians have largely ignored.

A characteristic opposition between Britishness as white and 'immigrants' as black and Asian which developed in the post-1945 period sustained an idea of Britain as an ethnically homogeneous nation, disrupted only by post-war developments (Webster 1998). Such an opposition obscured the history of immigration before 1945 — predominantly Irish and Jewish — when the mass immigration of Jews from Eastern Europe, after the pogroms of 1881-82, prompted a series of Aliens Acts from 1905 targeted primarily at limiting the entry of poorer immigrants — in practice predominantly Jews from Eastern Europe. Such an opposition also obscured the continuities between the pre-1945 period and post-1945 periods, both characterised by significant migration from Europe. In 1961, just before the passage of the Commonwealth Immigrants Act designed primarily to restrict black and Asian migration from the Commonwealth, the number of aliens resident in Britain, predominantly white Europeans, was larger than the number of those who had arrived from the Caribbean and the South Asian subcontinent (Walvin 1984, 11). Irish people, the largest group of post-war migrants to Britain, were never classified as aliens, and so excluded from these figures. Cypriots were also excluded because Cyprus was a British colony until 1960 when it became an independent republic within the Commonwealth. This colonial context may have shaped perceptions of Cypriots, for although Europeans were generally identified as white, Cypriots were not always seen as uncontestably so — studies of immigration in the 1960s variously defining them as 'white Commonwealth immigrants' and 'coloured Commonwealth citizens' (Webster 1998, xviii).

In this volume there is considerable attention to European migration and refugee movements to Britain after the Second World War — groups that, until recently, have received less attention in the literature than post-war Commonwealth migrants. Several chapters chart the significance of the Second World War in generating European migration to Britain, much of it enforced as people fled from Nazi persecution on the continent or were unable to return to countries which came under Communist rule from 1945. They also chart the government's role in the immediate aftermath of war in a context of serious labour shortage, in encouraging migration from Europe rather than colonies and former colonies; the blurring of these categories in migration from Cyprus and the continued significance of Irish migration (see chapters by Burrell, Evergeti, Ryan, Weber-Newth, Webster and Wilson), while Tony Morgan's chapter looks at Spanish migration in a later period. Through its attention to European migration the volume highlights the ethnic heterogeneity of the white population, challenging the opposition between immigrant/black and British/white. Through its focus on migration to post-war Britain, it pays attention to a range of other groups who arrived in the second half of the twentieth century. The case of those who were refused entry or settlement receives less attention. Notable among these in the immediate aftermath of war were Jewish Holocaust survivors who were allowed into Britain only in very limited numbers (London 2000, Chapter 9).

The diversity of groups arriving in Britain in the second half of the twentieth century was shaped by the policing of borders — who was allowed entry and settlement, who was refused entry, who was positively encouraged to enter. Such policing was subject to very considerable change in the course of the period. In the 1950s, the immigration status of many European immigrants and refugees as aliens was in contrast to the status of Commonwealth immigrants who had unrestricted right of entry under the government's 'open door' policy. Privately, however, there were attempts to find means to restrict black and Asian immigration, and both Labour and Conservative governments set up Committees to discuss this. Both met in secret (Malik 1996, 19-25). In the 1960s, a series of Acts, beginning in 1962, began to close the 'open door'. The 1962 Commonwealth Immigrants Act could be regarded as a watershed in the wider history of racial politics in Britain as the first legislation to restrict migration from the Commonwealth to Britain, targeted at black and Asian migrants, and establishing, for the first time, that British passport holders could be excluded from the right of entry. Coinciding as it did with increasing awareness of loss of imperial power, black and Asian migration to Britain was widely perceived as a threat to Britishness, collapsing boundaries between empire and metropolis, black and white.

The 1962 Act marked the beginning of a series of Acts that increasingly tightened and racialised immigration legislation. The 1971 Act was distinguished by a 'patrial' clause, where rights to abode in Britain were confined to those with a parent or grandparent born in Britain — a requirement that many white people, but few black people in the Commonwealth could meet. By the end of the twentieth century, the advocacy of tighter border controls focused particularly on asylum seekers. In 1991, the Home Secretary, Kenneth Baker stated that the purpose of the new Asylum Bill, which became law in 1993, was: 'to restrain the number of people who come to this country as asylum seekers'. In this context, refugee was a term increasingly associated with dishonesty in the notion of 'bogus' asylum seekers, and with criminality through the policy of detention in prisons. It became a term shunned by those arriving in Britain who might have used this as a self-description, because it had become a term of abuse in British society (Kushner and Knox 1999, xxx).

Decency and tolerance remained important to Britain's self-image throughout the twentieth century. Britain was not only constructed against Nazi Germany both during the Second World War and in subsequent public memories of war, but also against South Africa and its apartheid regime, and — especially in the 1950s and 1960s — against an America associated with the idea of racial conflict and conflagration. During the 1950s the idea of tolerance was strongly advertised in public, particularly by reference to a multi-racial Commonwealth, and the 'open door' policy on immigration from the Commonwealth. In the 1960s and 1970s, despite the increasing racialisation of immigration legislation, a reputation for decency was sustained by Race Relations legislation which sought to reduce racial discrimination and promote racial equality in Britain — the Act of 1976 outlawing both indirect and direct racial discrimination, and setting up the Commission for

Racial Equality. At a popular level, many groups, particularly in the voluntary sector, worked to welcome and support refugees to Britain, setting up local committees to organise campaigns on their behalf, as well as material support, including clothes and housing. But those involved in supporting refugees did so under increasingly difficult circumstances. Women's Aid to Former Yugoslavia, founded in 1992, was mainly involved in distributing aid to refugees in former Yugoslavia, since such limited numbers entered Britain (Kushner and Knox 1999).

By the end of the century, the 'open door' policy, by which Commonwealth migrants had unrestricted right of entry in contrast to many Europeans was reversed. Britain's membership of the European community and the Single European Act of 1986 which set a date for the abolition of internal frontiers meant that, from 1993, nationals migrating internally within the EC had access to an 'open door' through which they could seek work and take up residence in other member states. Initially the abolition of internal frontiers aroused little public comment, and those who migrated to Britain in this context were associated with a positive image of free movement of people. The additional enlargement of the EU in 2004 and 2007 changed this, leading to a marked increase in migration to Britain, mostly from Eastern Europe: an area which, since the eighteenth century had been constructed as 'backward' in relation to Western Europe and as 'a paradox of simultaneous inclusion and exclusion, Europe but not Europe' (Wolff 1994, 7). Between 2004 and 2007 more than 700,000 EU migrants registered for employment in Britain, over half of them from Poland. This new source of labour was initially welcomed, but the volume of migration was unanticipated and resulted in growing calls to restrict the entry of migrants from new accession states (see Ryan et al. 2007). In this context, the heterogeneity of whites in Britain was increasingly acknowledged and white migrants became more visible, especially through growing media coverage.

Gender

In recent years there have been growing calls for a gendered approach to migration which encompasses men as well as women. Pierrette Hondagneu-Sotelo has argued: 'this preoccupation with writing women into migration research and theory has stifled theorising about the ways in which constructions of masculinities and femininities organise migration and migration outcomes' (cited in Mahler and Pessar 2006, 50). When researching gender and migration, it is not uncommon for academics to look only at women, so that consideration of gender and women's migration become one and the same thing. This not only excludes men from such studies but also overlooks the complex interactions between men and women, within and between migrant groups and between migrant and indigenous groups, and the impact that these have for both masculine and feminine identities.

Despite an increasing recent interest in female migration especially among feminist researchers within the European context (Ackers 1998; Kofman et al. 2000; Zulauf 2001; Morokvasic 2004), Eleonore Kofman (2004a, 644) argues that 'mainstream theorisations have been slow to incorporate the relevance of gender issues'. The dominance of economic perspectives has resulted in a focus on the migrant worker as an individual economic actor. There has been a tendency to configure the migrant as a 'singular, bounded, intentional actor — the individual who confidently declares that: "I decided to travel overseas"' (Conradson and Latham 2005, 297). Many of these mainstream theories of migration, despite their apparent 'gender neutrality', construct this individual economic migrant as male thus tending to exacerbate the exclusion of women from analyses of migration.

Notwithstanding the impact of recent feminist research, there remains a tendency to consider women migrants within narrow domestic and familial contexts: such as playing supporting roles as wives and home-makers (Erel 2002). This reinforces the view that men are the primary economic migrants and women are either left behind or simply follow through family reunification. Thus female migration has tended to be defined in terms of dependency rather than employment and autonomy (Ackers 1998). Dichotomies based upon a constellation of the economic, male and workplace in opposition to the socio-cultural, female and family, frame the way migration is traditionally explained (Kofman 2004a, 647). Nonetheless, while mainstream theorizations of migration may assume a male migrant, his masculinity is simply taken for granted, rather than being a focus of analysis and research. Several chapters in this volume suggest that women's experiences of migration can only be fully understood by considering the wider context, both temporally and spatially, including their dynamic relationships with men. Similarly, men's relationships with women, in families, workplaces, in the host and native society are important to an understanding of how identities are formed and developed over time. Such an approach not only compares the experiences and migration pathways of men and women but also develops more dynamic and fluid conceptualisations of gender as a process that is relational, temporal and situational (Mahler and Pessar 2006).

While acknowledging that migration may take many varied forms, Bill Jordan and Franck Duvell (2003) have argued that it is rarely an isolated decision pursued by individual agents but rather a collective action involving families, kinships and other communal contacts. Mary Chamberlain's work on migration to Britain from Barbados, investigating questions of motivation and identity, tips the balance of analysis towards the home society, emphasising the importance of family histories and the idea of a 'culture of migration' where migration is seen within the family as the norm, and the image of a migrant searching for identity becomes irrelevant (Chamberlain 1997b). However, because of particular migration flows into Europe over the last fifty years, 'family migration' has often been configured as a secondary type of migration, an un-intended consequence of male economic mobility, as dependent wife and children arrive to join the male breadwinner (Kofman 2004b), as illustrated, for example, by Turkish workers in Germany. Recent research has begun to challenge some of the assumptions about this kind of guest worker migration (Faist and Ozveren 2004). Rather than simply following their husbands, women may play more active roles in family strategies around migration (Erel 2002).

A theoretical framework helpful in conceptualising and studying gendered identities and relations is 'gendered geographies of power'. Proposed by Sarah Mahler and Patricia Pessar (2006), it provides a way of understanding the geographical spaces and social locations within which migrants live, work and socialise and is divided into four building blocks: geographical scales (gender operates usually simultaneously on multiple spatial, social and cultural scales); social location (how groups and individuals are situated in multiple and intersecting hierarchies of gender, class, race, ethnicity, etc); agency (how individuals exert agency over their social locations) and imagination (images, meanings and values associated with gender, place, consumption, etc).

As the experiences of migrants discussed in this volume reveal, gender is a key factor in organising social life but it cannot be understood in isolation from other axes and hierarchies of differentiation:

> To advance migration studies a consideration of gender differences alone is often insufficient. Rather gender is entwined with other structures of difference, such as race, class, generation and sexual orientation and these must be factored into studies of gender and migration (Mahler and Pessar 2006, 37-38).

Instead of merely comparing the experiences of men and women migrants within specific social locations such as the workplace, it is necessary to explore how women's entry into paid employment may impact on men's roles within the home, and how women's economic role may intersect with and impact upon notions of masculine authority. Similarly, migrant men's expressions of masculinity within the home need to be understood in relation to experiences in the wider society including racism, homophobia, classism and ageism. Several of the chapters in this volume (Ahmad, Burrell and Herbert), do precisely that by examining gendered dynamics within families, the ways in which these are negotiated over time, and their relation to wider social practices and institutions. The complex intersections of gender and ethnic identity within specific social locations are clearly evident in relation to the work place. In this volume, Louise Ryan's chapter analyses nurses' negotiation of their roles and identities as Irish, professionals and women within hospital settings, Dolly Wilson shows how migrant men and women became marginalised within specific factories, while Ali Ahmad discusses Pakistani men's and women's complex relationships within highly gendered workspaces. Sarah Keeler explores how doing 'women's work' such as cooking and sewing impacts on the masculine identities of Kurdish men.

A focus on family relationships can reveal complex family dynamics surrounding migration, like the experiences of young Pakistani men marrying into families in the East End of London (Ahmad) or German women marrying British men after the Second World War (Weber-Newth). Venetia Evergeti's chapter examines how a Greek migrant's experiences of domestic violence impacted not only on her relationships in Britain but also with her relatives back home in Greece. Studies such as these reveal how gender dynamics intersect with age, class, and cultural expectations within changing social, economic and political settings. This kind of research involves going beyond the migrant as an economic actor but also approaching migrant families as complex, dynamic and differentiated groups.

Recent research on migration has helped to complicate previous assumptions about 'the family' as a bounded geographical unit. 'Families represent a social group geographically dispersed. They create kinship networks which exist across space and are the conduits for information and assistance which in turn influence migration decisions' (Boyd 1989, 643). Through transnational mobility, family members become extended through space and time as geographically dispersed relatives form part of diverse social relations linking migrants' societies of origin and settlement (Baldassar and Baldock 2000). Exploring life stories from the Caribbean, Chamberlain (2006, 110) argues that 'the idea of family and the meanings attached to it have emerged as the key elements in the narratives of belonging and identity', and that these narratives 'link families across the oceans and the generations'. Deborah Bryceson and Ulla Vuorela (2002, 3) observe that: 'By their very nature, transnational families constitute an elusive phenomenon — spatially dispersed and seemingly capable of unending social mutations'. This topic is discussed by both Evergeti and Ryan in relation to ageing and the changing relationships with families 'back home' in Greece and Ireland through the life course.

In terms of gendered geographies of power, many of the chapters in this volume focus not only on transnational relationships, but also on specific sites of migration within Britain, such as Pakistanis and Kurds in the East End of London and East African Asians in Leicester (Ahmad, Keeler and Herbert). These chapters reveal how migrants may have to negotiate their belonging and attachment to these locales. As Robert Putnam (2007) has argued, the advantages of migration are often experienced at the macro level, through the national economy, for example, while the costs and tensions are usually experienced at a micro level, in the workplace, local borough or neighbourhood. Richard Smith's chapter suggests a degree of local acceptance of Black soldiers in Britain during the First World War, but also demonstrates the opposition and hostility expressed by local residents. These local tensions can also be generated between migrant groups. As Keeler shows in her chapter, areas may become associated with one migrant population — for example Turks in 'Little Istanbul' — so that other migrants such as Kurds may experience these areas as hostile or alien.

Gendering Ethnicity

One of the aims of this volume is to explore the intersections of gender and ethnicity in the context of migration. Although there are now a variety of theoretical perspectives on ethnicity, it is broadly agreed that ethnicity has something to do with 'the classification of people and group relationships' (Eriksen 1996, 28). Thomas Eriksen defines ethnicity simply as 'relationships between groups whose members consider themselves distinctive' (1996, 30). This definition reveals the importance of self-ascription. However, until recently, there was little research on the process of self- identification and how people actively engage with notions of their own ethnic identity. In their research into the components that make up ethnic identity, James Nazroo and Saffron Karlsen (2003) emphasise the importance of self-description, traditional identity, participating in a community and external definitions.

The work of Richard Alba (1990) has demonstrated the complex and diverse ways in which white populations engage with their ethnic identities. Alba begins his analysis with the self-perception of ethnic identity which he defines as 'a person's subjective orientation toward his or her ethnic origins' (1990, 25). He also emphasises that, far from being essential or static, a person's perception and interpretation of their ethnicity may change over time and so it is important to acknowledge the fluidity of ethnic identity. While underlining the importance of self-perception, Alba (1990) argues that ethnic identity cannot be sustained as a private, individual position, rather it is in expressing one's identity that one is truly *being* ethnic.

> Such mundane actions as eating ethnic foods, enacting holiday rituals … and participating in ethnic social clubs give meaning to an otherwise abstract assertion of ethnic identity and breathe life into ethnicity as a social form (Alba 1990, 75).

For Alba, membership of ethnic social structures such as families, friendship groups or social clubs, enables ethnic identity to be expressed and experienced as a collective phenomenon. However, membership of an ethnic group does not imply that ethnicity is homogeneous — rather it may be experienced and defined very differently within a specific ethnic group (Castles and Miller 2003; Wimmer 2004; Lacy 2004). Ethnic identity interacts with other facets of identity such as sex, class, and occupational status. Articulations of identity emerge 'out of multiple social positionings and the interplay between these positionings in the formations of selves' (Gray 2004, 19). Ethnic identity thus cannot be seen as given or fixed, despite invocations of tradition rooted in the distance past, ethnicities are dynamic and change both temporally and spatially. Hence, as Ryan (2007b) has argued at length elsewhere, expressions of ethnicity will vary in different social contexts. For example, the way ethnic identity is expressed in the privacy of the home or in an ethnic social club may differ markedly from how ethnic identity is expressed in a more diverse environment such as the work place.

The significance of context and recognition by others also suggest the ways in which constructions of ethnicity can be constrained by wider social processes and structures. The work of Fredrik Barth (1969; 1996) has been influential in highlighting the interplay of self-description and ascription by others in the formation of ethnic identity. In recent years there has been a growing understanding of ethnicity as a two-way process so that ethnicity is increasingly understood as 'a product of both "other definition" and of "self definition"' (Castles and Miller 2003, 33).

One product of 'other definition' and 'self definition' in post-war Britain was solidarity between different migrant groups which extended to political organisation and was a notable feature of the Afro-Asian Caribbean Conference which opposed the 1962 Commonwealth Immigrants Act. In the 1970s, political activists adopted the term 'Black', with an upper-case 'B', as a political signifier to express the idea of solidarity between people of Asian, African and Caribbean descent as a result of shared experiences of British colonialism and racism. But the chapters in this volume suggest that solidarity, tensions and shared experiences and circumstances do not always divide along black and non-black lines.

One shared circumstance that crossed lines of ethnicity, including white and black ethnicities was location in the labour market. Low-paid and low-status work feature in many chapters here, which show this as an experience shared by Poles who settled in Britain in the late 1940s under the Polish Resettlement Act (Burrell), by European Volunteer Workers recruited from displaced persons camps in Germany and Austria in the late 1940s (Webster, Wilson), by East African Asians, many of whom came to Britain in the 1960s and 1970s as refugees (Herbert), and by Punjabis, Caribbeans, Pakistanis as well as Kurds (Ahmad, Keeler, Wilson). However, entrepreneurial activity was also characteristic of migrants from a number of groups discussed, including East African Asians, Pakistani migrants who used their factory wages to establish their own businesses, and Italians (Ahmad, Herbert, Wilson).

Gender emerges as a particularly complex factor in labour market activity, intersecting with ethnicity. At a time when the labour market position of both working-class and middle-class indigenous women was subordinate to that of men from their own class, migrant women sometimes had access to higher status jobs than their male counterparts. Ryan's chapter shows that some nurses felt that their occupational status protected them from being looked down on as Irish migrants. Caribbean women from the same generation were usually trained as State Enrolled Nurse. Irish nurses often trained to the higher status and better-paid State Registered Nurse, but in some instances access to this higher qualification had to be negotiated through ethnic stereotypes (Ryan 2007b). Even so, nursing gave migrant women, including Irish and Caribbean women, access to higher status work than many of their male compatriots. For a later period, Morgan's chapter shows the success of Spanish female professionals in the British labour market significantly exceeding that of their male counterparts.

Gender also emerges from these chapters as a significant factor in the way in which migrants, especially male migrants, experienced their positions in the labour market. When the Pakistani women in Ahmad's chapter take sewing jobs at home, this is sometimes not regarded as paid employment by their menfolk, but simply as 'what women do'. But sewing jobs, as well as jobs in catering are described by a Kurdish man in Keeler's chapter as tasks 'that men didn't do'. In both cases masculine jobs are defined against what is appropriately feminine behaviour, but while in the case of Pakistanis a denial that what women are doing is paid employment secures the status of males as providers, in the case of Kurds the task of sewing, when undertaken by males is seen as 'a big challenge to being a man'.

Such a challenge is also noted in chapters by Kathy Burrell and Joanna Herbert. What is striking about their discussions of Polish and East African Asian men is the significant role played by gender in experiences of downward mobility. Men in both groups, many of them taking low-paid work in British factories, felt the decline in their occupational status acutely. Downward mobility is usually understood in class terms, but these chapters demonstrate the very significant role played by gender as men experienced not only the loss of their pre-migration occupational status but also felt unable to live up to masculine ideals: material success and provision for their families. Polish men were undergoing this experience in the late 1940s and 1950s and East African Asian men in the late 1960s and 1970s, but downward mobility could nevertheless be regarded as an experience they shared across differences of ethnicity. It is interesting that in both cases women's work in jobs that also involved them in downward mobility (in the case of Poles), and in setting up family businesses (in the case of East African Asians) is acknowledged in male narratives only as supplementary to that of the main male wage earner or entrepreneur, or ignored altogether.

The Polish and East African Asian men discussed by Burrell and Herbert were predominantly forced migrants, but experiences of downward mobility were common to a wide range of groups arriving in Britain. Wilson's chapter demonstrates the extent to which perceptions of migrants as unskilled, as well as employers' reservations about placing them in positions of authority over indigenous workers, limited their chances of appointment to skilled, supervisory or professional posts. Women as well as men were affected by such discrimination, but women's experiences of downward mobility could also encompass the loss of status associated with a full-time housewife who did no paid employment. Jewish female refugees who came to Britain before the war under a British Ministry of Labour scheme could only enter on condition that they worked as domestic servants (Kushner 1990). Their history complicates the story of class relations in domestic service, for many had been middle-class employers of servants, or daughters in servant-employing households, in Germany and Austria before the rise of Hitler. On arrival in Britain, they had to don a cap and apron. Linda McDowell's study of Latvian EVW women shows that some experienced loss of status in a similarly gendered way, although in their case, this could involve a complex history of geographical as well as social mobility including a period as forced labourers in Germany as well as displaced persons in German camps before their recruitment to low-paid employment in Britain (McDowell 2005).

Shared circumstances and experiences across differences of ethnicity, including the very complex meanings attached to the idea of home and their changes over the life-course, run through these chapters. But so do very diverse experiences: different not only by ethnicity, gender, class, national identity and their intersections but also by many other factors. Not least among these are different moments within the period, which produced different experiences for established and new migrants of the same nationality, and between first and second generations. Newly hybrid, multiple, mobile and transnational identities that call into question the idea of a unitary national culture jostle in the stories migrants tell with fixed and singular identities. Burrell's chapter, for example, argues that despite the dominance of the image of the brave Polish soldier in the Polish community, which fixed an idea of national and ethnic identity and a strong attachment to this, many gender ideals had to be abandoned. In contrast Keeler's chapter argues that, for Kurdish men, migration tended to challenge ethnic essentialism but reinforce gender essentialism. Both chapters, however, also draw attention to diversity within the groups they interviewed.

Burrell's chapter also shows the influence of ageing in eroding a community focus on Second World War soldiers. In analysing the fluidity of identities — gender and ethnic identities and the intersections between them — several chapters in this volume take a life course perspective to map the dynamism of experiences and relationships over time. Chapters by Evergeti and Ryan use this perspective to explore changing relationships to people and places as migrants age. Evergeti describes how changing attachments to the homeland are defined through landscape, food, traditions and language. The sociological orientation of a life course perspective emphasises that relationships develop in the context of social roles and change in salience as the individual moves in and out of roles, for example changing jobs, starting a family, moving house:

> The lens of a life course perspective focuses attention on the social roles in which personal relationships are formed. Life course events and transitions usually involve a change in social roles and situations, often altering the basis for the social relationships that were formed in the context of the role (Larner 1990, 182).

Thus rather than simply focusing on a moment in time, it is important to consider how migrants' present attitudes, experiences, strategies and life choices may be shaped not only by their current situation but also by their changing relationships to people and places as they age. Of course, migrants' experiences and relationships are also informed by the wider social context, the political and public discourses surrounding immigration at any given time.

Narratives of Migration

During the twentieth century a wide range of public discourses circulated in Britain about immigration: social, political, cultural and legal. For the most part the voices of migrants and their descendants were excluded from these. For example, West Indian writers in Britain produced a substantial literature in the 1950s and 1960s, but their work was largely ignored by the British (Schwarz 2003). By the new millennium, however, migrant voices became increasingly evident in cultural discourse. Black British cinema, a label given to films that drew on the experiences and were mainly made by film-makers from the Asian, African and Caribbean diasporas, attracted a good deal of attention in the 1980s (Malik, S. 1996). In the new millennium, novels like Zadie Smith's *White Teeth* and Monica Ali's *Brick Lane* were highly acclaimed. From the 1970s, the voices of migrants were also widely recorded in scholarly literatures based on interview material, while local history groups and museum exhibitions encouraged the collection and publication of oral histories for a wider public.

Main themes of research on public discourses of immigration in Britain are its impact on national identity and who was excluded and who included in ideas of Britishness in different contexts. Main themes of research using interview material are the impact of migration on migrants' own identities and how far migration produces a new sense of self. Within disciplines such as sociology, geography and anthropology, in-depth interviews as well as participant observation have formed part of qualitative research that uses ethnographic methods and is often carried out in a local setting over many months (Mahler and Pessar 2006, 30). 'Ethnographers argue that migration is not merely a process best understood in economic and/or political terms; it is also a sociocultural process mediated by gendered and kinship ideologies, institutions and practices' (Mahler and Pessar 2006, 33). This type of approach is used in this volume by Ahmad, Herbert, and Keeler and to some extent by Burrell, Evergeti and Ryan.

Several chapters in this volume focus on public discourses of immigration, particularly as they circulated through government documents and in the media, and analyse their sexualized and racialised narratives of national identity (Smith, Webster, Wilson). Richard Smith's chapter on media portrayals of black masculinity during the First World War and its aftermath demonstrates considerable similarities to the perceptions of official policy-makers in the aftermath of the Second World War discussed by Wilson. In both cases attention focused on sexual relationships between black men and white women in a language of miscegenation which, Bill Schwarz has argued for the 1940s and 1950s, 'was the central issue in terms of white perceptions of race, defining the boundaries of England and signifying the inviolate centre which could brook no impurity' (Schwarz 1996, 197). But while this might suggest fixed ideas and considerable continuity over time, both Smith and Wilson also emphasise the contradictory, volatile and shifting nature of public discourse. Smith shows how an early First World War media image of black masculinity which focused on physical prowess was succeeded by increasing fears of miscegenation. Wilson argues that attention to miscegenation by official policy-makers in the 1950s gave way to anxieties about over-fertile black women in the 1960s: a shift that is also evident in media imagery.

The chapter by Wendy Webster suggests something of the complexity of the relationship between official and media discourses: one in which, in the late 1940s, the government attempted to shape public attitudes to European migrants through their interventions to secure favourable coverage in the media. Despite their efforts, however, she shows that media representations of European refugees were contradictory — portrayed both as criminal foreigners and as fellow-Europeans who had demonstrated their valour in fighting alongside the British: both images which had counterparts during the Second World War. There were no comparable government attempts to secure favourable media coverage for other migrant groups. Indeed Kathleen Paul, critiquing the view that, in the 1960s liberal politicians caved in to the clamour of an illiberal public for immigration control and were forced to legislate in 1962, argues that the government fostered an unfavourable public atmosphere for colonial migrants and, from March 1954, began a deliberate campaign to sway public opinion in favour of immigration control (Paul 1997, especially Chapter 6). European migrants were not so prominent in sexualized narratives of national identity as black and Asian migrants, but there were nevertheless some popular anxieties about their relationships with British women, particularly in the late 1940s perception of Polish men as Casanovas or Irish men as drunken and aggressive (Webster 2005, 153; Ryan 2001). There were also hierarchies within European migrants in which in late 1940s official discourses, Jewish migrants were at the bottom (Webster, this volume).

Personal narratives collected by interviewers have a complex relationship to public discourses, and can be understood as 'the product of relations between discourse and subjectivity' (Summerfield 1998, 16). Such an approach emphasises that people do not tell their stories outside public discourses, although personal narratives may challenge such discourses. The extent to which personal narratives draw on wider discourses is evident throughout this volume. Ryan argues that nurses drew on positive ethnic stereotypes about caring and hard-working Irish women to counter negative labels. Herbert argues that East African Asian men drew on ideas about masculinity to present themselves as autonomous agents, pioneering and determined, in a context where there they felt their male self-esteem was threatened. Inge Weber-

Newth shows that German war brides were anxious to repudiate a common image of fraternising women in late 1940s Germany — as good-time girls or prostitutes who became a metaphor for the moral decline of the nation — by emphasising their own respectability and the respectable context in which their relationships had been conducted. The way in which stories are shaped by wider discourses is also evident in the silences noted by Weber-Newth: German war brides' reluctance to talk about gender relations. She also comments on silences within public discourses: on looting and rape by British occupying forces.

In contrast to media interviews which usually focus on individuals, most academic research using interviews constructs a collective subject, apparent in the title under which the testimony of ex-slaves collected in the 1930s as part of the New Deal Federal Writers' Project were finally edited and published in 1977 by George Rawick — *The American Slave: A Composite Autobiography*. Such a collective subject is also apparent in sociological and anthropological texts of the 1920s and 1930s, when the interview method was first widely used in a range of academic work, including Robert Redfield's *The Life Story of the Mexican Immigrant* (1931). Academic work using interviews has sometimes been seen as a collaborative task undertaken by interviewer and narrator and as an empowering process — one which gives voice to those who were previously denied one. However, questions have also been raised about the power relations involved in interviews: the extent to which interviewers may control the form in which the interview is conducted and disseminated, their role in mediating, contextualising, editing and interpreting narratives, and the differential outcomes of interviews, which may increase interviewers' prestige or income without benefiting their subjects (Cotterill 1992; Luff 1999; Turnbull 2000). Complex questions about power relations are also embedded in the social context in which narratives are collected, notably in the case of *testimonio* which are sometimes edited in particular ways by Western anthropologists for Western audiences (Webster 2001a; 2001b).

Researchers of migration who use interview material, through their concern to present the perspective of migrants, contribute to shifts in the direction in which knowledge flows. The narratives they collect have a shaping influence, often a major influence, on the knowledge and understanding they produce (Ryan and Golden 2006). But there is no certainty that the interviewers' interpretation of narratives coincides with those of the narrators and interpretive conflicts may arise between researcher and narrator which raise difficult ethical issues. Narratives are also likely to be mediated and shaped by narrators' assumptions about the expectations of their interviewers, as well as the wider audience to which their narratives may be disseminated. These assumptions may, in their turn, be influenced by how far they perceive the interviewer as same or different — by, for example, gender, ethnicity, class, age and sexuality (Phoenix 1994; Ryan and Golden 2006). Stories elicited through interview processes are also told within the conventions of different interview contexts, which generate a range of autobiographical practices and a range of topics through the different subject positions constructed for speakers (Turnbull 2000). Interviews are a widespread practice in many societies that require people to produce narrative coherence in relation to many aspects of their lives: as users of health, education, counselling, and social services, as applicants for jobs or in encounters with the police or immigration officials (Webster 2001a). Migration, a central topic in life stories told by migrants to researchers of migration processes, may not be raised in interviews in other contexts.

Despite their collective subject, in-depth, qualitative studies are also often necessarily small scale, usually involving the study of one particular migrant or ethnic group. They generate rich data and can provide an insight into the processes of migration and personal agency. One of the chapters in this volume, Morgan's study of Spanish migrants, employs quantitative methods, including the results of a large postal survey and statistical analysis of census data. Morgan's chapter indicates the advantages of this kind of data for revealing changing trends within large populations. For example, his research indicates not only the increasing proportion of women within the Spanish population in Britain but also their changing levels of educational qualifications, employment patterns and home ownership. However, this chapter also indicates the value of qualitative research in the interpretation of quantitative data.

It is important to go beyond the single case study to undertake multi-sited ethnography, for example, to study transnational migration and the changing relationships between 'here' and 'there' or compare migrants and non-migrants, or undertake a comparative study of different migrant groups. Mahler and Pessar (2006) make a plea for funding sources to recognise the need to support larger research projects including longitudinal studies that cost significantly more than the single site, single group, short-term project. However, this type of research can also contribute to the on-going marginalisation of gender studies within the wider field of migration research. Both the subject matter, gender, and the methodology, micro, qualitative studies, may be used to label this area of research 'soft' and marginal. Within migration research there continues to be an on-going dominance of large-scale quantitative research and the seemingly convincing results generated by the analysis of large data sets. 'The hierarchy of methods yields differently valued research results' (Mahler and Pessar 2006, 31). As Hondagneu-Sotelo and others argue 'gender has encountered resistance and indifference in immigration scholarship' (cited in Mahler and Pessar 2006, 28).

Conclusion

The chapters in this volume demonstrate that gender — always intersecting with ethnicity — played a significant but variable role in ideas and images of migrants in Britain and in the experiences of migrants. Themes of gender and ethnicity were extensively deployed in official and media discourses about migrants as well as in the narratives migrants told. Gender and ethnicity shaped the experiences of migrants in Britain, but were also shaped and changed by the process of migration to varying degrees, influenced by factors like age, class, religion and generation and by developments within the period — the war and its aftermath, legislation on immigrants and asylum seekers, Britain's membership of the European Union. Situating their discussion of gender in the context of ethnicity, the chapters explore the impact of migration on men and masculine identities as well as women and feminine identities, and the impact on indigenous populations as well as migrant groups. The volume demonstrates the contribution that this approach makes to understanding histories of migration.

References

Ackers, L. (1998), *Shifting Spaces* (Bristol: The Policy Press).

Alba, R. (1990), *Ethnic Identity: The Transformation of White America* (London: Yale University Press).

Baldassar, L. and Baldock, C. (2000), 'Linking Migration and Family Studies: Transnational Migrants and the Care of Ageing Parents', in Agozino, B. (ed.), *Theoretical and Methodological Issues in Migration Research* (Aldershot: Ashgate), 61-91.

Barth, F. (1996), 'Ethnic Groups and Boundaries', in Hutchinson, J. and Smith, A.D. (eds), *Ethnicity* (Oxford: Oxford University Press), 75-82.

Boyd, M. (1989), 'Family and Personal Networks in International Migration', *International Migration Review* 23:3, 638-70.

Bryceson, D. and Vuorela, U. (eds) (2002), *The Transnational Family: New European Frontiers and Global Networks* (Oxford: Berg).

Castles, S. and Miller, M. (2003), *The Age of Migration: International Population Movements in the Modern World* (Basingstoke: Palgrave).

Chamberlain, M. (1997a), 'Gender and the Narratives of Migration', *History Workshop Journal* 53, 87-108.

—— (1997b), *Narratives of Exile and Return* (London: Macmillan).

—— (2006), *Family Love in the Diaspora: Migration and the Anglo-Caribbean Experience* (Edison, NJ, Transaction Publishers).

Conradson, D. and Latham, A. (2005), 'Friendship, Networks and Transnationality in a World City: Antipodean Transmigrants in London', *Journal of Ethnic and Migration Studies* 3:2, 287-305.

Cotterill, P. (1992), 'Interviewing Women, Issues of Friendship, Vulnerability and Power', *Women's Studies International Forum* 15:5-6, 593-606.

Donato, K., Gabbaccia, D., Holdaway, J., Manalansan, M. and Pessar, P. (2006), 'A Glass Half Full? Gender in Migration Studies', *International Migration Review* 40:1, 3-26.

Eriksen, T.H. (1996), 'Ethnicity, Race, Class and Nation', in Hutchinson, J. and Smith, A.D. (eds), *Ethnicity* (Oxford: Oxford University Press), 28-34.

Faist, T. and Ozveren, E. (eds) (2004), *Transnational Social Spaces: Agents, Networks and Institutions* (Aldershot: Ashgate).

Gray, B. (2004), *Women and the Irish Diaspora* (London: Sage).

Jordan, B. and Duvell, F. (2003), *Migration: The Boundaries of Equality and Justice* (Cambridge: Polity).

Kofman, E. (2004a), 'Gendered Global Migrations', *International Feminist Journal of Politics* 6:4, 643-665.

—— (2004b), 'Family-related Migration: A Critical Review of European Studies', *Journal of Ethnic and Migration Studies* 30:2, 243-262.

Kofman, E., Phizacklea, A., Raghuram, P. and Sales, R. (2000), *Gender, Migration and Welfare in Europe* (London: Routledge).

Kushner, T. (1990), 'Politics and Race, Gender and Class: Refugees, Fascists and Domestic Service in Britain 1933-1940', in Kushner and Lunn (eds).

Kushner T. and Lunn, K. (eds) (1990), *The Politics of Marginality: Race, the Radical Right and Minorities in Twentieth-Century Britain* (London: Frank Cass).

Kushner T. and Knox, K. (1999), *Refugees in an Age of Genocide* (London: Frank Cass).

Lacy, K.R. (2004), 'Black Spaces, Black Places: Strategic Assimilation and Identity Construction in Middle-class Suburbia', *Ethnic and Racial Studies* 27:6, 908-930.

London, L. (2000), *Whitehall and the Jews, 1933-1948: British Immigration Policy, Jewish Refugees and the Holocaust* (Cambridge: Cambridge University Press).

Luff, D. (1999), 'Dialogue Across the Divides: Moments of Rapport and Power in Feminist Research with Anti-feminist Women', *Sociology* 33:4, 687-703.

Mahler, S. and Pessar, P. (2006), 'Gender Matters: Ethnographers Bring Gender From the Periphery Toward the Core of Migration Studies', *International Migration Review* 40:1, 27-63.

Malik, K. (1996), *The Meaning of Race* (Basingstoke: Macmillan).

Malik, S. (1996), 'Beyond "The Cinema of Duty"? The Pleasures of Hybridity: Black British Film of the 1980s and 1990s', in Higson, A. (ed.), *Dissolving Views: Key Writings on British Cinema* (London: Cassell).

McDowell, L. (2005), *Hard Labour: The Forgotten Voices of Latvian Migrant Volunteer Workers* (London: UCL Press).

Morokvasic, M. (2004), 'Settled in Mobility: Engendering Post-wall Migration in Europe', *Feminist Review* 77, 7-25.

Nazroo, J. and Karlsen, S. (2003), 'Patterns of Identity Among Ethnic Minority People: Diversity and Commonality', *Ethnic and Racial Studies* 26:5, 902-930.

Panayi, P. (1999), 'The Historiography of Immigrants and Ethnic Minorities: Britain Compared with the USA', in Bulmer, M. and Solomos, J. (eds), *Ethnic and Racial Studies Today* (London: Routledge).

Parekh, B. (2000), *The Future of Multi-ethnic Britain* (London: Profile Books).

Paul, K. (1997), *Whitewashing Britain: Race and Citizenship in the Postwar Era* (Ithaca: Cornell University Press).

Phillips, C. (ed.) (1997), *Extravagant Strangers: A Literature of Belonging* (London: Faber).

Phizacklea, A. (1999), 'Gender and Transnational Labour Migration', in Barot, R., Bradley, H. and Fenton, S. (eds), *Ethnicity, Gender and Social Change* (London: Macmillan), 29-44.

Phoenix, A. (1994), 'Practising Feminist Research: The Intersection of Gender and "Race" in the Research Process', in Maynard, M. and Purvis, J. (eds), *Researching Women's Lives from a Feminist Perspective* (London: Taylor and Francis), 49-71.

Putnam, R.D. (2007), 'E Pluribus Unum: Diversity and Community in the Twenty-first Century. The 2006 Johan Skytte Prize Lecture', *Scandinavian Political Studies* 30:2, 137-174.

Ryan, L. (2001), 'Aliens, Migrants and Maids: Public Discourses on Irish Immigration to Britain in 1937', *Immigrants and Minorities* 20:3, 25-42.

—— (2007a), 'Migrant Women, Social Networks and Motherhood: The Experiences of Irish Nurses in Britain', *Sociology* 41:2, 295-312.

—— (2007b), 'Who Do You Think You Are?: Irish Nurses Encountering Ethnicity and Constructing Identity in Britain', *Ethnic and Racial Studies* 30:3, 416-438.

Ryan, L. and Golden, A. (2006), '"Tick the Box Please": A Reflexive Approach to Doing Quantitative Social Research', *Sociology* 40:6, 1191-1200.

Schwarz, B. (1996), 'Black Metropolis, White England', in Nava, M. and O'Shea, A. (eds), *Modern Times: Reflections on a Century of English Modernity* (London: Routledge).

Schwarz, B. (2003), *West Indian Intellectuals in Britain* (Manchester: Manchester University Press).

Summerfield, P. (1998), *Reconstructing Women's Wartime Lives: Discourse and Subjectivity in Oral Histories of the Second World War* (Manchester: Manchester University Press),

Turnbull, A. (2000), 'Collaboration and Censorship in the Oral History Interview', *International Journal of Social Research Methodology* 3:1, 15-34.

Walvin, J. (1984), *Passage to Britain* (Harmondsworth: Penguin).

Webster, W. (1998), *Imagining Home: Gender 'Race' and National Identity 1945-64* (London: UCL Press).

—— (2001a), 'Interviews', in Jolly, M. (ed.), *Encyclopedia of Life Writing: Autobiographical and Biographical Forms* (London: Fitzroy Dearborn).

—— (2001b), 'Sound Recording and Life Story', in Jolly, M. (ed.), *Encyclopedia of Life Writing: Autobiographical and Biographical Forms* (London: Fitzroy Dearborn).

—— (2005), *Englishness and Empire, 1939-1965* (Oxford: Oxford University Press).

Wimmer, A. (2004), 'Does Ethnicity Matter? Everyday Group Formation in Three Swiss Immigrant Neighbourhoods', *Ethnic and Racial Studies* 27:1, 1-36.

Wolff, L. (1996), *Inventing Eastern Europe: Map of Civilisation on the Mind of the Enlightenment* (Stanford: Stanford University Press).

Zulauf, M. (2001), *Migrant Women: Professionals in the European Union* (Basingstoke: Palgrave).

Chapter 1

'The Black Peril': Race, Masculinity and Migration During the First World War

Richard Smith

The First World War gave rise to an increasingly visible black presence in Britain. Employment prospects for black seafarers improved and African and Caribbean men arrived to seek work in war industries or to volunteer for military service. The experiences of the black British population during this period provide important insights and context to the inter-war moral panics centred on relationships between black men and white women identified by Bland (2005; 2006), Joannou (2004), Kohn (1992), Schwarz (1996) and Tabili (1996). Such a study also illustrates the impact of international conflict on community relations.

Far smaller than the black population established during and after the Second World War, the black presence through the First World War[1] was, nevertheless, of fundamental symbolic significance, underlining the instability and contingency of apparently fixed categories, such as 'race' and masculinity, and disturbing the normative place of whiteness. Wartime circumstances produced contradictory depictions of the black male subject in Britain and the wider empire. As white masculine ideals were undermined by the martial performance of white men, some portrayals of black men offered hope of renewed masculine vigour. However, although faced with rising casualties, declining voluntary enlistment and concern about the physical and mental condition of recruits, the military were reluctant to consider the enlistment of black men. Instead, misrepresentations of inferior black character were re-articulated to exclude black volunteers from the front line in an attempt to restore diminishing white hegemony.

Charting how these contrasting depictions of black men impacted on the home front, this chapter offers complementary readings to economic explanations for an increase in anti-black feeling (Jenkinson 1996) and greater understanding of wartime racialized, sexual anxiety identified by Rowe (2000). The study focuses on dock communities in East London, home to a significant black population between the wars,[2] and the north-western city of Manchester, which attracted black migrants seeking employment in the munitions factories. Drawing extensively on local newspaper coverage, comparisons are invited with the experience of Irish migrants, who arrived in considerable numbers in the 1930s. As Louise Ryan (2001)

---

1   For an overview of the black presence in Britain prior to the First World War see Fryer (1984) and Walvin (1973).

2   For more background to the black community in this area see Visram (1999).

demonstrates, local newspapers were pivotal in mediating racial identities and citizenship during this era of burgeoning mass culture.

The black masculine presence came to be viewed as both threatening and alluring. Welcomed at first, as government and media endeavoured to portray an empire united in struggle, black volunteers and war-workers faced growing antipathy and were increasingly regarded as a 'black invasion' or 'black peril'. In some circumstances, the black man on British streets embodied a dandy-like figure, whose presence served to threaten and destabilize imperial categories of race and gender. Anxieties around the black presence found expression through an increasing preoccupation with miscegenation, a contemporary pseudo-scientific term for the mixing of 'racial' and ethnic groups. The popular press routinely suggested such mingling had a dissipating effect on the British nation, contributing to violent attacks on black communities.

War, Empire and White Masculinity

Captain J.C. Dunn, a medical officer with the Royal Welch Fusiliers, recounted the consequences of poverty on the physiques of many British soldiers, noting the 'astonishing number of men whose narrow and misshapen chests, and other deformities or defects, unfitted them to stay the more exacting requirements of service in the field' (1938, 245). Such concerns about the physical fitness of recruits echoed misgivings about the state of British manhood expressed during the South African War (1899-1902) (see Davin 1978) but also evident in earlier imperial crises. Writing six years after the Jamaican Morant Bay rebellion of 1865, Charles Kingsley described the black West Indian peasantry as more robust than the 'short and stunted figures' of Britain's cities (cited in Lorimer 1978, 155). Later, the eugenicist Francis Galton would express concern that white Britons were 'less shapely than many of the dark-coloured peoples whom I have seen' (Galton 1903, 168).

For eugenicists, the First World War brought great unease, claiming the fittest and compounding the effects of the declining birthrate among the middle, upper and respectable working classes. This was epitomised in an article by Reverend James Marchant of the National Council for Public Morals, attacking the growing use of birth control:

> Some modern parents, modern advocates of little and good as applied to families, are deeply impressed by their own cheap and easy reason for shirking their responsibilities to the race ... this limitation of children looks more like lack of physical stamina, of the weakening of the moral fibre, of an impoverished sense of social responsibility, of the death of the spirit of self-sacrifice, than deep-seated foresight for the quality of the children to be ... Many noble men have been sacrificed and the race is now on to breed purer and stronger families. Quantity is the key — competition will improve the quality of the race.[3]

---

3   *Umpire*, 26 November 1916, 7.

Not only the physical condition, but also the character of white masculinity was brought into question. Since the 1880s, there was growing concern that the fruits of empire and domestic comfort produced ineffectual, morally weak men damaging to the imperial effort. As the army reformer, Viscount Wolseley, argued: 'Over-cultivation is calculated to convert manliness to effeminacy; it is conducive of luxury and love of ease ... indolent habits which kill all virile energy, and when that dies, not only the greatness of the nation but its independent existence are buried in the same grave' (1888, 692). By the turn of the century, this theme had been taken up vociferously by the populist journalist Arnold White (1901).

As men returned broken and shattered from the war, the physical decline of white British masculinity was further underlined, despite efforts to present the mutilated veteran as 'more of a man' (Bourke 1996, 58). Psychological conditions displayed by thousands of soldiers, alongside a general sense of helplessness in the face of technological destruction and military discipline, also diluted the basis of white masculine superiority founded on rationality, stoicism and self-control (Showalter 1987).[4] Around 200,000 soldiers were discharged from the army on psychiatric grounds (Stone 1985, 249). Many more were treated and sent back to the front line. Scholars such as Stryker (2003) and Meyer (2004) have begun to question the emphasis laid on the prevalence of psychiatric conditions, popularly known as shell shock, deployed to evoke the 'crisis of masculinity' identified by Showalter (1987, 171) in her influential study. They suggest masculinity, rather than being undermined, was re-articulated through a culture of suffering.

All these transformations in white British masculine character had the potential to call into question explanations of imperial authority and ascendancy. The figurative presence of the enfeebled British Tommy was evident in the development of Australian identity. National narratives suggested Australian rather than the British soldiers were responsible for decisive victories, due to the robust physique and independent character at the heart of settler mythology. Such representations were sufficiently persuasive for the dissemination of counter-propaganda to be considered by the imperial authorities (Andrews 1993). It is important to underline the specific and contingent quality of these fictive representations of white British masculinity. In her chapter on the Second World War, in this volume, Inge Weber-Newth shows that, in other circumstances, the British Tommy could embody altogether more potent and appealing qualities.

Imagining the Black Male Body

As heroic images of white masculinity were eroded, representations of the black male body were deployed to revitalise masculine identities. As Frantz Fanon would later comment, 'When the whites feel they have become too mechanized, they turn to the men of color and ask them for a little human sustenance' (1986, 29) a process evident in the post-war popularity of the African American actor and singer, Paul Robeson (Dyer 2004) and more generally among European responses to black

---

4   For an excellent overview of psychiatric responses to the war see Leese (2002).

culture during the 1920s and 1930s (Archer-Shaw 2000; Sweeney 2004). The place of Robeson in popular culture reflected, in part, white desire for spiritual and bodily vigour, unspoilt by the horror of modern war. But while apparently underlining white frailty, Robeson's mediated presence exemplified the contradictory, ambiguous and restorative qualities of black masculinity in the white imagination. On the Western Front, '*le soldat noir aimable*' (friendly black soldier) served as 'society entertainer' (Horner 1919, 50) a repository for emotions otherwise denied to white soldiers expected to sustain stoicism, rationality and self-control.

Through this lens, the black subject was looked upon as a child of nature, innately spiritual and untroubled by the cares of the modern world — a source of solace and perhaps envy to white civilisations in the depth of crisis. Ironically these representations of black masculinity, predicated on physical prowess and proximity to nature, can be traced to the emergence of colonialism, plantation slavery and post-emancipation economies in the Americas (Rich 1990); features, like the war itself, of modernity, rather than the primordial. Centred on such preoccupations, suggestions of hyper-sexuality, volatility and irrationality, were never far from the surface, capable of justifying the hierarchy of empire, while simultaneously reflecting or creating white masculine anxiety.

When black soldiers of the newly-formed British West Indies Regiment (BWIR)[5] appeared at the Lord Mayor's show in November 1915, press accounts were flattering, particularly about the men's physique. The *Belfast Evening Telegraph* pictured 'sturdy West Indian troops'[6] and the *Daily News* reported the arrival of 'huge and mighty men of valour' (*Times History*, 1919, 86). Between October 1915 and March 1916, the West Indian contingents were based in the south coast town of Seaford and a local newspaper reported the 'splendid impression' they made, declaring 'Some of them are magnificently proportioned'. A Barbadian private of six feet eight inches was singled out for special attention[7] and would have towered over members of the 'bantam' battalions being formed to accommodate British recruits who did not meet the minimum height requirement of five feet three inches (J. Winter 1985). The fascination with the physique of the West Indian soldiers was also evident in an account written by Alfred Horner, padre to the six and ninth battalions of the BWIR. Horner related how at a regimental boxing match 'several officers ... were absolutely astounded at the fine figure and splendid outlines of our men ... They look sometimes a little heavy and ill-built in their heavy kit, but remove that and ... it makes all the difference' (Horner 1919, 7-8).

---

5   The British West Indies Regiment was formed in October 1915 in response to popular feeling in the West Indies. The regiment comprised twelve battalions recruited for the duration of the war only and enlisted around 15200 men from Jamaica (9977), Trinidad and Tobago (1438), Barbados (811), British Guiana (686), British Honduras (528), Grenada (441), The Bahamas (439), St. Lucia (354), St. Vincent (305) and the Leeward Islands (225). For further reading see Howe (2002) and Smith (2004).

6   *Belfast Evening Telegraph*, 14 October 1915, 6.

7   *Newhaven Chronicle*, 14 October 1915, 6.

Black Men, Employment and Citizenship

These re-imaginings of black masculinity achieved added potency as black seafarers and war workers appeared in greater numbers on the streets of London, seaports and northern industrial cities. Black men 'knocking about English streets with their tool bags'[8] were regarded, at best, as an irksome, but necessary part of the war effort. As one writer in the *Empire News* stated:

> Remember we need black labour now, and need it badly. We want every hand we can get, every ounce of muscle, every effort, and we cannot afford to quibble about the colour of the skin ... when we get down to the bed-rock of things it is only by the strength of men — actual muscular effort and the sweat of the brow — that we can win this war.[9]

The writer argued black labour should be given menial tasks in mills and factories to free white workers for military service. The 'ordinary coloured labourer' was deemed 'deficient' in the 'coolness, courage and initiative' required in the 'Firing Line'.[10]

As Wendy Webster argues in this volume, attributed martial capability played a significant role in determining whether outsiders might be embraced by the nation. Misrepresentations of martial performance therefore help to explain the ambiguous treatment of black volunteers under nationality and military laws. The British Nationality and Status of Aliens Act (1914) stated that 'Any person born within His Majesty's dominions and allegiance' was already in effect a 'natural born British subject' (33). The *Manual of Military Law* (1914), however, stated 'any negro or person of colour' was an alien. Defined as such, the army stipulated black men should not comprise more than one in fifty of enlisted men nor hold higher than non-commissioned rank. However, military law permitted a black soldier 'all the privileges of a natural-born British subject' (471) while serving. These contradictory legal circumstances meant black volunteers were accepted according to the whims or prejudices of local recruiting officers. Even men who had paid their own passages from the West Indies or who had risked the crossing as stowaways were rejected. Black men accepted were generally allocated to auxiliary units or were transferred to the British West Indies Regiment, of which the majority of battalions were deployed in labouring, rather than front-line roles (Smith 2004).

These legal inconsistencies underlined that the Mother Country could be considered as no more than a temporary and symbolic homeland. The black man's share of the fruits of victory should be enjoyed 'beneath the sunshine of his native skies'.[11] There were limited calls to reward the contribution of black war workers with unequivocal citizenship rights. Lord Henry Cavendish-Bentinck, a Tory reformer and Member of Parliament for South Nottingham, argued 'the native labourer should be treated as a citizen of the British empire, and not as a helot whose only lot in life

---

8 *Umpire*, 17 September 1916, 6.

9 *Empire News*, 12 August 1917, 2.

10 'Memorandum from Military Members of the Army Council' to Commander-in-Chief, British Armies in France, 6 February 1917, National Archives WO32/5094.

11 *Empire News*, 12 August 1917, 2.

was to work for the white man'. He should be given 'the privilege of settling down in the country where he works after his agreement is finished'.[12]

Prior to the war, there had been growing trade union antagonism towards the use of non-white labour in the shipping industry (Tabili 1994). However, from the autumn of 1916, labour movement attention shifted towards the deployment of black labour in general, particularly towards proposals to introduce black labour in the munitions factories and unskilled reserved occupations. The Triple Alliance of mine, railway and transport workers passed a resolution calling for an end to 'the sinister movement to import coloured labour into this country'. The Alliance expressed 'irrevocable opposition to any and every effort in this direction' and urged 'the whole organized Labour Movement of Great Britain to take steps immediately to stop the movement'.[13]

For some protagonists in this debate, it was not just a trade union issue regarding cheap imported labour — the manhood, and indeed the viability and honour of the entire nation was being brought into question. Tellingly, Will Thorne, MP for West Ham South and leader of the municipal workers union, argued in Parliament in November 1916, that '[i]f all whites did their duty there would be no need for blacks'.[14] It was evident from observations made in Thorne's own constituency that many men in Britain were simply not fit to do 'their duty', either because of existing poor health or because they had already been invalided from the forces. Workers at Mansfield House, a university settlement in the Canning Town district of Thorne's constituency, reported a steady stream of discharged soldiers seeking welfare support. Some had been rejected by the military before even embarking for service overseas. Others had been wounded or had suffered serious disease. If they were fit to work at all, most were only capable of light work.[15]

Black Dandies

On the home front, men who appeared to expend time and energy on personal appearance, rather than contributing to the war effort, may have had their masculinity called into question, especially if they were not in uniform. In the popular imagination, the dandy had evolved from self-defining individualist to *fin-de-siecle* decadent (Moers 1960) and now signified a shirker evading military service. Thus a 'reformed dandy' who was featured in an East London newspaper having enlisted as an army ambulance driver, could boast 'I ... cast off my tight waist overcoat, patent leather shoes and plush hat in exchange for a more up-to-date style and at last succeeded in getting a whole new suit of clothes more creditable than any I have worn.'[16] But well-groomed black men, sauntering the wartime streets in fashionable attire, were less easily derided than their white counterparts. The black dandy presented a vivid contrast to the impoverished black population examined by the Committee for

---

12 Ibid.

13 *The Times*, 22 December 1916, 5.

14 *The Times*, 3 November 1916, 12.

15 *Mansfield House Magazine*, XXIV, 7/8, July/August 1917, 80-1.

16 *Stratford Express*, 12 May 1915, 1.

Distressed Colonial and Indian Subjects in 1910. Fashionable attire had historically been deployed by black colonial subjects to signify independent industry and identity able to transcend the discipline and poverty of plantation labour (Buckridge 2004). But more significantly, as Monica Miller (2005) has shown in her study of early twentieth century Harlem, sartorial innovation was a politics of expression that laid claim to urban space and had the potential to rise above or subvert racialized categories.

A pre-war observer could mock the West Indian dandy 'to be found leaning on his walking-stick at the corners of mean streets' who 'walk[ed] with a curious strut … like a half–lame peacock' (Henderson 1903, 91). But now images of physically striking and well-dressed black men became a source of anxiety, rather than ridicule. This mood was captured by a reporter writing for the *Empire News*, who tried to mask these concerns with irony and insinuations of femininity:

> The black dandy is a familiar figure in our city streets these days … the high-price tailor has the patronage of the black men in our midst. The forty-shilling suit … is an outrage on the coloured man's taste. Mention a fine, light-grey tweed, a fashionably tinted blue at about ninety shillings, and there is a chance of business. These men are as fastidious as a woman over the cut of clothes, the shape and colour of boots and the mode in hats … No wonder the feminine eye is charmed. Ask the girl you have seen coquetting with a black dandy what she means by it. You will promptly be told he looks like a gentleman, generous, and no commoner.[17]

Cutting a distinctive figure, akin to the heroic aesthete imagined by Baudelaire (1986), the black dandy contrasted spectacularly with the increasingly jaded images of wartime British manhood. Having insisted the contribution of black migrants was vital to the war effort, another correspondent in the *Empire News* was more equivocal when he chanced upon 'a finely-built, coal-black Hercules, accompanied by his small white wife'.[18] This recasting of the relationship between black skin and physical prowess and the proximity to white women, raised the urgency, on the part of the establishment, of censuring and policing imagined black male and white female desire and behaviour.

Black Men and White Women

Total war augmented the nation as a source and object of identity as citizens were called upon to defend an imagined common way of life. At the same time, men and women were presented with opportunities to break with the very values they had been enlisted to protect (Rose 1998). Women were already subject to disproportionate attention around the pivotal national markers of family and sexuality. They came under closer scrutiny as they appeared to take advantage of the greater independence and public presence possible in the wartime economy. From the early days of the war, the alleged predisposition of women towards men in uniform had been a

---

17 2 September 1917, 4.

18 *Empire News*, 12 August 1917, 2.

concern of civil and military officials, anxious to regulate the sexual behaviour of young women and to ensure men were not distracted from performing their national duty (Woollacott 1994).

But as the war tarnished the emblems of military masculinity, the black dandy became a potential alternative object of desire. Previously women's conduct had been policed in efforts to ensure they adhered to the obligations of national service — self-control and public-spirited self-sacrifice. Now energy was directed at re-stating the race and gender codes, categories and assumptions of imperial order. Relationships between white women and black threatened to undermine the white male authority upon which these hierarchies were premised, unleashing a wave of black male and white female irrationality. White women's 'treason to their ... gift of motherhood',[19] encapsulated the worst fears of those already unsettled by racial degeneration, the alleged dysgenics of war and falling birthrates among the middle and respectable working classes, suggesting the ultimate defeat of the British nation even if victory were gained on the battlefield. As such, the 'colour problem' was essentially miscegenation, or as the *Empire News* put it, 'The war has forced the colour problem into prominence. Where we formerly saw one black in a large city we now see hundreds, where we formerly saw one white woman married to a black, or living with him, we now see scores'.[20]

The *Empire News* demanded that women of all backgrounds be called to account if they took up with black men and argued for the development of policies to discourage marriage or cohabiting between black men and white women. Black men should only be allowed to settle if they were accompanied by a spouse of their own race and lived in districts barred to white women. White women, particularly of the lower classes, were believed to be 'easily tempted by free-handed Negroes earning good money'[21] while working 'in Government controlled factories, where they are proving to be most energetic workers on tedious and laborious jobs.'[22] References to 'good money' were calculated to engender resentment on two counts. Firstly, they implied black men were in a position to buy the sexual favours of white women and were pressing them into prostitution — underscoring white-black relationships as immoral. As Tabili (1996) has shown in her study of post-First World War gender and race relations, this was a common conflation in ports with a visible black presence. Secondly, many soldiers' families were dependent on meagre army pay and separation allowances which did not compare favourably with the marginal improvement in wages on the home front (Marwick 1991; Winter, D. 1979).

Having reluctantly extolled the virtues of black manhood to sustain the illusion of an inclusive imperial war effort, the press coverage became increasingly hostile. Manchester newspapers warned of 'The Black Peril' to reiterate the 'pronounced weakness' of black men 'for associating with white women'.[23] Parents of young women were said to be 'crying out ... that conditions should be returned to

---

19 *Empire News*, 12 August 1917, 2.
20 Ibid.
21 *Empire News*, 12 August 1917, 2.
22 *Daily Dispatch*, 8 August 1917, 2.
23 *Daily Dispatch*, 8 August 1917, 3.

normal',[24] an appeal that relied upon shared imaginings of a pre-war idyll for full effect. An 'Anxious Mother' wrote to the paper urging young women not to flout expected norms while their men risked death or injury at the front: 'It makes me feel sick to see so many of our white girls walking about with black men. These girls appear to have lost all sense of shame and self-respect. If they have not the sense for themselves then the Government should step in and remove a temptation which is daily becoming more hideous.'[25]

A British officer on leave in Manchester expressed astonishment 'at the number of niggers to be seen in the Brunswick Street locality', having 'one night ... counted as many as eleven[26] between All Saints' and Nelson St. ... four of them ... with white women'. According to the report these black migrants were 'for the most part to be young and of fine physique' and the officer went on: 'If they are Britishers, as is presumed, why are they not pressed into military service? The question is one which is repeatedly asked, seeing that the military authorities are clamouring for more and more men'.[27] Another correspondent took up the suggestion that black migrants should be directed towards the front line. 'The Father of Four Girls' from the Rusholme district of the city, pleaded for the government to 'compel some of us older men to go into the munitions factories before allowing this danger to exist' and suggested 'the place for many of these young fellows is in the army'.[28] Such a resolution to the 'colour problem' was unlikely to be greeted with enthusiasm by the military authorities who, as we have seen, disparaged the fighting qualities of black men and routinely rejected them at recruiting offices.

The Salvation Army commissioned an investigation 'into the danger attendant upon this coloured invasion'[29] in Manchester, part of a war against 'sin' encompassing black men, alcohol, dancing and the 'selling of bodies'. A female social worker in the Salvation Army reported that in a

> public-house named the _, ... young girls, from 16 years upwards, are night after night consorting with and listening to the persuasions of coloured men. No notice is taken by anyone. Can no one save them? It is heartbreaking ... we step aside to avoid collision with one of a number of black and white couples dancing up and down the middle of the room.[30]

That 'no notice was taken by anyone' suggests a degree of local acceptance of the black presence. But the insinuation of the Salvationist report was clear — white men served the nation as black men arrived to beguile and corrupt their unprotected, unsupervised wives and daughters. The destabilisation of white masculine ideals during the war also suggested white men might not provide credible protection, even

---

24 Ibid.

25 Ibid.

26 Seed (2006) has some useful observations to make about the numbers of migrants reported in sensationalist press coverage during this period.

27 *Daily Dispatch*, 7 August 1917, 2.

28 *Daily Dispatch*, 8 August 1917, 3.

29 *Daily Dispatch*, 8 August 1917, 3.

30 Ibid.

when present, a fear evident when black military prisoners mutinied aboard the *S.S. Orca* en route to the West Indies in September 1919. A senior officer reported the white soldiers under his command were 'Physically ... quite incapable of dealing with coloured men'.[31]

Containing Black Masculinity

Women who succumbed to the attentions of black men and displayed evidence of pleasure and autonomy, stood accused of ignoring the demands of national service, scapegoated for the apparent shortcomings of white men. However, black men, rather than white women, were presented as more transgressive. This contrasts with the more categorical pillorying of women in occupied German from 1945, described by Inge Weber-Newth in this volume. In an imperial setting, racial considerations overrode those of gender.

Providing 'rational amusements' so black men would have 'more to do ... than to lounge at corners outside public-houses'[32] was a milder solution to the 'colour problem' advanced in the press, which simultaneously projected stereotypes of black disorder and criminality. A correspondent in the *Umpire*, who had served for many years in South Africa,[33] demanded more extreme measures: 'our governing authorities should at once take the necessary steps for the proper control of these men ... it is astonishing to find them mixing with whites, and enjoying the full privileges of the people of England'. The correspondent restated the purported threat black men presented to the integrity of white women claiming, '90 per cent of the cases of rape ... and other indecent assaults on white women [in South Africa], are committed by the Kaffir'. He proposed a rigorous system of segregation overseen by a 'Commissioner for Native Affairs'[34] to implement measures adopted by the pre-Apartheid state, including separate public transport, exclusion from public footpaths and the prohibition of alcohol. Inferior, segregated recreational and medical facilities were already provided to non-white troops and auxiliaries serving under the British in Europe and were introduced under similar pretexts (Smith 2004).

The increasingly negative press coverage of black war workers did not go unanswered. *The Daily Dispatch* reported a meeting of black men intended to publicize the adverse British media coverage in their home colonies.[35] They may have been partially successful, for the Jamaican *Daily Gleaner* reprinted extracts

---

31 Hemsley, Maj. H.W. (1919), 'Memoranda on Voyage of SS Orca', 29 September, National Archives CO318/349/60449.

32 *Empire News*, 12 August 1917, 2.

33 The writer is possibly Sir Godfrey Lagden, whose lengthy service as a colonial administrator included Commissioner for Native Affairs in the Transvaal during its Crown Colony status to 1907 and Chairman of the South African Native Affairs Commission, established in 1903.

34 *Umpire*, 17 September 1916, 6. The *Umpire* was later renamed *Empire* (April-July 1917) and *Empire News* (from July 1917).

35 *Daily Dispatch*, 9 August 1917, 6.

from a number of the papers cited above, under the headline 'Coloured Men in Motherland' (4 September 1917, 11), although with no further comment.[36]

After reports of the Salvation Army investigation, two responses from local black men were published in the *Daily Dispatch*. A veteran of the King's Liverpool Regiment, wounded in France complained, 'after sacrificing two years of my manhood for King and country ... I was awarded the sum of 8s. 3d. In the firing line I counted over 100 negroes, and unfortunately some of my best friends have gone west. I blame the people of this country for being ignorant of the coloured race'.[37] Another correspondent, 'J.M.' pointed to the hypocrisy surrounding relationships between black and white people and suggested that 'persons who are keenly watching the behaviour of the coloured men and white girls do not realise that there are white men in all the colonies ... inhabited by blacks, and that some ... are absolutely mashed on the best of our girls'.[38] More pointedly, 'J.M.' highlighted how the perceived failure of some white men to meet the demands of military masculinity had contributed to heightened levels of sexualized anxiety: 'People speak of us being young and of fine physique, and fit for military service. In our coloured race every man who is under British rule is a loyal subject. There are no conscientious objectors'.[39] The belief that black men had risked their lives in the war, while white men had evaded military duty was to persist in the post-war era.[40]

Racial Violence and the Post-war Order

Despite their contribution to the war effort, black men were increasingly subject to physical hostility as shifting masculine identities were contested on the streets. In July 1917, black seamen's lodging-houses were attacked in Canning Town, East London. Two men and three women were found guilty of assault and damage to property, while a black seaman was fined for discharging an unlicensed firearm to scare off his assailants. The local newspaper reported the incident with the headline 'Baiting Black Men: Girls Infatuation Leads to Trouble' and alleged that 'In consequence of the infatuation of white girls for black men in the district some of the inhabitants are

---

36 The ill-treatment of black men in Britain was a key factor in post-war riots in Jamaica, which on at least one occasion resulted in revenge attacks on British sailors stationed on the island (Smith 2004, 143-4).

37 *Daily Dispatch*, 9 August 1917, 6.

38 Ibid. During the attacks on black communities in 1919, when miscegenation fears reached a peak, F.E.M. Hercules, leader of the Society of Peoples of African Origin, was less circumspect when he highlighted the presence of significant 'mixed-race' populations in the Caribbean and South Africa, largely the result, he suggested, of the sexual exploitation of black women by white men (*The Times*, 19 June 1919, 8).

39 *Daily Dispatch*, 9 August 1917, 6.

40 See for example CO318/349/60449 'Petition of J.A. Thompson and 43 other seamen to Col. Bryan, Acting Governor of Jamaica 29 August 1919' (enclosed with Governor's Dispatch, 1 October 1919).

greatly incensed against the black'.[41] This explanation was shared by the authorities, as this exchange between a magistrate and a police inspector makes clear:

> In reply to the Magistrate, Inspr. Ashton said the feeling in the neighbourhood was that the blacks were getting a little too big.
>
> The Magistrate: On account of the stupid conduct of the girls in going about with them? — Yes, sir.[42]

More serious attacks against black communities occurred during demobilisation in several of seaports and cities between January and August 1919.[43] During February, rioting broke out when black men were accused of luring white women into their homes in South Shields on Tyneside.[44] Outbreaks of fighting occurred in a number of East London districts with longstanding multi-ethnic seafaring communities. In April, black seafarers were attacked in Cable Street due to 'the attention paid by coloured men to the waitresses at some of the cafes'.[45] Women working in cafes and public houses frequented by sailors were regarded as particularly vulnerable to immoral pressure and two years earlier, a visiting black seaman from the United States had been stabbed to death after allegedly insulting a waitress in nearby Brick Lane.[46] In July 1919, a black Jamaican, John Martin, on leave from the Navy, was cleared of wounding and discharging a firearm the previous May, following unrest in Limehouse sparked by the association of black men and white women.[47]

The worst violence of 1919 took place in Liverpool and Cardiff and resulted in several fatalities. In both cities, black seamen and demobilized soldiers from the British West Indies Regiment were attacked. In Liverpool, violence erupted during May and was allegedly triggered when black men and their white partners publicly boasted about the 'superior qualities'[48] of the former. In June, riots were sparked in Cardiff when a crowd attacked vehicles carrying a party of black men and white women returning from a day trip.[49] The element of racialized sexual jealousy evident in these outbreaks of violence was now linked not only to doubts around white masculine martial capability, but also to fears about the place of white men in the post-war economy. Furthermore, as was evident in the response to media hostility, martial assurance and war service gave black men the confidence to begin demanding full and equal treatment as British citizens. In the words of William Samuel, writing to the Secretary of State for the Colonies after the unrest in Limehouse: 'our blood

---

41 *Stratford Express*, 7 July 1917, 6.

42 Ibid.

43 See Fryer (1984) and Jenkinson (1981) for comprehensive details.

44 Chief Constable, South Shields to Director of Intelligence, 17 November 1919, National Archives CO/318/352/70187.

45 *Seaman*, 11 April 1919, 2.

46 *East End News*, 23 March 1917, 6.

47 *The Times*, 1 July 1919, 4.

48 'Report of Superintendent "C" Division', 16 June 1919, National Archives CO/318/352/62494.

49 Chief Constable, Cardiff City Police to Director of Intelligence, 9 October 1919, National Archives CO/318/352/62494.

was shed on the battlefield for your safety ... we do not believe in walking along the streets of civilised London and been [sic] fired at like dogs without offering any resistance.'[50]

The destabilisation of masculine and racial hierarchies was evident in court judgements delivered in the wake of further minor unrest in Canning Town during August 1919. Black seamen who had served in the war were cast in a more favourable light than white, casual labour. Of three Jamaican seamen accused of discharging firearms over the heads of an angry white crowd, one was found guilty and fined twenty shillings. Another Jamaican, Thomas Pell, a long-term resident of the area who had been assaulted in the local disturbances two years previously, was attacked in the lodging house he owned. Property and personal effects were damaged.

The black seamen were portrayed in court as victims of a white underclass, who were depicted in terms often reserved for the subject races. A white man, William Grantham, leader of the attack on the lodging house, was reported to be 'behaving like a raving lunatic'. The solicitor defending the black men painted a scene in which a number of local butchers emerged from their premises 'brandishing choppers and other implements of their trade and threatened to kill the accused'.[51] The black men were forced to fire over the heads of the hostile white crowd in self-defence. Grantham, who had been stirring up racial antagonism in the area for several weeks, was sentenced to two months hard labour for assault and criminal damage. Grantham's wife was bound over for striking a black man on his doorstep in a neighbouring street. The magistrate described the attack as entirely unprovoked. In any case, he argued, Thomas Pell 'was a British subject ... entitled to protection as much as any other of His Majesty's subjects. After the gallantry of our subject races during the war it was a very shabby thing for loafers in the docks to turn upon them'.[52]

However, despite the sympathetic attitudes towards the black population from some quarters, racial violence contributed to the partial restoration of imperial racial constraints and the denial of full citizenship to many black migrants. It has been estimated that over 1,000 and perhaps up to 2,000 black men were repatriated by the Colonial Office, ostensibly for their own safety (Jenkinson 1987). However, the true motive was evident in the official discouragement of white wives from accompanying their black husbands. After the riots in Cardiff and Liverpool, a resettlement scheme was introduced to encourage black men to return to their countries of origin. They were paid an allowance for any dependents who accompanied them. At first, white wives were excluded from the scheme and although the Colonial Office later reversed this policy, white wives were instead issued with a formal warning advising them of the harsh conditions pertaining in the colonies.[53]

---

50 William Samuel to Secretary of State for the Colonies, 29 May 1919, CO318/352/32222.

51 *Stratford Express*, 16 August 1919, 6.

52 Ibid.

53 See for example 'Case of Theophilus Savis', CO137/735.

Conclusion

This discussion of black migrants in Britain during the First World War has highlighted the inconsistent, unstable and contested nature of race and gender identities. Furthermore, the chapter has taken into account the impact of international conflict on the identity formation of black communities in Britain. During the war, idealised representations of white masculinity, which lay prior claim to qualities such as fortitude and rationality, were brought under heightened scrutiny, due to appalling levels of physical and mental trauma and uncertainties over the availability of able-bodied recruits. These circumstances made way for more positive representations of black masculinity, typified by independent character and rearticulated stereotypes of emotional expression and physical prowess. However, possession of competence and aesthetic appeal suggested black men would become increasingly attractive to white women, particularly compared to the jaded portrayals of white manhood. This resulted in a renewal of pathologizing representations of blackness in the press and, ultimately, physical attacks on black communities. These preoccupations and ensuing events ensured the black contribution to the war effort and claims to citizenship were not fully recognized.

The experiences of the war also need to be seen in broader historical perspective which sees transitions in black and white masculine identities as an ongoing process of struggle and negotiation. In the post-First World War era, these identities would increasingly be informed by shifts in the imperial balance of power. After the Second World War and the rise of colonial independence movements, Britons felt themselves to be a beleaguered island race, rather than part of a vigorous imperial nation. As white men, once more appeared to lose the capacity to act and fashion the world in their own image, with the onset of black migration, fears of miscegenation were renewed.

References

Andrews, E.M. (1993), *The Anzac Illusion: Anglo-Australian Relations During World War I* (Cambridge: Cambridge University Press).

Archer-Shaw, P. (2000), *Negrophilia: Avant-Garde Paris and Black Culture in the 1920s* (New York: Thames & Hudson).

Baudelaire, C. (1986), 'The Painter of Modern Life', in *The Painter of Modern Life and Other Essays* (New York: Da Capo Press, originally published 1863), 1-41.

Bland, L. (2005), 'White Women and Men of Colour: Miscegenation Fears in Britain after the Great War', *Gender and History* 17:1, 29-61.

—— (2006), 'British Eugenics and "Race-Crossing": A Study of an Interwar Investigation', *New Formations* 60, 66-78.

Bourke, J. (1996), *Dismembering the Male: Men's Bodies, Britain and the Great War* (London: Reaktion).

British Nationality and Status of Aliens Act (1914) (Acts of Parliament, 1914, Chapter 16) (London: HMSO).

Buckridge, S.O. (2004), *The Language of Dress: Resistance and Accommodation in Jamaica, 1750-1890* (Kingston, Jamaica: University of the West Indies Press).

Davin, A. (1978), 'Imperialism and Motherhood', *History Workshop* 5, 9-65.

Dunn, J.C. (1938), *The War the Infantry Knew, 1914-1919* (London: P.S. King and Son).

Dyer, R. (2004), *Heavenly Bodies: Film Stars and Society* (London: Routledge).

Fanon, F. (1986), *Black Skins, White Masks* (London: Pluto).

Fryer, P. (1984), *Staying Power: The History of Black People in Britain* (London: Pluto).

Galton, F. (1903), 'Our National Physique – Prospects of the British Race – Are We Degenerating?, *Daily Chronicle*, 29 July, reprinted in *Sandow's Magazine of Physical Culture*, October 1903, 168.

Henderson, J. (1906), *Jamaica* (London: Adam and Charles Black).

Horner, A.E. (1919), *From the Islands of the Sea: Glimpses of a West Indian Battalion in France* (Nassau: Guardian).

Howe, G. (2002), *Race, War and Nationalism: A Social History of West Indians in the First World War* (Kingston, Jamaica: Ian Randle).

Jenkinson, J. (1981), 'The 1919 Race Riots in Britain: A Survey', in Lotz, R. and Pegg, I. (eds), *Under the Imperial Carpet: Essays in Black History 1780-1950* (Crawley: Rabbit Press), 182-207.

—— (1987), 'Repatriation to the West Indies: A Repercussion of the 1919 Race Riots in Britain', *Inter Arts: A Journal of Third World Cultures*, Spring, 11-13.

—— (1996), 'The 1919 Riots', in Panayi, P. (ed.), *Racial Violence in Britain in the Nineteenth and Twentieth Centuries* (Leicester: Leicester University Press), 92-111.

Joannou, M. (2004), 'Nancy Cunard's English Journey', *Feminist Review* 78, 141-163.

Joseph, C.L. (1971), 'The British West Indies Regiment, 1914-1918', *Journal of Caribbean History* 2, 94-124.

Kohn, M. (1992), *Dope Girls: The Birth of the British Drug Underground* (London: Lawrence and Wishart).

Leese, P. (2002), *Shell Shock: Traumatic Neurosis and the British Soldiers of the First World War* (Basingstoke: Palgrave).

Lorimer, D.A. (1978), *Colour, Class and the Victorians: English Attitudes to the Negro in the Mid-Nineteenth Century* (Leicester: Leicester University Press).

Manual of Military Law (1914) (London: HMSO).

Marwick, A. (1991), *The Deluge: British Society and the First World War*, 2nd Edition (Basingstoke: Macmillan).

Meyer, J. (2004), '"Not Septimus Now": Wives of Disabled Veterans and Cultural Memory of the First World War in Britain', *Women's History Review* 13:1, 117-138.

Miller, M. (2005), 'The Black Dandy as Bad Modernist', in Walkowitz, R. and Mao, D. (eds), *Bad Modernisms* (Durham: Duke University Press), 179-203.

Moers, E. (1960), *The Dandy: Brummell to Beerbohm* (London: Secker & Warburg).

Report of the Committee on Distressed Colonial and Indian Subjects (Cd. 5133) (1910) (London: HMSO).

Rich, P. (1990), *Race and Empire in British Politics* (Cambridge: Cambridge University Press).

Rose, S.O. (1998), 'Sex, Citizenship, and the Nation in World War II Britain', *American Historical Review* 103:4, 1147-1176.

Rowe, M. (2000), 'Sex, "Race" and Riot in Liverpool, 1919', *Immigrants and Minorities* 19:2, 53-70.

Ryan, L. (2001), 'Aliens, Migrants and Maids: Public Discourses on Irish Immigration to Britain in 1937', *Immigrants and Minorities* 20:3, 25-42.

Schwarz, B. (1996), 'Black Metropolis, White England', in Nava, M. and O'Shea, A. (eds), *Modern Times: Reflections on a Century of English Modernity* (London: Routledge), 176-207.

Seed, J. (2006), 'Limehouse Blues: Looking for Chinatown in the London Docks, 1900-40', *History Workshop Journal* 62:1, 58-85.

Showalter, E. (1987), *The Female Malady: Women, Madness and English Culture, 1800-1980* (London: Virago).

Smith, R. (2004), *Jamaican Volunteers in the First World War: Race, Masculinity and the Development of National Consciousness* (Manchester: Manchester University Press).

Stone, M. (1985), 'Shellshock and the Psychologists', in Bynum, W.F., Porter, R. and Shepherd, M. (eds), *The Anatomy of Madness: Essays in the History of Psychiatry*, Vol. II (London: Tavistock), 242-271.

Stryker, L. (2003), 'Mental Cases: British Shellshock – Politics of Interpretation', in Braybon, G. (ed.), *Evidence, History and the Great War: Historians and the Impact of 1914-18* (Oxford: Berghahn), 154-171.

Sweeney, C. (2004), *From Fetish to Subject: Race, Modernism, and Primitivism, 1919-1935* (Westport, Conn.: Praeger Publishers).

Tabili, L. (1994), *'We Ask For British Justice': Workers and Racial Difference in Late Imperial Britain* (Ithaca: Cornell University Press).

—— (1996), 'Women "of a Very Low Type": Crossing Racial Boundaries in Imperial Britain', in Frader, L.L. and Rose, S.O. (eds), *Gender and Class in Modern Europe* (Ithaca: Cornell University Press), 165-190.

Times History of the War (1919), Vol. XIX (London: *The Times*).

Visram, R. (1999), 'Kamal A. Chunchie of the Coloured Men's Institute: The Man and the Legend', *Immigrants & Minorities* 18:1, 29-48.

Walvin, J. (1973), *Black and White: The Negro and English Society, 1555-1945* (London: Allen Lane).

White, A. (1901), *Efficiency and Empire* (London: Methuen).

Winter, D. (1979), *Death's Men: Soldiers of the Great War* (Harmondsworth: Penguin).

Winter, J.M. (1985), *The Great War and the British People* (London: Macmillan).

Wolseley, Lord (1888), 'The Negro as a Soldier', *The Fortnightly Review* 44, CCLXIV, 1 December, 689-703.

Woollacott, A. (1994), '"Khaki Fever" and its Control: Gender, Class, Age and Sexual Morality on the British Homefront in the First World War', *Journal of Contemporary History* 29:2, 325-347.

Chapter 2

Britain and the Refugees of Europe 1939-50

Wendy Webster

In February 1945, Winston Churchill, speaking in the House of Commons to cordial cheers, expressed the earnest hope that Polish forces who had fought under the British flag might, if they desired, be offered citizenship of the British Empire. 'We should think it an honour' he stated 'to have such ... faithful and valiant warriors dwelling among us as if they were men of our own blood'.[1] In a parliamentary debate in 1947, European Volunteer Workers (EVWs) were described as 'ideal immigrants', and as 'first-class people, who if let into this country would be of great benefit to our stock', whose love of freedom signalled 'the spirit and stuff of which we can make Britons' (quoted in Kay and Miles 1992, 54). Recruited to the British labour force from displaced persons camps in Germany and Austria under a government scheme in the late 1940s, the term 'European Volunteer Worker' merged into one category a group whose diversity was perhaps their most notable characteristic. Predominantly from Eastern Europe, EVWs included a range of nationalities — chiefly Polish, Ukrainian, Yugoslavian, Estonian, Latvian and Lithuanian — in a scheme which was later extended to Sudeten Germans and Austrians. Although the majority were men recruited into mining, agriculture and textiles, 21,434 women came to Britain under this scheme — mainly to work in the textile industry in Lancashire and West Yorkshire.

The language of 'blood' and 'stock' was characteristic of debates about immigrants and refugees in Britain in the late 1940s (Paul 1995). As used in these speeches, such language assigned Europeans a racial identity that was marked by approbation. Britons themselves rarely identified as European except in a racial context, and particularly a racial context in empire where 'European' served as a synonym for white. But speakers in these parliamentary debates came close to transferring such imperial identifications of Britons to the metropolis, their approbation suggested that Poles and EVWs shared a common racial identity with Britons as fellow-Europeans.

The language of 'blood' and 'stock' also informed attitudes to intermarriage. Fears of 'miscegenation', surfacing in the metropolis in the first half of the twentieth century (see Smith, this volume) were important in immigration policy after 1945. In 1949 the Royal Commission on Population reported:

---

1   *The Times*, 28 February 1945.

Immigration on a large scale into a fully established society like ours could only be welcomed without reserve if the immigrants were of good human stock and were not prevented by their religion or race from intermarrying with the host population and becoming merged in it.[2]

As the Commission made clear, their fears were about marriages that crossed racial boundaries and EVWs, although mainly wanted as a flexible and mobile workers, were seen as 'suitable immigrants' at least in part because they did not arouse such fears.

Churchill's celebration of Polish warriors suggested another shared characteristic through which Poles were defined as fellow-Europeans: martial masculinity. The identification of continental Europeans as brave resisters against Nazi Germany was very apparent in wartime when Europeans of a range of nationalities who had escaped from occupied Europe to continue the fight from Britain formed part of a wider celebration of European resisters, especially from 1942. But anti-alienism was also apparent in responses to European refugees in Britain, and expressed particularly strongly in the early stages of the war. The Fifth Column scare, beginning in 1939, intensified in 1940 when, after the fall of France, the invasion of Britain seemed imminent and some 27,000 enemy aliens were interned, many of them German Jews who had only recently escaped to Britain from Nazi persecution. During the height of the scare, all foreigners were regarded as suspicious and threatening.

What was regarded as Churchill's pledge to Poles in his 1945 speech was fulfilled in 1946-47. The formation of the Polish Resettlement Corps and the passage of the Polish Resettlement Act meant that Poles who did not want to emigrate to other countries or return to Poland could settle in Britain (see Burrell, this volume). But contradictory representations of European refugees in Britain in wartime had their counterparts in the immediate aftermath of war when anti-alienism also surfaced in responses to Poles and EVWs in Britain. In 1948 a *Daily Mirror* editorial, under the headline 'Let Them Be Displaced', portrayed EVWs as black marketeers and criminals. 'In taking in Displaced Persons wholesale', the editorial declared, 'we have had a bad deal. Too many are living or working in some dubious way. Some, no doubt are in the Black Market. They live on our rations — and live very well. They add to our discomfort and swell the crime wave. This cannot be tolerated. They must now be rounded up and sent back'.[3]

The celebration of martial masculinity shared by Britons and continental Europeans continuing the fight meant that women were generally marginalized in wartime media imagery of refugees in Britain. They remained marginalized, like women in migrant groups to Britain, in the post-war period. But as the extent of wartime displacement became apparent through the millions of people who ended the war in DP camps, media imagery of refugees on the continent often foregrounded women as symbols of the suffering of Europe under Nazi invasion and occupation and in its aftermath.

---

2   Royal Commission on Population (1949), *Report* Cmnd. 7695 (London HMSO), para. 329.

3   *Daily Mirror*, 20 July 1948.

This chapter explores the significance of European refugees in stories of British national identity told in wartime and its aftermath, especially in the media. In what contexts were refugees viewed as fellow-Europeans and in what contexts as suspicious, threatening or criminal foreigners? How was British identity defined in relation to different groups of refugees from Europe? In addressing these questions, the chapter focuses on the complex interplay of gendered and ethnic imagery in these definitions.

Warriors and Spies

In 1939 *The First Days*, a British documentary film recording the early days of the Second World War in London, showed men and women queuing to register as aliens. 'They are', the commentary stated, 'a part of London, part of its broad culture, its tolerance'.[4] The idea of London as a tolerant city was extensively developed in a film that celebrated its citizens as friendly, warm and peace-loving: part of a wider image of Britain projected during the war that emphasised British decency and tolerance. The treatment of refugees was important to this image. In wartime, when air attacks on refugees on French and Belgian roads became a common image of Nazi brutality, Britain was increasingly represented as a haven for those who fled Nazi oppression, and a British tradition of asylum for refugees frequently invoked both in wartime and its aftermath. In a radio broadcast in May 1945 — the last of the VE special programmes entitled 'London Victorious' and written by Louis MacNeice — a Frenchman describes what London means to the 'men of Europe who escape their tyrants'. He states: 'she is asylum, sanctuary'.[5]

Sonya Rose has argued that a restrained version of exemplary British masculinity characterised by quiet reticence — what she calls 'the temperate hero' — was constructed in the Second World War in opposition to 'hyper-masculine' Nazis (Rose 2003, Chapter 5). The heroes of two early wartime feature films that showed Britons aiding Europeans to escape German oppression exemplify such heroism. *Night Train to Munich* (1940) shows Gus Bennett (Rex Harrison) protecting and aiding Czechoslovakians, obscuring the pre-war history of British-Czechoslovakian relations including consent to Hitler's demand for the annexation of Czechoslovakia's border regions by the Third Reich. In *Pimpernel Smith* (1941), Professor Horatio Smith, aided by a team of Cambridge undergraduates, ostensibly goes on an archaeological dig to Germany, but is actually on a mission to get persecuted artists, intellectuals and scientists across the German border. Leslie Howard who directed the film and was cast in the role of Professor Horatio was the son of Hungarian Jewish refugees but, as Antonia Lant observes, 'could invoke, through his mere presence, the idea of a unified nation (Lant 1991, 111). In *Pimpernel Smith* he plays a quintessential Englishman, quiet and pipe-smoking, his Professorial absent-mindedness providing good cover for his enterprising and determined rescue operations. He is committed to non-violence.[6]

---

4 *The First Days* (Humphrey Jennings and Harry Watt, 1939).
5 'London Victorious', BBC radio, Home Service, 18 May 1945.
6 *Night Train to Munich* (Carol Reed, 1940); *Pimpernel Smith* (Leslie Howard, 1941).

Before September 1939 in the context of appeasement, the British Board of Film Censors withheld approval from a range of films that they considered anti-Nazi propaganda, including films that showed religious persecution in Europe — of Christians and Jews — and films that showed refugees entering Britain as a result of such persecution.[7] This policy changed immediately war was declared. *Night Train to Munich* and *Pimpernel Smith* were both explicitly anti-Nazi. They were set in the period leading up to the declaration of war when the official British policy was appeasement, and read back anti-Nazi action into this period. In the same week that *Night Train to Munich* was released, the press featured a range of stories about Europeans seeking to escape to England from the Nazis, including the Albanian and Dutch royal families.[8] In 1943, *Nations Within a Nation* — a short documentary produced for the Ministry of Information — showed nine European governments in exile in Britain and identified 1940 as a year when 'Britain ... resumed her historical role, and gave asylum to the friends of liberty whose enemies had cast them out'.[9]

This celebration of a British tradition of asylum was highly selective, for 1940 was also a year that marked a wartime high-point of anti-alienism: a moment when the story of a decent and tolerant nation came under considerable strain. Before May 1940, tribunals set up to review cases of enemy aliens exempted the vast majority from internment. But in May 1940 a policy of mass internment was introduced. Italy's entry into the war on the side of Germany in June 1940 not only swelled the numbers interned, but also prompted anti-Italian riots in a number of British cities (Colpi 1993, 172-3). Mass internment meant that those shown queuing to register in *The First Days*, or rescued from Germany by Professor Horatio in *Pimpernel Smith*, might find themselves behind barbed wire in a camp, with no knowledge of when they would be released.

The extension of internment was demanded in sections of the British press which increasingly attributed Germany's swift conquest of Europe to Nazi sympathisers — enemies within who acted as subversive agents and agitators — and rehearsed the dangers of a Fifth Column in Britain. On 24 May 1940, just before the beginning of the Dunkirk evacuation, the *Daily Mail*, urging the 'rounding up of enemy agents', demanded: 'All refugees from Austria, Germany and Czechoslovakia, men and women alike, should be drafted without delay to a remote part of the country and kept under strict supervision' (quoted in Gillman 1980, 132). The dangers were attributed particularly to Nazi sympathisers and enemy aliens, but fears of Fifth Column activity often extended to all aliens in Britain. Mass Observation reported in May 1940 that stories of aliens acting as Fifth Columnists in Holland meant that: 'the enemy in our midst is easily visualised. The always latent antagonism to the alien and foreigner began to flare up. Nearly everyone, as previous research has shown, is latently somewhat anti-Semitic and somewhat anti-alien. But ordinarily

---

7   British Board of Film Censors, Scenario Notes on *In the Steps* (16 December 1938); *Passport for a Girl* (31 May 1939); *The Fugitive Smuggler* (17 July 1939); *Pastor Hall* (17 July 1939).

8   See, for example, *Daily Mail*, 28 and 29 June 1940.

9   *Nations Within a Nation* (British Paramount News, 1943), National Archives (NA) INF 6/587.

it is not the done thing to express such sentiments publicly. The news from Holland made it the done thing all of a sudden ... ' (quoted in Rose 2003, 94).

In demanding the rounding up of 'enemy agents' the *Daily Mail* identified these with refugees from Austria, Germany and Czechoslovakia. They thus cast those who had recently fled from Nazi persecution in the unlikely role of agents of their persecutors. Officially there was some attempt to distinguish between refugees and enemy agents in preparations for internment in 1938 when the Home Office proposed separate camps for internees and refugees noting that: 'among the enemy aliens ... will be a number who have been admitted on the ground that they are refugees from their native country for racial, religious or political reasons' (quoted in Gilman 1980, 27). But these plans were never implemented and many Jewish refugees found themselves on the same trains — often bound for the Isle of Man where the largest internment camp was based — and subsequently in the same internment camps as Nazi sympathisers. Moreover, since the government began to transport internees on ships to Canada and Australia, passages were shared by ardent anti-Semites and Jews.

While enemy aliens were interned, refugees who arrived in Britain from occupied Europe were increasingly lauded as brave allies continuing the fight. Celebration of their anti-Nazi resistance formed one element of a range of tributes to the courage and heroism of brave continental Europeans which was particularly apparent in a cycle of feature films from 1942 (Chapman 1998, Chapter 12; Murphy 2000, Chapter 4). Feature films showed resistance across a very wide range of European countries — Austria, Belgium, Czechoslovakia, Denmark, France, the Netherlands, Norway, Yugoslavia — defining 'Good Europeans' by their resistance to Nazi Germany, and often portraying Britons and continental Europeans united against a common enemy, working together in relationships of mutuality, trust and cooperation. Such imagery came close to endowing Britons and continental European resisters with a common European identity. Indeed, the definition of 'good Europeans' was so routinely constructed against Germany, that it was Germans who were implicitly shown as 'not-European'.

Many wartime feature films about resistance on the continent foregrounded brave European women, often through a father-daughter pair who work closely together and sometimes masquerade as collaborators.[10] Male and female resisters in these films did not always conform to the idea of 'temperate heroism'. Andre Delange (Eric Portman) the hero of *Uncensored*, set in Belgium, finds that invading Nazi troops have used flame-throwers to burn women and children alive. He later encounters one of the perpetrators of this massacre and bayonets him to death, confessing to a Roman Catholic priest that he has 'killed a man in cold blood'. Most British wartime media productions offered unprecedented support for clandestine European resistance movements using terrorist methods — sabotage and murder — and for violent revenge against Nazi atrocities.

Films that showed European refugees and exiled armed forces continuing the fight from Britain also characterised them by a desire for revenge. The documentary

---

10 See for example *Uncensored* (Anthony Asquith, 1942); *Secret Mission* (Harold French, 1942); *Tomorrow We Live* (George King, 1942).

Diary of a Polish Airman (1942) traces the airman's wartime life before he is killed in action through his diary entries, showing how, as the Germans surround Warsaw, he continues the fight initially from France and then from Britain. One entry declares that: 'The murderers of Warsaw women and children WILL be punished'. The film suggests a shared martial masculinity between Britons and Poles of mutual respect, sacrifice and effort. The diary records that Polish airmen shot down over 200 planes and, just after the airman's arrival in Britain, that: 'Here at last we have found a real ally and real strength. The RAF is ready to meet the Germans and we Poles do our best in defeating them'. It ends with the Polish airman's death and the statement that 'others will finish this diary'.[11] A survey of 36 viewers found that 19 of them 'strongly approved' of the film, which was thought to show not only 'the courage and patriotism of Poles', but also their 'hatred for the Germans and desire for revenge'.[12]

A rare wartime portrayal of a female refugee made clear that women continuing the fight from Britain did not always conform to temperate femininity. In *The Gentle Sex* (1943), the question of violent revenge is central to the portrayal of Erna Debruski (Lilli Palmer). The film focuses on women in the Auxiliary Territorial Service (ATS), and Erna is initially introduced by the narrator (Leslie Howard) as 'this foreign-looking one whose face is so lost and yet so angry' — she is Czechoslovakian, but could stand for any refugee from occupied Europe who has experienced Nazi atrocities. Later her fellow-soldiers in the ATS learn the reasons for her anger. In a long set-piece speech Erna vehemently attacks the Nazis and is told by a fellow-soldier to 'Keep calm!' She replies:

> My country is gone, I am calm. My father was shot for fun I am calm. My younger brother was handsome but I'll never forget his face after they were done with him ... I'm calm when they take my Paul ...

At the end of the film, watching a German aeroplane shot down, Erna is elated and the final comment from the authoritative voice of Leslie Howard as narrator makes clear why: 'Sweet violent revenge — you're getting what you want Erna'.[13] Howard's final comment, however, suggests that there are other, more appropriate femininities even for women who have a tragic knowledge of the war, expressing his hope that, once the war is over, Erna will marry and find happiness by making a home for her husband and for children.

The idea that European refugees were particularly determined to resist Nazi Germany because of their first-hand experience of ill-treatment and persecution by Nazis and their fears for the safety of their families was not extended to Jews, who were rarely incorporated into imagery of refugees continuing the fight from Britain. A radio play broadcast in 1942 — *The Fingers of Private Spiegel* — told the story of a German serving in the Pioneer Corps who has secured British naturalisation before the war, after abandoning a career as a violinist in Nazi Germany because of his opposition to the Nazi regime. He is heard in flash-back objecting to Nazi

---

11 *Diary of a Polish Airman* (Concanen, 1942).

12 NA, INF 1/293, Home Intelligence Special Report No. 28, 22 August 1942.

13 *The Gentle Sex* (Leslie Howard and Maurice Elvey, 1943).

anti-Semitism: 'There is too much marching, too much shouting ... and they talk of banning the works of Jewish composers ... it's absurd. Why are we to give poor old Mendelssohn the cold shoulder?' But Private Spiegel is not identified as Jewish.[14]

In 1942, British media gave substantial publicity to German atrocities against Jews, especially through reporting a speech in Parliament by the Foreign Secretary, Anthony Eden, where he stated that the German authorities were now carrying out 'Hitler's oft repeated intention to exterminate the Jewish people in Europe'.[15] Eden's statement was followed by a one-minute silence in Parliament for the victims. But by 1943 the BBC's policy on coverage of Jews confined this mainly to occasional 'favourable notices of Jews' in news bulletins. An announcement of the death of Brigadier F. H. Kirsch on the nine o'clock news in April 1943, for example, referred to his 'distinguished career in the last war' and identified him as the 'Chairman of the Palestine Zionist Executive', while an item on a British anti-tank detachment in May 1943 noted that it was 'commanded by a Jewish officer'.[16]

The BBC's decision to confine mention of Jews to brief and occasional news items was part of a wider decision to limit discussion of Jews — including discussions of anti-Semitism as well as news of German genocide against the Jews — because of fears of stimulating anti-Semitism in Britain.[17] In April 1943 the Director General of the BBC delivered the final word: 'the present time is not opportune for dealing with the Jewish problem in our programmes'.[18] As Sonya Rose's work has shown, this did not mean that Jews became invisible in the media, for in the correspondence columns of newspapers like the *Leicester Evening Mail* and *Glasgow Herald*, letter-writers suggested that Jews were black marketing and avoiding national service. Jews were also seen as an unmanly people through associations with ostentation and cowardice (Rose 2003, 97-101). News items on the BBC, however brief and occasional, at least acknowledged the Jewish contribution to the war effort. Such letters articulated anti-Semitism mainly through the idea that Jews were reluctant and unwilling to make any contribution.

The virtual exclusion of Jews from wartime accounts of the British war effort is particularly notable because of the extensive efforts in wartime to produce inclusive imagery. Such imagery encompassed a very wide range of groups, showing unity across differences of gender and class in Britain and unity across differences of race and ethnicity in empire, while imagery of Europeans continuing the fight from Britain meant that refugees were also incorporated. The shared martial masculinity of sacrifice and effort attributed to British armed forces and European refugees and exiled armed forces did not extend to Jews whose contribution to the war effort was scarcely acknowledged in the media, and never shown on film. Through the internment policy in 1940 and the persistence of anti-Semitic items in the wartime media, Jews were portrayed as spies and shirkers, not warriors.

---

14 *The Fingers of Private Spiegel*, BBC radio broadcast, Home Service, 9 December 1942.

15 *The Times*, 18 December 1942.

16 BBC Written Archives Centre (WAC) R34/277.

17 See WAC, E188/2.

18 Memorandum from Sir Richard Maconachie, 27 April 1943, WAC, E188/2.

Suffering, Chaotic and Corrupt Europe

In *The Lost People* (1949), Captain Ridley (Dennis Price) gestures around a former theatre in Germany, now converted into a dispersal centre for refugees under British administration where Ridley is the officer in charge. The war is over, but it has made millions of Europeans into refugees. 'Something we'll never see again', Ridley tells his Sergeant (William Hartnell). 'The whole of Europe under one roof'.[19]

In the late 1940s, British imagery of suffering on the continent foregrounded women. In her autobiography, Mai Zetterling — the Swedish actress who came to Britain in 1943 — noted: 'I must have trudged, looking pathetic, through more bombed cities and rehabilitation camps than any other living actress' (Zetterling 1985, 83). Zetterling played Lili in *The Lost People*: one of the refugees who comprise the 'whole of Europe' at which Captain Ridley gestures. She also played Hildegard in *Portrait From Life* (1948): the woman in a portrait seen in a War Artists Exhibition by Major Lawrence (Guy Rolfe) which prompts his search through many DP camps to find her.[20] Hildegard is Jewish and has spent the war in Auschwitz. She has a number tattooed on her arm — a symbol of Nazi atrocities which also characterises many DPs in *The Lost People*. But, like Lili, Hildegard's wartime experience is not explored.

Christine Geraghty has demonstrated the extent to which, in 1950s British cinema, the figure of the European woman presented a particular configuration of sexuality and politics, combining sexual experience with a tragic knowledge of the war (Geraghty 2000, Chapter 6). But, in Zetterling's performances, it is Lili's and Hildegard's innocence and not their sexual experience that is associated with their wartime suffering. In *Portrait From Life*, Major Lawrence's narrative voice describes his tour through a range of camps in search of Hildegard as 'like a nightmare'. DP camps are shown teeming with desperate people and as places of black market activities, corruption, quarrelling, spying and violence. But Hildegard is set apart from this — portrayed as a child-like figure in imagery that emphasises her innocence. She is first shown in a wood outside the DP camp, and subsequent sequences show her in rural scenes outside the camp, or teaching small children in a schoolroom. The image of her innocence is reinforced when she recovers from amnesia through being reunited with childhood toys — a doll and a music box. The *Daily Express*, reviewing the film, described Hildegard as a 'touchingly lovely waif'.[21]

The Lost People develops similar imagery of a DP dispersal centre and Zetterling's character is similarly set apart from this. Lili spends much of her time on the airy and spacious roof of the theatre engaged in romance with Jan (Richard Attenborough), away from the turbulent and noisy interior. She has been raped in previous camps, but Jan asks her to marry him, and until their marriage they sleep on the roof on opposite sides of a dividing buttress. Lili is not only a victim of the Nazis, but also of divisions within the camp — at the end of the film a fellow DP, mistaking her for somebody else, murders her. The theatrical setting of the dispersal centre reinforces

---

19 *The Lost People* (Bernard Knowles 1949).
20 *Portrait From Life* (Terence Fisher 1948).
21 *Daily Express*, 17 December 1948.

the theme of star-crossed lovers, and when Lili is murdered, her body is carried by Ridley onto the stage.

In September 1945, *Picture Post*, publishing an article on 'Europe's millions of displaced persons' called it 'Report on Chaos'.[22] Refugees in DP camps were not only shown as victims of Nazi atrocities, but also as violent, desperate and threatening in a generalised image of Europe where chaos and corruption were as significant as suffering. *The Lost People* is careful to establish that the refugees in the dispersal centre are of a very wide range of European nationalities. However, they share similar characteristics regardless of nationality — prone to shouting, hysteria, fighting and sometimes violence. There is constant quarrelling and squabbling within and between different national groups, but Captain Ridley settles their disputes through his moral authority. In *The Way From Germany* (1946), a documentary made by the Crown Film Unit, refugees are shown leaving Germany — in wagons and trucks, on foot — and although they appear orderly and the narrative voice emphasises that they are making for their homes, it also refers to their 'blind aimless movement' and the way they spread chaos through the countryside which is brought under control by the military police.[23]

German refugees were increasingly included and often foregrounded in this generalised image of European suffering and chaos. The 'Save Europe Now' campaign, begun in September 1945 on the initiative of the publisher, Victor Gollancz, publicised the threat of mass starvation in Germany, and drew attention to the millions of Germans who had become refugees at the end of the war through flight from the advance of Soviet forces and expulsion from Poland and Czechoslovakia. In reporting of this crisis, there was often slippage between descriptions of conditions in Germany and Europe more generally. An editorial in the *Daily Mirror*, for example, advocating the need to solve the German refugee problem, emphasised that this was 'not out of any sympathy for the German people', highlighting this point through the headline: 'Feed the Brutes?' But it argued that: 'The longer Europe is allowed to sink into the bog, the longer it will take to raise up — the longer the occupation will have to go on'.[24] As this editorial suggests, media coverage of the German refugee crisis often made a sharp division between German refugees and those of other European nationalities, with German refugees attracting more controversy than any other group (see Weber-Newth, this volume). Appeals for aid made by Save Europe Now were highly contentious. But even those sections of the press, like the *Daily Mirror*, which thought Germans undeserving of any sympathy, increasingly acknowledged that a resolution to the crisis was necessary for the sake of Europe. Newspaper accounts referred not only to the threat of mass starvation, but also of disease, rioting and further war, urging action to avert catastrophe and prevent chaos spreading (Frank 2006).

The turn to an image of suffering Germany, however contentious the schemes for relief, meant that Germany was increasingly incorporated into the wider image of a suffering continent. Imagery of Germany and Europe also increasingly converged

---

22 *Picture Post*, 8 September 1945.
23 *The Way From Germany* (Crown Film Unit, 1946).
24 *Daily Mirror*, 5 October 1945.

in an emphasis on wartime collaboration with Germans. Collaboration had been obscured in the wartime resistance narrative, but once the war was over it became characteristic of imagery of refugees in DP camps in Europe. War criminals who masquerade as refugees are a prominent theme in *Portrait From Life* where Major Lawrence is responsible for exposing an impostor DP, who taking advantage of Hildegard's amnesia, has also masqueraded as her father, but is in fact an SS officer. In *The Lost People*, the question of wartime records constantly arises in relation to DPs and is a source of quarrelling between them, especially within national groups, as accusations and counter-accusations of collaboration pass to and fro. In contrast, the question of what Captain Ridley did during the war does not arise: it is simply assumed that he played an honourable role. These images blur wartime distinctions between enemy aliens and 'good Europeans' and set Britons apart from Europeans.

The liberation of concentration camps and war crimes trials in 1945-6 drew increasing attention to questions about wartime moral conduct — of nations as well as individuals — producing very substantial publicity for German war crimes, particularly through newsreel. Hildegard in *Portrait From Life* offers a rare example of the incorporation of Jews into post-war imagery of suffering Europe. There were generally few references in the British media to the Jewishness of victims or survivors of concentration camps. Belsen, where the majority of dead and survivors were Jewish, was a strong focus of British media coverage since it was liberated by the British. But references to Jews were rare in newspapers and newsreels, and Jewish suffering subsumed into the generalised portrayal of European suffering, which identified victims of the Nazis as people of all nationalities and religions (Reilly 1998, 77).

When Captain Ridley gestures around the dispersal centre and tells his Sergeant that the whole of Europe is under one roof there, he does not include himself in this description. *The Lost People* offers a particularly sharp opposition between continental Europeans as quarrelsome, turbulent, noisy and chaotic, and British restraint, order and self-control. Gender is also deployed to dramatise ideas about differences between Britons and continental Europeans, foregrounding women in imagery of suffering Europe while the British — as occupying forces and administrators in Germany — are male. Britain is thus positioned as masculine in relation to continental Europe in an image which emphasises benevolent paternalism. In *Portrait From Life*, it is a British officer serving in occupied Germany who acts to rescue Hildegard from the DP camp and restore her to her rightful father. In *The Lost People*, Captain Ridley bears a strong resemblance to imperial administrators as shown in interwar British films like *Sanders of the River* (1935) set in Africa.[25] Like Sanders, Ridley is constantly confronted by conflicts between people — in this case continental Europeans — who are rendered child-like through the notion that their disputes are 'squabbles'. Like Sanders, Ridley represents fairness and firmness against their squabbling, and settles their disputes single-handedly through his moral authority. As in *Sanders of the River*, a tiny number of British — in *The Lost People* only Ridley and his one trusty Sergeant — control a chaotic mass of people by virtue of this moral authority.

---

25 *Sanders of the River* (Alexander Korda, 1935).

The final sequence of *The Lost People* shows Ridley lecturing the refugees from the stage of the theatre. Their squabbles have ended in the tragedy of Lili's death. As the camera moves closer to him, ending in a close-up of his face, he tells them: 'You can live in peace and harmony if you want it badly enough. I've done all I can. I can't do any more. Nor can Lili. Now it is up to you'. British moral authority is untainted — indeed very much enhanced — by its wartime role. It is a place of stability in contrast to war-torn Europe.

Post-war Warriors and 'The Scum of Europe'

In the immediate aftermath of war, official discussions and statements about the recruitment of Poles and other refugees to the British labour market through the Polish Resettlement scheme and the EVW scheme defined these groups in terms of the white ethnicity they shared with Britons as fellow-Europeans. Such definitions were most prominent in the context of discussions of the possibilities of recruitment of colonial labour. A government working party, reporting on such possibilities in 1948, set out the range of Europeans recruited to the British labour market since the war. But of a proposal to bring in colonial labour, it recommended only a very limited and experimental scheme for women to work as hospital domestics, noting that 'a large majority of any workers brought here would be coloured, and this fact has been borne in mind throughout our discussions'.[26] Kathleen Paul suggests that a central factor in the ideas of policy makers about who should enter Britain after 1945 was 'the perceived significance of skin colour and the resultant 'races' which different skin colours were presumed to denote' (Paul 1998, 228). In the late 1940s European refugees, as well as Irish and Italian migrants, were favoured in recruitment schemes over black and Asian Commonwealth migrants.

One reason for the government's preference for Europeans was their association of black and Asian migration to Britain with miscegenation. If such migration produced fears of a collapse of boundaries between empire and metropolis, black and white, it was particularly through the breaching of internal frontiers that collapse was imagined. In contrast, the possibility that EVW men might intermarry with white British women was canvassed as a positive aspect of EVW recruitment, recommended in a parliamentary debate in 1947 in these terms:

> We are suffering from the falling birth-rate of the late 20's and 30's and have no fewer than 200,000 numerically surplus women. I believe that is an unfortunate sociological factor ... On the assumption that we should take mainly single men, there are the strongest possible reasons for having an infusion of vigorous young blood from overseas at the present time.[27]

However, when intermarriage was envisaged between European refugees and Britons, it was seen in the same gendered terms as miscegenation where the question

---

26 Report of Working Party on Employment in the UK of Surplus Colonial Labour, 1948, NA, CO 1042/192.

27 *Hansard*, 29 February 1947, Col. 758.

'Would you let your daughter marry a negro' was recurrent in the British media in the 1950s (see Webster 2005, Chapter 6). Indigenous British men's relationships with migrant and refugee women — whether black or white — prompted little attention (see Burrell, this volume).

The British government's caution about admitting colonial labour was not matched by similar caution about admitting war criminals. A Ukrainian Waffen SS division came to Britain as prisoners-of-war in 1947 and were converted into EVWs in 1948 (Cesarini 2001, Chapter 6). War criminals of a range of other nationalities also entered Britain under the EVW scheme (Cesarini 1997). In 1948 the *Daily Mirror* carried a front-page story on the 8,000 Ukrainians in Britain who had arrived in Britain in the spring of 1947 as prisoners-of-war, but had their status changed to that of EVWs. The reporter quoted what a police inspector had told him about his encounter with Ukrainians: 'Some of them, who speak a little English, after getting drunk, tell us they fought against us in the Ukrainian Division of the Wehrmacht. Some of our local boys did some fighting too, and naturally they don't like that sort of talk'.[28]

Doubts about the war records of EVWs were a consistent undercurrent in popular responses and DPs recruited to the British labour market, like those in continental DP camps, were often associated with corruption and black marketeering as well as wartime collaboration. A Committee set up by the Ministry of Labour found that popular opinion about EVWs included the view that they were Fascists who had fought for the Germans, 'some of the scum of Europe' and 'the Jews of Europe'.[29] In fact, as Tony Kushner's work has shown, the EVW recruitment scheme placed Jewish survivors in DP camps at the bottom of its desirability lists (Kushner 1998, 233). People from the Baltic States — Estonia, Latvia, Lithuania — were placed at the top, above those from the Ukraine and Poland (McDowell 2005). Such a racial hierarchy — identical to that adopted in the Australian scheme for recruiting European DPs — replicated the Nazi hierarchy (Webster 2006).

In an unprecedented move, and one that was never subsequently extended to any other group of migrants, the Ministry of Labour set up a Committee on Publicity for the Education of Popular Opinion on Foreign Workers to shape public attitudes — not only to EVWs but also other European migrants — through interventions to secure favourable coverage in the media. A Public Relations Officer was appointed to orchestrate such publicity.[30] A documentary about EVWs made by the Central Office of Information and also shown on television — *Code Name: Westward Ho!* (1949) — was one product of the Ministry of Labour's efforts.[31] It rehearsed a number of objections to EVWs through a range of British voices commenting on their arrival and employment. These hostile voices accuse EVWs of black marketeering and fighting with the Germans and call them 'the scum of Europe', but are

---

28 *Daily Mirror*, 19 July 1948.

29 NA, LAB 12/513.

30 Publicity for the Education of Popular Opinion on Foreign Workers, Minutes of Committee Meeting, 5 December 1947, NA, LAB 12/513.

31 *Code Name: Westward Ho!* (Mary Beales, 1949), shown on BBC television on 25 October 1949 and repeated on 1 September 1949; NA, INF 6/731.

countered by other British voices stating that 'really, they're like us' — a main message of the film.

Questions about war records were raised not only in the case of EVWs — a scheme which recruited many Poles to the British labour market — but also in the case of Poles involved in the Resettlement Scheme. One Trade Union official reported that 'when urging the employment of Poles he was frequently met at meetings with the statement that Poles were ex-Fascists'.[32] The Communist Party of Great Britain claimed that at least one-third of Poles in Britain had fought with the Germans and published a leaflet entitled *No British Jobs for Fascist Poles*. Anti-Catholicism — an historic thread in anti-alienism — also occasionally surfaced in reaction to Poles settling in Britain (Hanson 1995, Vol. 1, 144-206, Vol. 2, 342). There was nevertheless some support for Churchill's description of 'faithful and valiant warriors'. A letter to the *Lancashire Evening Post*, for example, noted that:

> No British soldier who has fought alongside the Polish troops in the Eighth Army in Africa, at Arnhem, Monte Casino etc. would deny that they are entitled to the same consideration as any of our own lads ... The services rendered by the 400 Polish pilots who fought in the Battle of Britain will never be forgotten by decent minded people.[33]

Questions about refugees' war records meant that martial masculinity — celebrated in wartime as a common characteristic uniting Britons and refugees who continued anti-Nazi resistance from Britain — became highly problematic. The blurring of wartime distinctions between enemy aliens and 'good Europeans' was compounded by revelations about the sufferings of Germans which, however contentious, raised the possibility that Germans might not only be the perpetrators of war crimes, but also the victims of war.

Female refugees did not raise questions about a problematic martial masculinity, and although rarely visible in the wartime media, became a little more visible in the context of post-war government concerns about popular responses to EVWs. *Code Name: Westward Ho!* uses a romantic plot to establish EVWs' settlement in Britain and increasing attachment to their new life, and to endorse the view, expressed by a female British voice: 'really they're like us, they want a home of their own'. It ends with marriage between two EVWs. *I Was A Stranger* — a BBC documentary on EVWs — was not a product of Ministry of Labour initiatives, and first conceived as a story about a Ukrainian lawyer and his wife arriving with their teenage daughter in a proposal demonstrating considerable ignorance of the EVW scheme which rarely recruited married couples and never admitted children.[34] Like *Code Name: Westward Ho!* it uses a romantic plot that leads to marriage between two EVWs, and it ends with the birth of their child.

It is perhaps significant that both these documentaries show EVWs marrying one another. EVWs did marry each other or other migrants in a variety of partnerships: Ukrainian-Polish, Polish-Irish, Ukrainian-Italian (Colpi 1991, 146). But a number of refugees also married Britons, with 4,000 British-Polish marriages recorded at

---

32 Letter on Polish labour, 8 September 1947, NA, LAB 12/513.

33 *Lancashire Evening Post*, 14 November 1946.

34 WAC, T4/25.

the end of the Second World War (Patterson 1977, 224). In 1941 Beverley Nichols, writing in the *Sunday Chronicle*, saw Polish men bringing 'new colour and romance to the North' (quoted in Rose 2003, 257), but once the war was over Polish-British marriages sometimes attracted local hostility, and the British wife of a Polish man might be told to 'go and live in Poland', while what Nichols had identified as the romance of Polish men was often given a more hostile label: 'Casanova' (Nocon 1996, 81).

Changes to the story-line of *I Was A Stranger* from the initial proposal involved a focus on a female refugee as a symbol of the sufferings of Europe. Like Hildegard in *Portrait From Life*, Wanda (Cecile Chevreau), a Ukrainian shown initially in a DP camp in Germany, has a number tattooed on her arm. The number is shown in close-up at the outset of the programme and there are frequent references to Wanda's fear of numbers, and her consciousness of the tattoo which she continuously touches. Her tragic wartime experience is not explored, but the number establishes that she is a victim of the war. Despite these changes to the story, the programme maintains the focus of the initial proposal on EVWs developing local patriotism for Rochdale. At the outset of the programme Ivan — Wanda's fellow-DP — dismisses the poster displayed in their DP camp as propaganda. It shows a man and a woman marching along an arrow pointing to a map of Britain with the slogan 'new life'. However, by the end of the programme, Ivan tells Wanda: 'our home is a place called Rochdale'. The programme heavily emphasises that the local community, initially suspicious and occasionally hostile, increasingly accepts Ivan's view of Rochdale as their home.

Stories of increasing acceptance by local communities in Britain were never told of Jews. Anti-Semitism, historically a strong thread in British anti-alienism, persisted once the war was over. There were anti-Jewish riots in a number of British cities in 1947 (Kushner 1996). In contrast to the considerable efforts made by the government to ensure that EVWs were accepted, anti-Semitism in Britain was regarded by the Foreign Office as a reason to exclude Jews from the EVW scheme in a memorandum instructing that: 'the situation in Palestine, and anti semitics (*sic*), clearly prevent the recruitment of Jews' (quoted in Kushner 1994, 235). Very few Jewish survivors of the Holocaust were admitted to Britain — most of them under a scheme allowing 'distressed foreigners' to join relatives in Britain. In this context the Foreign Secretary voiced anxieties about 'the concentration of large numbers of refugees, especially Jewish refugees, in the towns', suggesting that to avoid such concentration, young Jewish men should be encouraged to work in agriculture and Jewish women steered into hospital work.[35] Thus, in official policy-making, fellow-Europeans were defined not only against black and Asian groups in empire, but also against Jews.

---

35 NA, LAB 8/99.

Conclusion

In wartime and its aftermath there were two main contexts in which continental Europeans were officially identified in Britain as fellow-Europeans. One was the celebration of a Europe united in resistance to Nazi Germany. The other was the recruitment of a range of continental Europeans to the British labour market. In both contexts European refugees were prominent: those who escaped from occupied Europe and were shown continuing the anti-Nazi fight from Britain, and those who came to Britain under the post-war Polish Resettlement scheme and the EVW scheme.

Such identification of a range of groups as fellow-Europeans was more apparent in official discussions and statements about post-war recruitment schemes than in popular attitudes, and particularly prominent in the context of comparisons between the recruitment of European refugees to the British labour market and the recruitment of colonial labour. One important element of this comparison was official approbation of intermarriage between refugee men and British women in contrast to concerns about interracial marriages. Despite government efforts to shape opinion on European refugees through interventions in the media, popular attitudes remained diverse, and included some hostility to British females marrying refugee males, as well as the identification of refugees as Fifth Columnists, criminals and Fascists.

A martial masculinity, common to Britons and Europeans resisting Nazi Germany, was another way in which refugees were identified as fellow-Europeans and particularly characteristic of wartime imagery. But in the aftermath of war, the martial masculinity of refugees became increasingly problematic in the context of suspicions that some had fought alongside Germans, not Britons. Imagery of continental Europe, which in wartime had focussed on united resistance to Germany, increasingly developed themes not only of wartime collaboration, but also of suffering, chaos, corruption and the threat of future war. Refugees were often central to these themes which produced a view of an entire continent characterised by tragic, difficult and threatening problems with little distinction between different nations. The idea of suffering Europe foregrounded females, positioning Britain as masculine in relation to Europe: acting as a benevolent paternalist bringing order, control and aid to a continent in distress.

Jews were not identified as fellow-Europeans either by policy-makers or in the British media. Jewish refugees were not associated with determined resistance to Nazi Germany despite their flight from Nazi persecution. Instead substantial numbers were interned in 1940 as enemy aliens. In imagery of the British war effort that was otherwise inclusive, the Jewish contribution received little attention. Portrayed as spies or shirkers and as an unmanly people, Jews were excluded from the idea of martial masculinity. In official policy-making, fellow-Europeans were defined not only against black and Asian groups in empire but also against Jews, and very few Jewish Holocaust survivors admitted to Britain after 1945. The idea of suffering Europe marginalized Jewish suffering which, when mentioned, was subsumed into a wider image of European suffering.

Acknowledgement

I would like to thank the Leverhulme Trust for the award of a Leverhulme Fellowship in 2007-9 for work on Englishness and Europe 1939-73. This chapter draws on research done as part of that larger project which explores the significance of Europe to English identity in the period from Dunkirk to Britain's entry into the EEC.

References

Cesarini, D. (1997), 'Lacking in Convictions: British War Crimes Policy and National Memory of the Second World War', in Evans, M. and Lunn, K. (eds), *War and Memory in the Twentieth Century* (Oxford: Berg).

—— (2001), *Justice Delayed: How Britain Became a Refuge for Nazi War Criminals* (London: Phoenix Press).

Chapman, J. (1998), *The British at War: Cinema, State and Propaganda 1939-1945* (London: I.B. Tauris).

Colpi, T. (1991), *The Italian Factor: The Italian Community in Britain* (Edinburgh: Mainstream).

—— (1993), 'The Impact of the Second World War on the British Italian Community', in Cesarini, D. and Kushner, T. (eds), *The Internment of Aliens in Twentieth Century Britain* (London: Frank Cass).

Frank, M. (2006), 'The New Morality: Victor Gollancz, "Save Europe Now" and the German Refugee Crisis, 1945-46', *Twentieth Century British History* 17:2, 230-256.

Gillman, P. and Gillman, L. (1980), *Collar The Lot! How Britain Interned and Expelled its Wartime Refugees* (London: Quartet Books).

Geraghty, C. (2000), *British Cinema in the Fifties: Gender, Genre and the 'New Look'* (London: Routledge).

Hanson, J. (1995), *Sympathy, Antipathy, Hostility: British Attitudes to Non-Repatriable Poles and Ukrainians after the Second World War and to the Hungarian Refugees of 1956* (PhD dissertation, University of Sheffield), 2 vols.

Kay, D. and Miles, R. (1992), *Refugees or Migrant Workers? European Volunteer Workers in Britain 1946-1951* (London: Routledge).

Kushner, T. (1994), *The Holocaust and the Liberal Imagination: A Social and Cultural History* (Oxford: Blackwell).

—— (1996), 'Anti-semitism and Austerity: The August 1947 Riots in Britain', in Panayi, P. (ed.), *Racial Violence in Britain in the Nineteenth and Twentieth Centuries* (London: Leicester University Press).

—— (1998), 'Remembering to Forget: Racism and Anti-racism in Postwar Britain', in Cheyette, B. and Marcus, L. (eds), *Modernity, Culture and 'the Jew'* (Cambridge: Polity).

McDowell, L. (2005), *Hard Labour: The Forgotten Voices of Latvian Migrant Volunteer Workers* (London: UCL Press).

Murphy, R. (2000), *British Cinema and the Second World War* (London:

Continuum).

Nocon, A. (1991), 'A Reluctant Welcome?: Poles in Britain in the 1940s', *Oral History*, Spring 1996, 79-87.

Patterson, S. (1977), 'The Poles: An Exile Community in Britain', in Watson, J. (ed.), *Between Two Cultures: Migrants and Minorities in Britain* (Oxford, Blackwell).

Paul, K. (1995), 'British Subjects and British Stock: Labour's Post-War Imperialism', *Journal of British Studies* 34, 233-76.

—— (1998), 'From Subjects to Immigrants: Black Britons and National Identity, 1948-62', in Weight, R. and Beach, A. (eds), *The Right to Belong: Citizenship and National Identity in Britain, 1930-60* (London: I.B. Tauris).

Reilly, J. (1998), *Belsen: The Liberation of a Concentration Camp* (London: Routledge).

Rose, S. (2003), *Which People's War? National Identity and Citizenship in Wartime Britain 1939-1945* (Oxford: Oxford University Press).

Webster, W. (2005), *Englishness and Empire, 1939-1965* (Oxford: Oxford University Press).

—— (2006), 'Transnational Journeys and Domestic Histories', *Journal of Social History* 39:3, 651-666.

Zetterling, M. (1985), *All Those Tomorrows* (London: Jonathan Cape).

Chapter 3

Bilateral Relations: British Soldiers and German Women

Inge Weber-Newth

The Allied military occupation of Germany in 1945 enabled encounters with 'the other' at a time when international migration was limited and borders were less permeable. On a large scale it brought together people from different nations who would not otherwise have met in conditions of extreme hardship and difficulty. Inevitably, contacts between members of the Allied forces and the civilian population led to encounters between the sexes and sexual encounters. Many of these liaisons resulted in marriage and the subsequent emigration of thousands of German women, mainly to the USA, but also to France and Britain. In all, about 10,000 women followed their British fiancés or husbands to the UK between 1947 and 1950. In Germany relationships between Allied servicemen and German women officially remained a taboo. Whereas the hard-working *Trümmerfrauen* (rubble women) became a symbol of Germany's successful post-war reconstruction, women who engaged in liaisons with men from the Allied forces were considered unruly and morally reprehensible (Heineman 2005). In a climate of collective guilt and repression they were silenced. Even 50 years after their emigration German women in Britain find it difficult to talk about their memories of this period.

Research into the relationships between the occupying troops and German women and their subsequent migration is relatively recent and focuses almost exclusively on German-American relationships. This has certainly been stimulated by the large numbers of women who migrated to the USA[1] but can also be seen both as a reflection of the powerful political relationship that developed after the war and of the cultural transformation Germany underwent as part of its process of post-war reconstruction. Several authors argue that German women played an important but undervalued part in forging this political and cultural process (Goedde 2003; Höhn 2002; Willoughby 2001; Kleinschmidt 1997). In contrast, German-British liaisons have received no more than passing mentions in academic publications on the era of occupational politics. As migration to the UK did not enjoy social status (and political recognition) comparable to migration to the USA it took place rather inconspicuously, in the shadow of the much more glamorously perceived transatlantic migration. Although the occupation of Germany was based on jointly formulated aims, their application

---

1   Estimates of the number of German women who married Americans and migrated to the USA during the post war era vary considerable: Willoughby (2001): 3,500; Shukert and Scibetta (1989): 20,000; Kleinschmidt (1997) and Domentat (1998): 180,000.

varied considerably between the occupying nations. This chapter concentrates on developments in the British zone of occupation. It draws on a variety of official and non-official contemporary sources and also on interviews with 14 women carried out in the late 1990s, 50 years after their migration to the UK. The interviews, which were part of a research project that analysed various groups of German migrants who came to Britain in the post-war era (Weber-Newth and Steinert 2006; Steinert and Weber-Newth 2000), add a subjective viewpoint to the more structural/ factual account of historical events.

Acknowledging Eisenstadt's (1954, 4) observation that migration is influenced by factors and processes that occurred before the actual event of migration, this chapter begins by focusing on the historical context that provided the exceptional conditions for the development of relationships between British men and German women. It shows how these private encounters in the British occupied zone became political, causing reactions within the occupying military authorities and within sections of German society. The public representation of German women in relationships with Allied men as 'bad' — rather than victims of war — had a profound impact on women's personal lives and is reflected in the migrants' interviews. The chapter then moves on to consider aspects of life in Britain as perceived by the group of German war-bride interviewees. Experiences of the political and economic conditions under which the women lived during the post-war period varied considerably. However, as will be shown, they had to develop strong survival skills to enable them to cope in cultural climates that marginalized them, both in Britain and back in Germany.

'Keeping Them Apart': The Non-fraternisation Policy

During the Second World War, the propaganda machinery in Germany and the UK created strong images of the enemy. An intriguing example of the British government's efforts in conditioning their soldiers' thoughts and behaviour for the imminent invasion is the pocketbook *Germany* which the Political Warfare Executive, a branch of the Foreign Office and the government's propaganda unit, issued in late 1944. It was intended to prepare the soldiers for their encounter with a 'strange people in a strange country' (ibid. 5). Every serviceman received the booklet, which explained in very simple and general terms what to expect in Germany and how to behave in the 'enemy country'. They were told to anticipate destroyed cities and desperate people, but were warned not to show any sympathy, as the Germans deserved their fate for the crimes they had committed. In a passage that mixes strong views on race with an unintentional sense of humour, they were told that they would deal with a brutal people who, although 'more fleshy and less wiry' (ibid. 19), looked like them.[2] Focusing clearly on the enemy it reads: 'the deeper you dig into the German character, the more you realise how different they are from us' (ibid. 27). These cultural observations were followed by text preparing the servicemen for the non-fraternisation rule. It pointed out that the instructions they would receive in Germany

---

2   A similarly strong language was used to describe the German 'mind': unbalanced, a mixture of sentimentality and callousness. In addition Germans were seen as not good at controlling their feelings and as having a streak of hysteria (Germany 1944, 21).

would keep them totally apart from the local population. Field Marshal Montgomery, in charge of the British zone of occupation with its 23 million inhabitants, spelt out to the troops what this meant in practical terms: 'You must keep clear of Germans … You must not walk with them or shake hands or visit their homes … in short, you must not fraternise'.[3]

The rule of total separation was not initially planned to deter relationships with German women. It was mainly formulated to protect Allied troops from being infiltrated by Nazi propaganda (which also included women agents), and as a means of collectively punishing the population who were seen as solely consisting of convinced Nazis. As such the rule was an important symbol of the demarcation between victor and vanquished. Violations of the rule — the troops were warned — would be penalised and, if necessary, tried before a military court.[4] The policy was intended to remain in operation until the Germans had been fully re-educated in democracy.[5]

As the unconditional surrender on 8 May 1945 was seen by most of the German population as defeat rather than liberation, the Allied troops were not generally welcomed (Frevert 1986, 247). Hence, the military rule of separation did not pose a problem. On the contrary, during the first few weeks a harsh regime was practised and the occupiers took what they saw as their rights as a victor. Looting property and the rape of women were parts of this, and did not take place solely in the Russian zone (Meyer and Schulze 1984, 62; Shukert and Scibetta 1989, 124). There were, however, indications that the rule of non-fraternisation was not being followed strictly. The reliance of the Allied administration on German staff, and their daily contact and interaction with the population at large, made keeping to the rule difficult from the start. As time went on, and soldiers at all levels became more familiar with the country and its people, a softer and more understanding attitude inevitably developed.

It became clear that the reality of the Germans' everyday life did not match the images of an aggressive military machine that had been transmitted to the Allied troops during the war. The occupying forces dealt with a feminised population largely comprising women, children and the elderly.[6] Nearly four million men had been killed and 11.7 million were in captivity (Frevert 1986, 246). The remaining male population was either too young or too old to have been conscripted into the German army. The absence of men resulted in women bearing sole responsibility for the survival of their 'residual families' under the extremely harsh post-war conditions with shortages of necessities such as food and fuel (Thurnwald 1948).

---

3   The National Archives, FO 1060/8,74 (March 1945).

4   A confidential memorandum by Montgomery to all British officers provided a list of examples of serious cases (e.g. association with women or girls) and minor cases of fraternisation (e.g. small gifts to Germans, such as a piece of chocolate to children). The appropriate punishments ranged from trial by Court Martial to 7-14 days' pay forfeiture. FO 1060/8,74.

5   For a detailed discussion of the non-fraternisation rule see Kleinschmidt (1997), 16-82.

6   The so-called *Frauenüberschuß* (women surplus) of about 7 million meant that in some areas tow-thirds of the population was female Frevert (1986, 246).

Carrying out their daily duties, the forces saw the impact of war on the German population as chronicled in much detail by Victor Gollancz (1947) for *The Times*, *The Manchester Guardian* and *The Observer*[7] (see also Webster in this volume). They were unable to link impoverished women with Nazi cruelty or to identify them as guilty parties. Explicit warnings from the military leadership that female Nazis might intentionally seek out contact with Allied men were largely disregarded. With this softened response, the notion of Germany's collective guilt amongst the Allied forces began to fade (Kleinschmidt 1997, 42-83).

Against the background of desperate post-war poverty, which Axel Schild characterises as an extraordinary time where 'otherwise law-abiding citizens had to steal coal in order to survive' (*Der Spiegel* 2005, 48), corruption was inevitable and soon became endemic. Particularly in the cities most affected by Allied bombings, sexual contact became a frequent, perhaps *the* most frequent, form of fraternisation. In the opinion of a British officer, the non-fraternisation rule was reduced to one word only — sex.[8] For many women selling sex had become a means of survival. As one anonymous author wrote in her diary, all her 'thoughts, feelings, desires and hopes were concentrated on food' (Anonyma 2005, 11), and most women spent their energy organising just that.[9] The process was called 'sleeping for food': soldiers paid for the women's services with cigarettes[10] out of their weekly rations, which then enabled the women to obtain necessities on the black market. But sex was also traded directly for food or medicine from military allocations or army shops. Clearly, moral frameworks had very little relevance in a society that was to a large extent confronted with destruction, death and the fight of women and children for survival. The breakdown of moral and cultural norms that affected the ability to distinguish clearly between personal and public possessions can also be related to the female body as 'now everything belongs to everybody' (Anonyma 2005, 11). Both young German girls and married women got in touch with members of the occupation forces, often with the agreement of their families. Sometimes they were openly forced into prostitution: *Der Telegraf* reported how a 16-year-old girl was sent by her parents to sleep with soldiers in return for food and cigarettes (19 April 1946). A conservative estimate indicated that 10-20 per cent of the entire female German population had turned to prostitution (Shukert and Scibetta 1989, 136). The number of women who prostituted themselves could be seen as a measure of the extent of deprivation, a phenomenon that is also reflected in a comprehensive study of post-war conditions in Berlin (Thurnwald 1948). The author acknowledged that the supply of material goods by the Allied forces certainly played an important role in the survival of German families. Illustrating her findings, she drew on the example of a ten year old boy who wished to find an 'Englishman' for his mother, so that she would not need to starve any more (ibid. 197). However, despite the dramatic

---

7   The newspaper articles were re-published in book form as *In Darkest Germany* (1947).

8   Charters C.J. Imperial War Museum, Department of Documents, Con Shelf.

9   According Meehan (2001, 130) the daily ration provided for the population in Hamburg in May 1947 was 850-1,000 kcal.

10   According to a British officer 'the going rate for a *Fräulein* being twenty Players', Mayhew (2002, 19).

division of post-war society into winners and losers, haves and have-nots, not all sexual relationships between Allied men and German women were based purely on material motives. In reality the spectrum of relationships was diverse, motives not always clear-cut and the boundaries between romance, love and prostitution were blurred (ibid. 147).

In July 1945 Field Marshal Montgomery hinted indirectly at the loss of military control in his zone. In his speech he accused German girls of undermining the morale of the troops through their supposedly provocative behaviour. They 'seemed to be carrying out an organised strip-tease campaign to break down the will of the British soldiers' (*New York Times*, 22 June 1945). It soon became impossible to carry on ignoring the violations of the military ban, particularly in light of media coverage ridiculing the situation, such as 'Germany is not on its knees; it's lying down' (*Paris Presse*, 2 August 1945), accompanied by photographs of Allied-German couples enjoying the summer around the lakes in Berlin. A private letter by a British serviceman hints at the extent of cases the military authorities were faced with: 'in one district alone 19,000 officers and men are awaiting court martial and it is impossible to deal with them all'.[11] Even if these numbers were a true reflection of soldiers and officers facing military courts, it has to be noted that, of course, not all servicemen ignored the ban.

Attempts to differentiate between the levels of Allied involvement remain impressionistic and tainted by the different perspectives of the commentators. However, Willoughby (1998, 157) asserts, without providing evidence, that there seemed to be consent that the British forces generally exhibited more self-control than the US forces in obeying military rule. Reasons that might have contributed to a comparatively lower involvement of British forces with German women were linked less to national or cultural characteristics than to having directly experienced events such as the London Blitz, and fewer opportunities to meet Germans. The fact that many young US servicemen were conscious of their family connections with Europe and keen to meet German women may have contributed to this phenomenon. But the relatively liberal access of German women to American military clubs, in contrast to the British clubs which were 'out of bounds' for any German national, may also have played a role.

Finally, and perhaps also influenced by the different policy applied in the Russian zone, which encouraged good relations with the population (*The Times*, 6 July 1945), Montgomery urged Churchill to relax the rule. He explained in a letter written in July 1945 that the 20 million Germans in the British zone could not be re-educated whilst the occupiers did not talk to them and concluded: 'the Germans have had their lesson ... continuing with our present rigid rules we are merely making our task more difficult'.[12] Relaxation of the non-fraternisation rule took place gradually, allowing the occupiers as a first step to be friendly to children, then to talk to adults in public places. The last step, the total lifting of the rule, was announced in October 1945. One interviewee remembered the day as a great relief and took the opportunity to announce her engagement to 'her Ally'. However, it remained

11 Charters C.J. Imperial War Museum, Department of Documents, Con. Shelf.
12 The National Archives, FO 1030.289 (6 July 1945); PRO Premier 3/194/6 (6 July 1945).

illegal for a further year for British servicemen to live in the same house with Germans or to marry a German.

Irrespective of the official line, it is obvious that the lifting of the non-fraternisation rule took place under the pressure of common sense. After only five months of occupation, the encounters of ordinary German women and Allied servicemen had started to break down long-held stereotypical views of each group. Their, initially forbidden, private relationships had played an important role in undermining military authority so that it was no longer credible to ignore the extent of disregard for the ban. A policy, carefully planned in the distant headquarters of London, misjudged reality and had to be abandoned. However, Kleinschmidt (1997, 117) argues that global political factors may have also contributed to the abandonment of the non-fraternisation rule: he refers in particular to the first signs of the developing Cold War that necessitated a change of attitude towards the former enemy. Subsequently a more differentiated picture of the collective guilt of all Germans during the Nazi period emerged with the classification of perpetrators into different categories. The re-education of Germans had become the most important Allied strategy.

The Image of German Women

In military circles contact with German women continued to be seen as a dangerous influence on the troops. Of particular concern was the drastic rise in venereal diseases (VD) amongst the servicemen. The warnings of the *British Soldier's Pocketbook* that VD 'strikes at every fourth person between the ages of 15 and 41' (ibid. 31), and that most German women will be infected (ibid. 34), had obviously failed badly. Although Sir Jack Drummond, nutritional adviser to the government, saw the spread of VD amongst the Occupation troops as an indicator of the sheer hunger amongst the population: 'I would go so far as to say that one can be taken as the measure of the other' (cited in Meehan 2001, 115), tackling the roots of the problem was not the main goal. It was regarded as a public health issue and led to the creation of a special department in Berlin (*Zentralstelle zur Bekämpfung der Geschlechtskrankheiten*), whose aim it was to track female carriers of the disease (Timm 2005, 51). Under its aegis police raids were made on certain areas of the city, followed by forced medical examination of suspected women.[13] A poster campaign also showed a strong tendency towards blaming women as the only source of infection. The campaign appealed to the soldiers to stay away from any temptations in Germany and rather think of their 'ordered' lives after release from the Army. The posters, which polarise women into the good wives and fiancées back home in the UK and the threatening seductresses and prostitutes in Germany, are an interesting example of continued official stereotyping.

The behaviour of German women was even discussed at the National Council of Women conference in Hastings where delegates voiced their concern about the moral well-being of the young soldiers. They were concerned with the question as

---

13 The women's magazine *SIE* reported such an action in Berlin. Accordingly, 302 women and girls were medically examined in a local health centre. The result was: 11 infected women, 34 suspected of VD and 13 virgins (20 October 1946).

to whether it was responsible to send them to Germany, where they were subject to 'unprecedented moral dangers'. A delegate who had visited Germany with the *Women's Voluntary Services* explained (in the language of consumption) that German women were 'very easy meat. They were extremely attractive and knew much better than English women did how to put their sex over. They also regarded our English boys as free meal tickets' (*The Halifax Daily Courier* and *Manchester Guardian*, 14 October 1948). The construction of German women as sexually uninhibited may have derived from assumptions about sexual socialisation during the Nazi era, which was seen as permissive (Herzog 2005). It facilitated the view abroad and amongst the Allied troops that all women entered sexual relationships out of their own free will. References to the Nazi *Lebensborn* programme were used to support this opinion.[14] A lone voice in criticising the armed forces rather than the women was the Assistant Chaplain-General of the British Army of the Rhine. In a speech he made to a gathering of senior officers of the Control Commission in Berlin, he accused the troops of exploiting Germans for financial gain and material needs and to giving way to lust and easy temptation. 'Unless it pulls itself together', he warned, 'the Rhine Army as well as other Britishers, will leave a shameful heritage behind ... Germany will become a danger not as a military power but as the cesspool of Europe' (cited in Meehan 2001, 114).

The unusually high number of illegitimate children[15] born after the war whose fathers were Allied soldiers highlighted a further social problem (Domentat 1998; Shukert and Scibetta 1989). Apart from being socially stigmatised, women in such circumstances were left to deal with the practical and financial burdens of single parenthood without help. The Allied occupation authorities distanced themselves from any responsibility to the mothers of these children, rejecting all claims for support or maintenance payments. In 1947 and again in 1951, the bishops of the Church of England appealed to Westminster to examine the problem, but to no avail.[16] Reports of the National Council of the Unmarried Mother (NCUM) between 1947-1953 show that they regularly dealt with requests from German women to help them find the father of their children and to get financial support.[17] Later the NCUM was supported by the German Welfare Council in London (DSA) on the matter.[18] The unusual case of the soldier who, after his return to England, placed an advert with *Der Kurier* (4 February 1949) to search for his pregnant girlfriend made headlines in Germany. The 21 responses he received indicate the desperation of these women.

---

14 For example, on 2 July 1945, *Life* magazine published the photo of a young German woman with a baby commenting that she was unable to withstand the *Lebensborn Programm* and it was hoped that she and other German women would not now turn to American men.

15 In Berlin in 1946 the number of illegitimately born children whose fathers were Allied soldiers amounted to 95,000. The rate of abortions at the same time was 22 per cent above average (Domentat 1989, 146).

16 Church of England Record Centre (CERC) London, Church Assembly. Report of Proceedings. Autumn Session, 15 November 1951.

17 Women's Library, National Council of the Unmarried Mother (NCUM), 30th Report, May 1949-1950.

18 Deutscher Sozial Ausschuß (German Welfare Council), Annual Report, London 1956. The report mentioned that 'the men were sometimes willing to accept their responsibilities'.

The public debate about 'women without moral standards' also had its supporters amongst the German population, mainly men returning home from captivity. Humiliated as soldiers and alienated from their families, they also had to come to terms with the loss of their traditionally unquestioned superior male role and with relationships formed between the victors and German women (Heineman 1999). Apart from organised violent rape carried out by German soldiers there is also ample evidence that German soldiers had numerous relationships with women in countries which the German Army had invaded (for example, Drolshagen 2000; Bunting 1995), but they denied their women folk the same claim for sexual self-determination.[19] Double standards and entrenched attitudes to gender, which claimed a natural right for the possession of women, continued to prevail amongst many men. Hence the sight of a German woman with a foreign man sometimes prompted verbal abuse or violent attacks on the woman and hair clipping.

Fanatical Nazi-groups, which refused to accept defeat, were mainly responsible for placards seen in public places in Berlin and anti-fraternisation propaganda such as 'He [the German husband] lies in a mass grave, she in a strange bed. He fell for the fatherland, she for cigarettes' (cited in Biddiscombe 2001, 620). Such examples indicate not only wounded male pride, but also the persistence of Nazi ideology. However there were larger sections within the population who held the view that women in relationships with the former enemy were betraying their nation and disregarding the Nazis' laws of racial hygiene and purity. A war-bride reflecting on the reactions in her neighbourhood noted in her autobiography that 'there were those who cut us dead because we received an Englishman' (Baker 1990, 139). Even German church officials with their newly regained power showed little understanding for women in relationships with 'foreign' men. Harsh judgements were made on women who, in the language of a Catholic priest, 'were not ashamed to provoke foreign men like whores with their provocative dresses and manners and who would not only humiliate themselves but the whole nation' (cited [in German] in Kleinschmidt 1997, 154). Thoughts of this kind cannot have been supported by all men, and were certainly not restricted to men only, but they were widespread and deeply engrained in the psyche of many ordinary Germans. They are evidence of the inability of the post-war society at large to reflect critically on their role and involvement in the Third Reich. In contrast to those morally charged voices, the following diary entry offers a sobering view of the state of German men returning from war: 'Again and again I notice these days that my feelings and the feelings of all women towards men is changing. We feel sorry for them, they appear so wretched and powerless. The weak gender. A kind of collective disappointment is spreading under the surface amongst women. The male-dominated, glorified Nazi-world is moving — and with it the myth of manhood ... At the end of this war, next to other defeats, there is also the defeat of men as gender' (Anonyma 2005, 51).

19 Drolshagen (2000) focuses predominantly on love relationships of German soldiers in occupied France and Norway; Bunting (1995) deals with the German occupation of the Channel Islands.

Reactions, Perceptions and Motivations

An analysis of the interviews with war-brides who came to Britain suggests that the public debate of the late 1940s and the negative portrayal of women remained a burden for many decades. As has also been observed in interviews with Polish migrant women (Burrell in this volume), it was noticeable that, whilst German women talked freely about non-intimate aspects of their lives during and after the war, they were distinctly uncomfortable talking about their special relationships back in Germany. They did not initiate discussion on this topic and questions about it were only hesitantly or indirectly answered. It seemed that feelings of shame persisted even decades later. Remarks such as 'one had to be careful', 'one did not want to get a bad reputation', or a passing comment such as 'I left the car at the corner of the street, because of the neighbours', indicate that they were aware of the negative connotations of the German-Allied relationships but wanted to distance themselves from them. One woman said directly that she was not 'one of them'. To distance themselves from 'those women' who were walking the streets or formed relationships in bars and clubs, they deemed it important to emphasize that they had met their husbands at work or in work-related contexts. Women from middle-class backgrounds especially stressed their special status, having been selected to work for the occupying forces because of their previous knowledge of English and their good education. Some were keen to point out that their cross-national love developed very slowly and mainly at his, not her, initiative. They were anxious not to be associated with those 'weak and calculating' women, who had entered relationships with Allied servicemen because of material advantages. In one case a woman even said that she was initially disinterested in the attentions of the British man who later became her husband 'because I felt so sorry for our own soldiers'. However, another interviewee expressed very clearly the pride she felt in being selected as an Allied girlfriend: 'half of my class went out with an Englishman … all those who were a bit smarter'.

The particular characteristics that attracted women and men personally to each other are beyond the possibility of analysis here and will always border on the clichéd. Some interviews indicate though, perhaps not surprisingly, that it was the perceived difference that attracted the women to Allied men. The following words of a war-bride convey particularly well her fascination with the seemingly exotic occupier who embodied a whole new world: 'And on these paths which were freed from the rubble by women I saw these creatures for the first time, I looked at them as if they were coming from a different star. They were Allied soldiers and officers, smartly dressed, well groomed, they smelled nicely'. It was the obvious contrast with the women's personal circumstances that made these men attractive. The healthy-looking young Allied serviceman represented a masculinity that the defeated and demoralised German soldier in poor physical condition did not have. As Richard Smith notes in this volume, British soldiers were not always depicted in such positive and healthy terms, suggesting how constructions of masculine vary in different contexts of war. Apart from a fit body in a clean uniform, these British soldiers were perceived by the war-brides as having a polite and confident behaviour and the ability to provide materially ('As he was allowed to shoot, he brought us game for dinner', or, 'I occasionally found a chocolate bar in my drawer'). This played an important part in the construct of the Allied man who was able to offer a brighter future. On the other hand, a group of new British husbands, interviewed by the British magazine *Illustrated*, stressed that they perceived their German wives as 'so simple, natural, unsophisticated, docile ... and they don't use any make-up' (5 July 1947).

The interviews also provide insights into more complex reasons that contributed to the women's decisions to migrate. A picture emerges that is closely linked to past experiences and a clear vision for their future. The wish to marry young and to have a family and children was as strong as the fear of 'remaining a spinster'. War losses meant that statistically only one in three women was likely to have a German husband. The comment 'I didn't want to be hungry any more' hints at the more pragmatic reasons for marriage to a British man. However, in most interviews the loss of home and belongings, the break-up of families and the dispersal of those who had survived were talked about at length. Seven of the fourteen women interviewed originated from the former Eastern German territories that were ceded to Poland and the Soviet Union and, as refugees they were unable to return to their former homes. They also felt alien in West Germany and were barely tolerated by the local population with whom they were competing for scarce resources. The prospect of starting a new life in Britain, for these displaced women in particular, might not have been a difficult choice. 'We had lost everything, where should I have stayed?' was the answer of a war-bride whose strong wish was to build a new home, to settle down and to belong again.

Immigration and Reception

Couples wanting to get married had to wait until August 1946 at which time marriage between a German and a British national became officially permitted. Yet it was not an easy process, as Germans were still classified as 'enemy nationals' and regarded with suspicion. The British government applied strict controls on all marriages with enemy nationals, and adherence to these conditions was carefully observed by the authorities. German women had to pass a medical examination, fill in numerous forms and submit several documents — a process one interviewee described as the 'paper war'. To prevent hasty decisions, the bridegroom had to observe a six-month delay, during which he had to travel back to the UK to discuss his plans with his family (*Manchester Guardian*, 31 March 1947; Marholz 1994, 67). If the German bride wanted to accompany him — which was recommended in order to form a picture of her future home — she had to apply for a short term 'exit visa'. As they were enemy nationals, all cases were individually checked by the Home Office (*British Zone Review*, 3 August 1946). The process was equally onerous when a woman wanted to follow her fiancé after he had finished his service in Germany. Couples who tried to circumvent the process by smuggling the partner into the UK were punished (*Manchester Guardian*, 26 November 1946). The authorities suspected that cunning German women would misuse the marriage as a way of entering Britain and obtaining British citizenship. A former British officer who examined the applications of women for emigration stated in his interview that 'they just wanted to get away from Germany'. Undoubtedly, some women chose this path to gain entry to Britain, perhaps less motivated by feelings of love than by the wish to leave Germany and to find work independently. It should be noted that at this time the British government was actively involved in the recruitment of foreign labour for selected sectors in the undermanned industries and tried to benefit from this urge to leave Germany. Special work schemes offered young German women a limited stay in Britain if they worked in these undermanned sectors (Weber-Newth and Steinert 2006). According to a 'British official' cited in the *Bolton Evening News*, most of the German girls saw the work schemes as an alternative path of entry and would sign a contract 'with half an eye for a British husband' (15 April 1950). The article also mentioned that 'many girls were of a much better social standing than their profession would suggest', which indicated that they were prepared to accept a low social position temporarily for a possible later socio-economic gain.

Even though these war-brides were the subject of public discourse and Allied political decisions, their arrival in Britain did not arouse much attention. The arrival of other migrant groups from former Commonwealth countries and workers from Eastern Europe at the same time attracted much more reaction in the media. An exception is an extended article on the arrival of a group of German war-brides in the Tilbury Docks, written in a very sympathetic tone: 'The women I saw were mostly of the poorer classes, women who had borne the brunt of the heavy bombing of industrial cities during the war and the starvation after it ... Most of them were very young, ... some with small children ... and all of them poorly dressed in a kind of finery, their faces drawn with anxious excitement ... ' (*Manchester Guardian*, 20 October 1947). The article closes with the comment that not all women were met by their fiancés and subsequently had to return. However, some women returned voluntarily, a fact mentioned by the press a few times.[20] According to a former British officer, many war-brides returned within the first few years because they had married men with whom they were incompatible.

The few written reports from visits to Britain by German clergymen who were involved with the pastoral care of Germans abroad suggest that many cross-cultural couples experienced problems. A Caritas report in 1949 stated that they did not have accurate numbers for the German wives of British servicemen 'but many marriages are not alright'.[21] Two Protestant pastors reported even more negatively that 'only a small part of the war-brides were happy' (ibid.) or 'a particular tragedy are the marriages formed in England'.[22] Some 50 years on, the interviews neither confirm these assessments nor do they refute them. On the whole they give the impression that the women interviewed in this sample were quite content with the way their lives had turned out in Britain. However, difficulties during the first few years of their acculturation were mentioned frequently. Several women remembered their initial

---

20 'Fräulein Ilse says Duty at Home', *Daily Express*, 20 January 1948; 'German Girl Returns with Fiancé', *Bolton Evening News*, 21 January 1948; 'A Fräulein came to England', *Daily Express*, 30 March 1948.

21 DCV 372.16. Übersicht über das Problem der seelsorgerischen deutscher Zivilarbeiter, Mai 1949.

22 KFZ Büttner E.IV.11b, Pastor Dumont, Bradford, an Böhler, 9 November 1953.

surprise at the social conditions in Britain and none had anticipated the extent of the post-war austerity with food rationing and severe shortages in accommodation. An example was the young middle-class woman from Berlin who shared with her husband and his family a run-down flat without running water in London's East End, which she described as the 'most primitive environment'. After two years of marriage, she found herself a 20-year-old divorcee with a child, both British nationals and unable to return to Germany. Reflecting on that time she said critically that she was too young and too inexperienced to have been able to resist the courting of her boyfriend or to realistically assess the nature of her future life in Britain. This story is perhaps extreme but not exceptional — most women had expected an improvement in their socio-economic conditions. They hinted how hard it was for them to accept that the reality of post-war Britain did not correspond with the idealised image they had formed through their relationship with the victorious Allies back in Germany. One interviewee summarised the image she and others naively held of England at the time: 'We thought they would all live like lords'.

The interviews also provide insight into how migration impacted on these German-British liaisons at an inter-personal level, and how both partners had to negotiate their new positions in the UK. A few women indicated their initial disappointment when they realised that they had married into a different social class and their privileged status as Allied girl-friend did not continue: 'There are differences you only notice later ... that you marry into the family and the whole circle'. Subsequently, some women not only commented on their loss in social standing, but also on their husband's lack of ambition. Perceiving themselves as socially mobile and highly motivated, they had expected their husbands to actively support them in breaking out of the class confinements and to better themselves. Instead many husbands had to come to terms with their own return from abroad and their changing roles. Their re-orientation into civilian life after years in the Army was not always a smooth process and sometimes presented major challenges as the structured support provided by the Army had to be replaced with their own initiative to find new employment. Some men were not trained or qualified for any civilian jobs and had to be content with menial work as caretakers, factory workers or salesmen. Compared with their previously 'powerful' positions as victorious occupiers this meant a loss in status and could be seen as male defeat. Subsequently, several couples were forced to re-negotiate their gender roles. Their husbands' unemployment, poorly paid jobs and longstanding illnesses required a number of women to abandon the traditional family structure and take up paid work. However, in retrospect they felt empowered and proud of themselves as: 'it then all depended on me, I earned much more than my husband'. Another woman who became the sole provider for the family said proudly: 'I had to take care of my three men, my young sons and my husband who was unemployed'. Work was taken up in different domains according to previous training and qualifications: as cleaners or shop assistants, or in contexts where women could use their language competence such as in the London Press Exchange, the German Embassy or for multinational companies.

While individual effort and initiative overcame many obstacles, it was more difficult to influence the larger cultural context of society. The women's reception during the late 1940s took place in a climate that was still heavily influenced by the experiences of the war and the revelation of war crimes committed by Germans. Large segments of British society held negative feelings towards Germans. The results of a Mass Observation study[23] carried out in 1946 show that about half of the respondents had hostile feelings towards Germans and absolutely no sympathy for them. This attitude was clearly reflected in the media, where portrayals of the German as the enemy and images of the Germans as Nazis persisted for many years after the war (see also Webster, this volume). The women were painfully aware of the anti-German climate — they referred to examples in the media, TV films or headlines in newspapers, where Germans were depicted in a negative light. A few also mentioned specific episodes they experienced in their neighbourhoods, such as a front door daubed with a swastika. Such incidents contributed to their feelings of not being welcome as a German. The extent of harassment they felt seemed to depend also on the ethnic and social composition of their neighbourhoods — women who lived in ethnically diverse areas or in parts which were described as 'Irish' or 'Greek' felt ethnically much more accepted than those in traditionally 'English' areas (within London).[24] But there were also a couple of women who emphasised how welcome they felt at the time as a 'foreigner' in northern England and Scotland.

In these circumstances the women considered it necessary to mask their ethnicity and to lead unassuming and inconspicuous lives. In the course of their interviews they all mentioned that adaptation to British cultural norms and appearing 'British' to the outside world became important for them. They used strategies such as keeping their voice down in public, trying to disguise their accents and giving their children English names because 'everything German was being avoided in those days and we didn't want to cause any trouble'. According to one interviewee, not to appear German even led to a 'renouncing' of nationality. As her hometown became Polish after the war, she simply claimed to be Polish. A readiness to adapt and to be flexible were the skills women rated as most important for integration. If, despite this, they found themselves the subject of aggression, some women could rely on their husbands' protection, as in the case of the husband who reproved someone in a pub who held his young German wife responsible for the leg he had lost in the war. Despite the general feeling of not being acknowledged as 'German' by British society, a couple of women paradoxically believed that their particular 'ethnic traits' had helped them gain a privileged position at work: 'He soon asked me to keep his books, as he appreciated German accuracy (...) later I became the key-holder of the pharmacy'. In a similar vein, another woman assumed that she got a job because of her 'German reliability'. As Louise Ryan also argues (in this volume), on an individual level these stereotypical beliefs seemed to boost the women's self-worth and confidence.

In retrospect most women saw the time between their arrival and the end of the 1960s as the most difficult years of their acculturation. Today, they say, the image

---

23 IWM Harvester Mass-Observation Archive, February 1948, File report (No. 2565): Attitudes to the German People: A review of attitude changes among British public during the war.

24 German communities which had been extensive prior to the First World War no longer existed after the Second (see Panayi 1996).

of the ugly German who threatens Britain and whom the British cannot trust has disappeared. The fact that these migrants' settlement was geographically dispersed helped them to establish their lives in relative ethnic anonymity. One woman still remains cautious though: 'when travelling by train I always take something to read in English, not in German, and I heard that others do the same (…) we don't want the anti-German sentiments to reappear.'

Not only the first generation of migrants, but also their children were affected by the post-war anti-German climate. Re-enacting the war against Germany on the streets and in playgrounds as well as reading war comics was part of the culture in which these children grew up. To a greater extent than their mothers, children were directly confronted with anti-German remarks at school or in neighbourhoods when playing with their British friends. An interviewee remembered that her son was particularly upset at always having to play the 'baddy' in the game 'Brits and Germans'. Another war-bride had kept a Christmas card given to her son by a group of fellow class-mates that was covered in swastikas and said that he should be sent to a concentration camp. Her son later left Britain to live in Germany. Other children reacted by refusing to speak German in the presence of a British person.

Apart from narratives about their families, the impact of war can be singled out as the topic women were most concerned about in their interviews. They reflected extensively on their experiences during the war and the hardship they endured during the immediate post-war period. Although they had different stories to tell, the main theme was how they had to cope with loss, privation and suffering. The flight from East Prussia towards the West by horse and cart in freezing temperatures was vividly remembered, as were the Allied bombings of Dresden or Hamburg. They lamented that, as Germans, they were exclusively depicted as the culprits of war and never seen as victims. With the exception of those British forces who were amongst the first to arrive in Germany at the end of the war, British people had little knowledge about the state of Germany at that time and little understanding of the suffering of Germans. War-brides from the former Eastern territories felt particularly bitter that their circumstances and fate were not given a voice, whereas considerable empathy was expressed publicly for refugees of other nationalities (see also the discussion of German victimhood by Webster in this volume).

As mentioned above, the conditions of their migration as wives of British husbands led to a dispersed settlement that allowed relatively little contact with other Germans. Whilst this undoubtedly accelerated their integration into British society, for many years the war-brides missed the opportunity of turning to an ethnic community for practical help and emotional comfort. The only form of community life (on a very small scale) was offered by the few German Catholic and Protestant churches that existed in some areas in Britain. Both the absence of German ethnic communities and the anti-German hostility of the post-war years contributed to the relatively quiet and unassuming lives these German women had to live in Britain. In contrast to their husbands, who would spend time with male friends in pubs or at sporting events, the women turned their energy to the domestic sphere where they were able to express their ethnicity freely. German-ness was recreated in homes where the children were spoken and sung to in German. No effort was spared to obtain the correct ingredients for a German meal on special occasions or to have the appropriate accessories to celebrate festivities such as Easter or Christmas à la German. Homes, particularly living rooms, were often furnished and decorated with enormous effort in traditional German style and proudly presented to the interviewer. This, however, was sometimes accompanied with comments on their superiority as home-makers and mothers in comparison to British women, such as 'English women waste a lot' or 'we always dressed smarter'. It seems that the recreation of a private 'German' space (even referred to as 'my refuge') and the importance attached to it, served as compensation for the denial of being acknowledged as 'German' in the public sphere. It can also be argued that comments on the women's superiority in the domestic context were an assertion of their ethnicity in an otherwise relatively powerless position.

It is not surprising that, despite having lived in Britain nearly all their lives, these war-brides described themselves as 'mostly' German, even if they held British passports. Their self-declared German-ness was mainly connected with sentiments and memories of their original *Heimat*, where they had spent their childhood and youth. Their view of the Federal Republic was more ambivalent: they admired Germany's economic and social standing and proudly identified with its achievements after the war. On the other hand, some realised that they did not belong there any more. 'Their' Germany had become too modern and too 'Americanised' — they preferred everyday-life in Britain where it was generally calmer and less competitive. One woman expressed her ambiguous identity: 'I feel German when in Britain but British when in Germany'. Despite having faced severe problems as Germans initially, most of the war-brides in the study did not consider returning. Having made their homes and raised their families in Britain they feel they belong here.

Conclusion

The migration of thousands of German brides to the UK in the early post-war period was a consequence of the gendered actions of war and subsequent occupation, and a war-bride's entry into Britain was determined by her husband's status. Traditionally, the structure of marriage migration is seen as 'secondary migration' (Han 2003, 26), a concept that implies notions of dependency and inactivity. However, the lives and actions of the women discussed in this chapter question such one-dimensional assumptions. The present analysis has shown that to negotiate the complicated migration process these women showed strong agency and courage.

Despite the influence of war propaganda, German women and British men overcame notions of the enemy and national stereotyping to engage in personal friendships and intimate relationships. The gendered nature of their encounters, together with the harsh economic situation that existed in the immediate aftermath of the war, provided the background for these relationships. In accepting the 'otherness' of their British partners, German women left Nazi racial ideology behind — and for their part, the men risked court martial for breaking military rules. Within a very short period of time the large number of relationships challenged military power and contributed to the abandonment of the non-fraternization rule.

The women paid a high price for their actions. Whilst both men and women 'benefited' from these relationships (in different ways), German women endured being treated as morally degraded and negatively stereotyped as prostitutes and seductresses. Their moral stigmatization by unreconstructed fellow Germans, the Allied military authorities and those who had little insight into other people's living conditions permanently marked their lives. However, their actions in finding ways to help themselves and their families during extreme material shortages demonstrated strong survival skills, as did their determination to start a new life in a new country.

Overcoming restrictive British immigration laws, the women arrived in a country where memories of the war were raw and would endure for many decades. The existing anti-German climate made them feel unwelcome and they needed to develop strategies to avoid drawing attention to their ethnicity. These strategies included cautious behaviour in public, even to the extent of masking their nationality. In the absence of German ethnic communities to turn to for support and comfort they led private lives in which domesticity was cultivated and in this area their ethnicity found its expression. Their often idealised views of Britain as a country offering the opportunity for a brighter future did not correspond to the reality of life in the post-war conditions in Britain and demanded their adjustment to new situations. The destabilising effects of their husbands' return to Britain as civilians and the inevitable effects this had on the dynamic of their marriages exacerbated the situation. The women's initial expectations of devoting their lives solely to motherhood and family life in secure economic situations were challenged, and apparently fixed gender roles had to be re-negotiated. Women in this study adapted to the circumstances with which they were confronted and took on extensive responsibility when necessary. They learned English to a high level, worked hard to bring up their children, often bilingually, and many established themselves in good jobs making use of their language skills. They never severed their links with Germany and, as early post-war migrants, paved the way for intercultural encounters at a time when these were far from routine. This group of German women can hardly be described as inactive and dependent 'secondary' migrants. They deserve visibility in their own right and respect for their achievements, which were different but no less important than those of their compatriots who remained at home.

References

Anonyma (2005), *Eine Frau in Berlin, Tagebuchaufzeichnungen vom 20. April-22. Juni 1945* (Frankfurt/M: Eichborn Verlag).

Baker, G.E. (1990), *Shadow of War* (Oxford: Lion Publishing).

Biddiscombe, P. (2001), 'Dangerous Liaisons: The Anti-Fraternisation Movement in the U.S. Occupation Zones of Germany and Austria, 1945-1948', *Journal of Social History* 34:3, 611-647.

Brauerhoch, A. (2005), *Fräuleins und GIs* (Frankfurt/M: Stroemfeld Verlag).

Bunting, M. (1995), *The Model Occupation, The Channel Islands Under German Rule, 1940-1945* (London: Harper Collins).

Domentat, T. (1998), *'Hallo Fräulein', Deutsche Frauen und Amerikanische Soldaten* (Berlin: Aufbau Verlag).

Drolshagen, E.B. (2000), *Nicht ungeschoren davongekommen. Die Geliebten der Wehrmachtsoldaten im besetzten Europa* (München: Econ, Ullstein, List Verlag).

Eisenstadt, S.N. (1954), *The Absorption of Immigrants: A Comparative Study* (London: Routledge and Kegan).

Frevert, U. (1986), *Frauen-Geschichte Zwischen Bürgerlicher Verbesserung und Neuer Weiblichkeit* (Frankfurt/M: Suhrkamp Verlag).

Goedde, P. (2003), *GIs and Germans: Culture, Gender and Foreign Relations, 1945-1949* (New Haven and London: Yale University Press).

Gollancz, V. (1947), *In Darkest Germany* (London: Victor Gollancz).

Han, P. (2003), *Frauen und Migration* (Stuttgart: Lucius & Lucius).

Heineman, E.D. (1999), *What Difference Does a Husband Make? Women and Marital Status in Nazi and Postwar Germany* (Berkeley: University of California Press).

—— (2005), 'Trümmerfrauen, Amiliebchen und die nationale Identität der Bundesrepublik' in Allied Museum (ed.), *Es begann mit einem Kuss, Deutsch-Alliierte Beziehungen nach 1945* (Berlin: Jaron Verlag), 44-49.

Herzog, D. (2005), *Sex after Fascism: Memory and Morality in Twentieth-Century Germany* (Princeton and Oxford: Berghahn Books).

Höhn, M. (2002), *GIs and Fräuleins: The German-American Encounter in 1950s West Germany* (Chapel Hill: University of North Carolina Press).

Kleinschmidt, J. (1997), *Do Not Fraternise! Die schwierigen Anfänge deutsch-amerikanischer Freundschaft, 1944-1949* (Trier: Wissenschaftlicher Verlag).

Macckinnon, M. (1987), *The Naked Years, Growing up in Nazi Germany* (London: Chatto & Windus).

Marholz, E. (1994), *How Many Miles to Harrogate* (Kent: Carey Publishing).

Mayhew, M. (2002), *The Pathfinder* (London: Transworld Publishers).

Meehan, P. (2001), *A Strange Enemy People: Germans Under the British 1945-50* (London: Peter Owen).

Meyer, S. and Schulze, E. (1984), *Wie wir das alles geschafft haben, Alleinstehende Frauen berichten über ihr Leben nach 1945* (München: C.H. Beck'sche Verlagsbuchhandlung).

Panayi, P. (1996), *Germans in Britain Since 1500* (London and Rio Grande: Hambledon Press).

Shukert, E. and Scibetta, B. (1989), *War Brides of World War II* (Harmondsworth: Penguin).

Steinert, J.D. and Weber-Newth, I. (2000), *Labour and Love, Deutsche in Großbritannien nach dem Zweiten Weltkrieg* (Osnabrück: Sekolo).

—— (eds) (2003), *European Immigrants in Britain 1933-1950* (München: K.G. Saur).

Thurnwald, H. (1948), *Gegenwartsprobleme Berliner Familien, Eine soziologische Untersuchung an 498 Familien* (Berlin: Weidmannsche Verlagsbuchhandlung).

Timm, A.F. (2005), 'Denk Darüber nach! – Soldaten, Veronikas und Geschlechtskrankheiten im besetzten Berlin', *Es begann mit einem Kuss, Deutsch-*

Alliierte Beziehungen nach 1945, Allied Museum (ed.) (Berlin: Jaron Verlag) 50-56.

Weber-Newth, I. and Steinert, J.D. (2006), *German Migrants in Post-war Britain, An Enemy Embrace* (Abingdon: Routledge).

Wendel, E. (1994), *Hausfrau at War, 1939-45, A German Women's Account of Life in Hitler's Reich* (Durham: The Pentland Press).

Willoughby, J. (2001), *Remaking the Conquering Heroes, The Social and Geopolitical Impact of the Post-War American Occupation of Germany* (New York and Basingstoke: Palgrave).

Chapter 4

Male and Female Polishness in Post-war Leicester: Gender and its Intersections in a Refugee Community

Kathy Burrell

This chapter investigates the impact of wartime forced migration on gendered experiences among a Polish refugee community in post-war Britain. While the gendered nature of migration generally is now widely acknowledged (Donato et al. 2006; Buijs 1993), and indeed the gendered nature of all social practices (Butler 1990; Indira 1999; Pessar 2006), forced migration is arguably an even more transformative experience for migrants than economic migration, and so brings more potential for gendered change. Men and women often experience war, trauma and exile differently and have varying difficulties settling afterwards. Separate research into Vietnamese, Chilean and Palestinian forced migration, for example, suggests that male refugees suffer more acutely from a loss of prestige and a narrowing of public life, while female refugees lose social networks but 'compensate' by gaining a widening of their public lives (Kibria 1990; Eastmond 1993, 48-9; Abdulrahim 1993, 64-5). At the same time, the trauma of forced migration may lead to greater determination to hold on to the values and customs of the homeland, and recreate the same gendered structures in the new country. Whichever way, forced migration highlights the significance of gender either as a site of rupture or an anchoring space for the familiar.

Gender then, is extremely important for analysing migration, but as Sarah Mahler and Patricia Pessar (2006, 29) observe, it cannot be considered in isolation from other key social identities and constructs, intersecting closely with class, ethnicity/nationality and age. For forced migration, and more specifically migration resulting from war — the focus of this chapter — the gendered nuances of nation and age/generation are also particularly significant. Masculinity usually dominates the public persona of nationhood (Nagel 1998), but in war, masculinity becomes even more closely associated with the nation, and with militarism, heroism and violence. Femininity, on the other hand, supposedly translates into stoicism and vulnerability — the protected rather than protecting gender. It follows that the gendered roles learnt or rejected in war will have a lasting legacy on post-migration gendered relations. The trauma endured through war and forced migration also has a significant influence on ageing and the life course, already inherently gendered processes (see Arber et al. 2003). In many cases, powerful experiences such as war can break down gendered divisions by promoting strong generational identities shared by men and women who went through similar traumas at similar points in their lives. The life course however, tends to remain highly gendered in the aftermath of forced migration, resulting in contrasting experiences of old age and widowhood between men and women.

As the Polish refugee case-study illustrates, these variable intersections all point to the complexity of migration and its gendered nature, the fluidity of gendered constructs, and the difficulty in separating out gender, nation and life course in particular when researching migration.

The Polish Case-study

This chapter is based primarily on in-depth interviews undertaken with nearly thirty people from Leicester's Polish population — refugees who settled in and around the city after the Second World War and their children born there afterwards (see Burrell 2006a). Questions were asked about experiences of war and migration and 'community' life in Leicester, but the interviews were deliberately kept as unstructured as possible, with respondents encouraged to talk about what mattered to them most. All names used here are pseudonyms, and the respondents were afforded full anonymity. For many, it was the first time they had discussed their experiences of being refugees with an outside figure. Relying as it did on people's willingness to talk about sensitive times in their lives, my sample was not necessarily representative; while efforts were made to achieve a gender balance in the sample, for example, two-thirds of the interviews were carried out with female respondents. Approximately three-quarters of the interviews were held with first generation refugees, with the remainder held with second generation respondents. In addition, three further interviews were accessed from a pre-recorded local radio interview and a local oral history project, two of which were made with a self-proclaimed community statesman. Clearly, the interview material used here was created in different circumstances, with the respondents much more aware of the public communication of their discussions. In some ways, however, this potential limitation has been very useful, allowing the representation of community life to be considered from a different angle.

Before considering the impact of war and migration on the gendered lives of the respondents, it is important to note that these first generation Poles were largely socialised in a very nationalistic environment in interwar Poland. The interwar Second Republic was Poland's first opportunity to exercise national independence since 1773, having been partitioned until the First World War by Russia, Prussia and Austria (see Davies 1981). Within this new regime, gender for ethnic Poles was largely defined within a national parameter — nation, church, family. Men were to protect the country's new borders and support the economy, and women were to look after the family, all under the moral guidance of the Polish Catholic church. Although this era saw an increase in female participation in the public sphere and in education particularly, these values shaped public discourse throughout the interwar period. This was the environment in which the respondents were embedded when they found themselves caught up in war.

The circumstances which resulted in over 160,000 Polish born people being recorded in the 1951 British national census are now well documented (Holmes 1988, 212; Burrell 2006a; Lane 2004; Webster, this volume). As a result of the Nazi and Soviet invasions of 1939, Polish society found itself not only at war, but vulnerable to mass population displacement and deportation. While occupation pushed the armed forces out of Poland, causing the Polish army to be reformed first in France and then again under British command, over 1.5 million civilians from western Poland were deported to Nazi camps in 1939 and 1940, with a further 1.7 million civilians on the eastern side deported to Siberia by Russian troops in 1940 (Zubrzycki 1956, 52; Sword 1996a, 25-7). Survivors of these Soviet deportations were released in 1941 and those deemed to be of suitable age and fitness formed the Second Polish Corps under General Anders, later fighting in the famous Battle of Monte Casino in Italy. The remaining deportees stayed in Polish Red Cross camps for the duration of the war, spread throughout India, Africa and the Middle East. At the end of the war, after the Yalta peace agreements signalled Poland's position in the Soviet sphere, the Polish Resettlement Act allowed the Polish troops, and their scattered families, to settle in Britain rather than risk returning to Poland under the new Communist regime. In addition, the European Volunteer Workers (EVW) schemes brought a further 14,000 displaced Poles, victims of Nazi deportation, to Britain, though these people were categorised as workers rather than refugees (Tannahill 1958, 30). This new Polish population in Britain was faced with the double challenge of building new lives in a new environment, while coming to terms with the trauma of war and exile.

Not surprisingly, these experiences of war and subsequent settlement have been highly gendered. Men and women have had clearly designated roles in both war and peace and particular norms governing gendered relations have been sustained. At face value at least, the interviews portray a binary division of male and female Polishness, with both linking very significantly to national identity and rhetoric of national survival. A closer analysis, however, shows that these gendered experiences have in reality been far more fluid than initial portrayals suggest, and that tensions have arisen around the mutability of experience and the fixity of gendered ideals.

These gendered nuances have been generally missing in the historiography of the Polish population in Britain. Bogusia Temple (1994; 1995; 1999) has been the only researcher to really engage with the gendered nature of Polishness in Britain, and many accounts have neglected gender entirely, offering normatively 'masculinised' histories of Polish settlement without acknowledging this gendered bias (see Stachura 2004). Lane (2001, 51), for example, when discussing 'out marriage' refers only to Polish men marrying non-Polish women — the possibility that Polish women may also have married 'out' is not even countenanced. Temple, on the other hand, while providing illuminating insights into Polish women's lives, has not really considered Polish masculinity in any depth. This chapter, therefore, aims to probe more deeply the gendered aspects of Polish forced migration and settlement in Britain, and will focus on key areas of gendered intersections in the experiences of the respondents; war, nation and forced migration; settlement, community and social relations; generation and life course.

War, Nation and Forced Migration

Although previous work on Polish migration has focused on the dominance of the Second World War in Polish émigré testimonies, establishing the war as possibly the quintessential experience of first generation Polish refugees (Burrell 2006b; Winslow 1999; Temple 1996), the gendered nature of these wartime pasts has not yet been thoroughly examined. War, however, is highly gendered. As Nira Yuval Davis (1997, 93-4) notes, men are routinely constructed as naturally linked to warfare and war zones are imagined as male spaces. In times of war men find themselves cast as soldiers, charged with upholding an idealised version of manhood in order to protect the nation (Dawson 1994), an elevated position which may or may not survive later settlement. Women, on the other hand, are expected to be 'bearers of the collective' (Yuval-Davis 1997, 26), reproducers and nurturers of the nation, even if in practice they too engage in warfare as fighters (Anthias and Yuval-Davis 1989). Women's bodies also symbolise the boundaries of the nation, in war and peace, differently from men's. In war they are perceived as more vulnerable to violence (Mostov 2000, 90-1), and in a new nation they provide the means for biological and national continuation away from home. Even the telling of war is gendered. Alessandro Portelli (1998, 28) notes the ease with which men hang their life stories on war narratives, while Penny Summerfield (1998) highlights the difficulties women have in recounting past experiences that deviate from public discourses of war. However, while the relationship between war and gender may appear clear, much research in this area has shown that the experience and reality of war actually works to erode gender boundaries, turning women into fighters and men into victims (Anthias and Yuval-Davis 1989; Mostov 2000). In the case of the Polish refugees, war may have reinforced traditional gender roles in many respects, but it also undermined them in others.

Polish male experiences of war were brutal. Men accounted for most of the military deaths of the war; according to Davies (1981, 439), for example, the first invasions in 1939 left 'some 60,000 *men* killed, and 140,000 wounded' from the Polish forces (my emphasis). High ranking (male) officers were singled out and murdered by Soviet troops in the Katyn massacre, the bodies of 4,000 discovered in mass graves from a total of 15,000 'missing'. As Davies (1981, 452) states: 'only one man from the 15,000 was ever seen alive again'. The key battles of the war fought by Poles such as Monte Casino and the Warsaw Uprising are again associated with male losses, although women did fight in the Home Army (Armia Krajowa). Male civilians were also victims of deportation to labour camps and of forced conscription into the German army. The spaces of national combat, however — that famous battle 'for your freedom and ours' — seem to have been filled disproportionately by the bodies of Polish men. Once again men were called upon to die for the national cause, although this time they could do so under the Polish flag, charged with defending their fledgling national independence. The link between masculinity and nationhood had thus been reinvigorated, and Polish men, by fighting for the nation, could be heroes rather than victims. As Jarosław narrated, 'I took part in the defence of

Poland, I volunteered for the army. I was in the war from the first day. I was still a young man at that time and everything seemed to be exciting'.[1]

The experiences of the civilians who were deported to Siberia in 1940, the most common background of the people interviewed, illustrate further the significance of gender during the war. As the Katyn massacre showed, Soviet forces on the eastern side of Poland initially targeted men almost exclusively, arresting those deemed most threatening to the new status quo — men with high profile roles in the military and in different public institutions, the police especially, but also, engineers, foresters, some smallholders, and predominantly male academics and teachers (Sword 1996a, 13). Once this selection had been made, the families of these men were then designated for deportation (Sword 1996a, 14). Non-adult male deportees were largely chosen to be sent away by virtue of their association with a high ranking male, arguably invisible to the occupying forces as 'risks' in their own right. This pattern was apparent in the interviews, with women and those deported as children linking their own fates within their narratives with the key men in their families. Agata recounted the following:

In 1939 I got married, and my husband, first husband, he was from Silesia, and he was an engineer, with a degree. And when the war started the Russians came, and at night knocked on the door, and when we opened it he says "dress yourself and you come with me", to my husband, and they took him. They did that to every Pole in the same position, and they took them at night so that nobody knows about it ... one lady, the Russians took her husband, and she was waiting for him, so she stayed there with the children, and then after a while she heard that he was shot.[2]

Rather than wait for the Russians to come for her, Agata fled through Czechoslovakia soon after. Janina, who was deported, reported a similar situation: 'My father had to flee to Lithuania, with him being in the police force he would have been shot as soon as the Russians came, so he had to flee. It was just my mother, my three year old brother and myself, I was eighteen months old'.[3] It was the same for Anna who was also deported: 'We had to suffer for my father, because my father was in the police force'.[4] Not just invisible to the Russians, it is surprising how many historical accounts simply categorise these women and children as 'dependents', reinforcing their value as being relative to their male associates.

Until their release in 1941, gender seems to have made little difference to the experiences of the Polish deportees in Siberia. Women and men were both subjected to hard labour, although several of the respondents made a point of reinforcing the unnaturalness of *women* being forced to work in the gulags, emphasising that women, even pregnant women, were made to work in the camps. After 1941 gender again became a dominant issue. The Polish Second Corps was established using predominantly male survivors, while female and child survivors stayed in relative

---

1   Radio Leicester interview in 1995 with Jarosław. He came to Britain in 1946 aged 25, name has been changed.
2   Agata came to Britain in 1946 aged 25. Interviewed in Leicester, 2 February 2001.
3   Janina came to Britain in 1948 aged 10. Interviewed in Leicester, 26 February 2001.
4   Anna came to Britain in 1948 aged 18. Interviewed in Leicester, 16 February 2001.

safety in the Red Cross camps. Whilst the men were fighting for the nation therefore, the women were embodying the nation in a different way, just as they were supposed to have done during the partition era (Pietrow-Ennker 1992). Once again they provided a Polish environment for children to grow up in, although this time they created a Polish home away from home, rather than safeguarding Polish domestic space within the former boundaries of the Polish state. This time, as with conflicts since, they turned the refugee camps into private, feminised, and highly nationalised places (see Giles 1998, 90-1). Anna, who spent several years in a Red Cross camp in Africa, spoke about its 'motherly' environment:

> In that camp there were over 4,000 Polish women and children, there wasn't very many men at all, only disabled men. I started schooling there, with nothing, no teachers nothing … Whichever woman was educated or had experience in teaching, they were organising the schools for children, it comes naturally for women to take care of the youngsters. We had no text books, nothing at all, those people were teaching us what they knew, they passed their knowledge like mothers do … But somehow the atmosphere was motherly. Those women who were teaching, they were really teaching from the heart.[5]

These gendered divides appeared very clear in many of the interviews. Men fought while women tended to the needs of the next generation, once again reviving the partition era role of 'Matka Polka', simultaneously Polish mothers and guardians of mother Poland (Pietrow-Ennker 1992). These divisions, however, were not sustained in *all* of the interviews; gendered experiences of war proved to be far more fluid for other respondents. As Yuval-Davis asserts, the construction of warfare as a male sphere is largely mythical — women have always been present in war zones. During the partition era, for example, women in Poland were not simply 'mothers', but also actively resisted foreign occupation alongside men (see Jaworski 1992, 56). Polish women may have been largely written out of the history of Second World War combat, as the previous references to the casualties incurred by 'men' from Davies demonstrate, but they did serve as army members and worked and fought as underground resisters. This particular wartime narrative, however, was far less prominent in the testimonies. Jolanta came to Britain in 1948 as a member of the Second Polish Corps, but, unlike the male respondents, in her interview she did not talk about her army experiences in any depth. Instead she remarked that 'you see in the Polish army, the women came in the second groups, they were in the lower levels of the army'.[6]

Serving women were not the only people to have been sidelined in war. Only free and 'fit' men could participate in the battle for the nation. Slave labourers, German conscriptees, and, above all, disabled men could not join in the liberation struggle. As Anna's account shows, in her camp 'there wasn't very many men at all, only disabled men', disabled men not being 'real' men. If disabled men found themselves demasculinised in war, then so did male children — as Mahler and Pessar (2006, 35) remind us, children are gendered too. The situation was particularly difficult for the male interviewees who spent their early teens in Red Cross camps. Many felt

---

5   Interview with Anna.
6   Jolanta came to Britain in 1948 aged 39. Interview in Leicester, 26 August 1999.

the frustration of not being able to fulfil their male duties and being restricted to the civilian sphere. Jerzy, for example, lied about his age in order to join the forces:

> To join the army I was too young, I was thirteen, but being thin I went back two weeks later and lied about my age and they took me. When they corrected my age and they couldn't keep me I had to go again back to civilian life. My mother and my relatives were found and I had to join them.[7]

If deviations from the dominant gendered divisions of war were marginalised in the interviews, other silences were also apparent, especially regarding sexualized violence during the war. In a war where over 65 per cent of those who were affected were civilians (Matlou 1998, 133), it is interesting that the interviews did not include any direct references to rape. Research into the experiences of Latvian women, for example, has confirmed that rape was a very real part of Soviet invasion (McDowell 2005, 53-4). Sexual violence was only discussed via second hand information, through people narrating experiences which had been told to them. Zofia spoke about her mother's friend's encounters with the Soviet forces, as relayed to her by her mother:

> It wasn't a proper army, they were just peasants, but they went around raping and stealing. One of my mum's friends was nearly raped, and what they did, they threatened the soldier that they would tell his officer, and these Russian soldiers were scared of their officers, who were a bit more, who didn't go around raping to the extent that the peasants did.[8]

Of course, the respondents may have had no experiences of sexual violence, but it is impossible to know how readily this would have been narrated if they had.

The power of the male narrative of war has been one of the most recognisable characteristics of the Polish community in Britain. It is not the various histories of child deportees, of women fighting, of disabled men working in the refugee camps, or of systematic rape by Soviet troops which have been remembered in post-war Britain, but rather the brave Polish soldier who fought for the Polish nation, only to be betrayed by his western allies at the Yalta peace conference (see Stachura 2004). This is not to say that Polish soldiers were not brave, but rather that the historical identity of the community has been constructed disproportionately from this masculine image. Britain as a host nation has managed, albeit belatedly, to embrace the historical contributions of Polish airmen in the Battle of Britain and Polish intelligence in decoding Enigma; London had been a relatively proud host of the very male Polish Government in Exile. Across the country the different Ex-Service*men*'s Clubs have been extremely powerful stakeholders in both external and internal community relations. When the Polish experiences of war are remembered in Britain, they are commemorated in term of the loss of soldiers at key battles, with memorial services held around the decorated graves of key servicemen. Memory of deportation to Siberia is still very strong among those who experienced it, but this

---

7 Jerzy came to Britain in 1948 aged 20. Interview in Leicester, 26 February 2001.

8 Zofia was born in Britain to Polish parents in 1961. Interviewed in Leicester, 12 February 2001.

memory is far less public, shared within families rather than performed to a British audience (see Burrell 2006b). While the image of Polish immigrants was for a long time 'dumb Polak' in the United States, in the UK post-war Polish migration has been almost exclusively associated with the male Polish soldier.

Settlement, Community and Social Relations

Just as war and forced migration were highly gendered experiences for the Polish refugees, settlement, community and social relations developed in post-war Leicester in a significantly gendered manner. The legacy of war ensured that the ex-servicemen were at the centre of community life, vying only with the parish as the main source of authority within the local population. In Leicester, as in countless other industrial cities and towns, the beginnings of community life itself grew from the social gatherings of demobbed airmen, meeting together in the city centre to provide mutual networks of contact and support (see Burrell 2006a, 143). Once established, and buoyed by the arrival of women and children in the later 1940s, the mechanisms of community followed a familiar pattern of gendered public/private divisions of labour: men performing the visible duties of community life, supported by the behind the scenes work of the women (Temple 1994; 1995). While it was largely men who ran the committees, made speeches, led sermons and periodically issued official statements to the local press, women cooked, cleaned, danced, sang, painted eggs for Easter and taught 'Polishness' in the Saturday school — in many ways a continuation of their refugee camp roles. Jolanta, the former servicewoman, spoke about her husband's community roles, juxtaposing them to her duties of keeping the shop, house and family: 'My husband was a member of different groups, he played the organ, and I was keeping the shop and the house, the children, I had my mother with us as well'. Ewa also spoke about how her husband went to the Ex-Servicemen's Club while she stayed at home with the children.[9] These divisions were not absolute, men also sang and danced, women also participated in decision-making, but the overall sense is of a community with a very strong male lead. This is perhaps unsurprising given the imbalance in the gender ratio — Andrew Nocon (1996, 80) states that in 1954 within the Polish population throughout the UK there were three men for every woman.

For a group who had endured the traumas of war and displacement, it is also important to note the significant continuity that stable gender relations could bring to the settlement process. Wendy Webster (2000, 273) shows how among female European Volunteer Workers, highly gendered roles were not portrayed as oppressive, but rather comforting and a way of building a new home for the whole community. Magda, for example, spoke about the importance of having a large family for feelings of security, even if this was something which marked them out as different from the rest of British society.[10] Certainly all of the respondents had very strong views on

9   Ewa came to Britain in 1948 aged 14. Interviewed in Leicester, 27 August 1999 and 24 February 2000.

10   Magda came to Britain in 1948 aged 16. Interviewed in Leicester with Ewa, 27 August 1999 and 24 February 2000.

what Polish women should be, and of Polish mothers in particular. The strength of the Polish mother, and her ability to keep order in the family, was a recurrent theme. Magda also spoke about the tight supervision the women kept over the children of the community: 'But the children were at home, usually mothers made sure that they behaved properly that they were obedient ... The mothers, they made sure they learned everything, they checked everything ... Polish mothers didn't like them to go out in the street on their own and play just unsupervised'.[11] Piotr reinforced the image of the mother as key, and at the heart of running the household: 'Women are looked upon as mothers. They say it's a man's world, but it isn't, because the women run the men around their fingers. The man went out and brought the money, and the woman ran the household, she divided the money as she needed it'.[12]

In fact, this ideal of the Polish mother was so strong and underpinned by the church's teachings on morality, it was difficult for women who deviated from this norm (Temple 1999, 18-19). One single mother spoke of her problems in feeling accepted in the community, having broken the moral codes of community life (see Burrell 2006a, 172-3). Interestingly, a nun who was interviewed chose to speak about her sister's life (marriage, children), rather than her own. The role of Catholicism in determining gender roles generally has, of course, been greatly debated and critiqued (see for example Daly 1968); this specific example, however, illustrates how these powerful constructions of womanhood have worked hard to polarise women as Marys or Eves, even if this dichotomy of good woman/bad woman does not work in practice (see Forum Polek 1988, 33, 174).

While Polish women found the role of mother the only easy path to follow within the community, Polish men had a much freer set of ideals to conform to. Interestingly, Polish men depicted themselves in a far more sexualized way, with several interviewees keen to talk about their attractiveness to local women. For these men, their sexual identity was an important aspect of their personal narratives of migration and settlement, something that is often lost in migration studies generally (see Manalansan 2006). Jarosław spoke about meetings with English women, although he himself settled down with a Polish woman: 'When I was stationed in Bruntingthorpe there were about eight hundred men, but men only. So we came to Leicester for dances, the cinema, seeing girls ... Many of my colleagues married English girls in Leicester. My wife was Polish'.[13] Bogdan talked about how he met his English wife: 'I had girlfriends you know [laughs] ... I married a Leicester girl. I met her in the college. And well, you know, during the breaks, we met in the room for coffee and so on'.[14]

Sexual identity, however, also demonstrates the mutability of the supposed binary divide of gendered identities within the refugee community. Polish men may have been expected to be healthy, attractive and heterosexually active, but the sexualization of Polish women has not been so straightforward. Far from being only Marys or Eves,

---

11 Interview with Magda.

12 Piotr came to Britain in 1948 aged 12. Interviewed in Leicester, 24 January 2000.

13 Radio Leicester interview with Jarosław.

14 'Highfields Remembered' interview with Bogdan, Leicester, 18 October 1994. He came to England in 1945 aged 26, name has been changed.

new waves of marriage migration from Poland were by the late 1950s transforming community gender ratios, introducing a new type of Polish woman into community life (see Sword 1996, 40-1, 204). As Sheila Patterson (1964, 338) has noted, the Polish daily newspaper regularly carried matrimonial requests from women who were visiting from Poland, women who were highly prized as attractive and fertile, if admittedly suspiciously received for coming from the hated Communist regime, but who were thus neither deviant Eves, nor yet matronly Marys. The development of the Miss Polonia UK beauty contest, certainly established by the 1970s and continuing now, further complicates the idealised notion of Polish womanhood in Britain. The highly sexualized depictions of often second and third generation Polish women on the contest's internet sites appear to be acceptable from the point of view of national pride and community depiction — beautiful women representing Poles in Britain — but these women are hardly stylised as 'safe' motherly types (see also Wu 1997).[15]

This sexualization, clearly quite ambiguous in some cases, was also more problematic in terms of the external reception and image of the new Polish settlers. What was perceived as healthy interaction with English women by the Polish newcomers was seen as something more dangerous by some local people. While Polish men were never on the receiving end of the same degree of sexualized, racialised suspicion that West Indian men were subjected to (see Webster 2000, 262 and Smith in this volume), even their whiteness could not prevent the flourishing of some local fears about predatory Polish men and the danger of inter-ethnic sexual relations. Magda spoke about how one incident involving a Polish man developed into a wider stereotype of Polish men being seen as rapists, and how this impacted upon her husband: 'One soldier in Bucks raped a girl. This led to the common opinion that all Poles were rapists, or Fascists. My husband was avoided due to this stereotyping. They had to report to the police regularly. In shops they were called "bloody Poles" and "bloody foreigners".'[16] In her research into female Latvian EVWs, Linda McDowell (2005, 81) discovered that Latvian women had also been negatively sexualized, this time by the British state, with women subjected to invasive tests for diseases such as VD when they arrived. Inge Weber-Newth (this volume) also discusses how German war brides were subjected to medical examinations before they could marry British men. Again, as with the prevalence of rape, this was not something discussed by any of my respondents, but the possibility remains that some of the Polish EVWs at least had similar experiences.

These gendered and sexualized norms and values were obviously important in underpinning the workings of settlement in Britain, lending a familiar structure to community and family life. But in spite of the attempt to define male and female roles, the reality of the post-refugee experience encouraged greater fluidity in the realm of gender ensuring, for example, that many accepted and idealised gendered rituals and relations could not be maintained. Traditions and patterns of marriage and childbearing were affected enormously by the economic difficulties of a new life in

---

15 The key websites can be accessed at http://www.misspolonia.co.uk/index.php and http://www.misspoloniauk.com/index.php. Last accessed 29 April 2007.

16 Interview with Magda.

Britain. Weddings, for example, could not carry the same theatrical, all-encompassing status they would have commanded in Poland. As Piotr observed, 'because of the rationing, the girls used the parachutes for the things, because there was no materials. No it was very sober things, a meal yes, but no honeymoons because they were working, it was very difficult'.[17] Jarosław spoke about the economic problems pregnancy presented: 'We had to depend on the wives working. So, if any of our wives got pregnant at that time, it was a disaster! My wife was more or less earning the same in the hosiery as I did in the factory. But somehow we managed'.[18]

As this last point illustrates, gender relations, out of necessity, were far more complex than being simply male provider, female nurturer. Polish men were able to find work quite easily in Leicester, but usually this work was low paid, physically hard, and often represented a decline in status from their working lives, or expectations, in Poland. Many found the new environment and the nature of the work difficult to adapt to and struggled to fulfil the duties they expected of themselves as men. Striving to support his family and realise the potential he felt he had lost by leaving Poland was an important theme in Jerzy's account:

> I tried to get further education but that was not possible at the time. We were given two jobs, farm labourer or building labourer. I chose building labourer and I lasted for three months, I lost all the skin on my hands from lugging bricks, but in the meantime I entered night school for book keeping and accounts ... I put my sister through school.[19]

The loss of dignity, prestige and even identity that male refugees experience has been closely documented (see McSpadden 1998, 247). Forced migration and settlement in a new country directly challenges the confidence that men have in their position in society and within the family. Many of these Polish men were, in Magda's words, 'shell-shocked and damaged from the war', not fulfilling what a man should be economically, physically or psychologically. As Wiola explained, her sister had to work hard to support her family because her 'invalid' husband was unable to do so: 'My sister worked for twenty five years, part-time work, she was bringing up the family. In a shoe factory and then later on in the seventies she was in a factory in Wigston, and her husband was a war invalid, he wasn't able to work so she had to supplement the family budget.'[20]

This issue of women working is an important one. Work, of course, has been a central part of the lives of most post-war female migrants in Britain, voluntary migrants (see for example Ryan 2007; Anthias 1992) and refugees alike. As McDowell (2004, 47) has found with Latvian women, and to a certain extent Weber-Newth (this volume) with German war brides, Polish women in Leicester, as elsewhere in Britain, worked as a matter of course, just as many of them, depending on class and regional background, would have done in Poland (see Pietrow-Ennker 1992, 13; Żarnowska 2004). Even those who had family members to help with childcare still

---

17 Interview with Piotr.

18 Jarosław was also interviewed by the 'Highfields Remembered' project, Leicester, 9 January 1995.

19 Interview with Jerzy.

20 Wiola came to Britain in 1948 aged 16. Interviewed in Leicester, 26 August 1999.

took part-time work after their children were born. Furthermore, many women also had to accept a drop in status in their new work spheres in order to find employment at all. As Jolanta narrated, after she and her husband sold their continental shop, she had little choice but to take the kinds of jobs she would never have done in Poland: 'It was 1964 when we sold that shop, and I was fifty two years old. There was no time to start to do something clever. I worked in the factory, in the canteen, washing, serving, my English was enough for that'.[21] Working mothers, therefore, were not seen as a deviation from gender norms at all, but rather contributing to the shared project of building a new life, although as Temple (1995, 69) notes, and as Wiola's testimony shows, their wages were still seen as supplementary rather than central, even if they were in reality the principal earners.

In the new context of male vulnerability, female strength was an essential component for successful settlement. As women moved in public spaces through employment, furthermore, many of the interviews stressed the important roles that men played in the domestic sphere. Rather than being out at the Ex-Servicemen's club all the time, four separate female respondents spoke about how their husbands or fathers 'helped' at home, sometimes cooking, often looking after children and in particular decorating their houses, essentially homemaking too.

Postscript: Generation and Life Course

At the time of writing, the post-war Polish refugees have been in Britain for between 64 and 67 years. During this time many aspects of community life have changed, but the most significant change has been the ageing of the refugees themselves. The issues of ageing were important themes in the collected interviews, and many of the respondents spoke about community life in terms of the past, 'the good old days' which have now gone (see Burrell 2006a, 145-6; Winslow 2004, 92). During their interviews the respondents spoke about friends dying, about the proliferation of Polish graves in the cemeteries, and about funerals as social events. Perhaps the most important theme to emerge was the problem of isolation among the ageing refugees, and the need for ethnically appropriate care to cater for their needs (see British Refugee Council 1988). To some extent, these issues have been addressed on a national scale, with the Refugee Council recording in 1988 nine specifically Polish care homes scattered throughout the UK, half of the total of all care homes established for East European refugees (British Refugee Council 1988). At a local level, in Leicester as elsewhere, the day care centre, a relatively new community structure, now occupies a key place in community life, providing, according to the woman who runs it, another 'home' for the elderly Poles — somewhere where they can speak to other people in Polish and eat Polish food.

Perhaps unsurprisingly, this change in the age structure of the community has also brought with it changed gender dynamics. As many Polish men married younger women from Poland, and because women live longer than men generally, time has altered the gender ratio substantially. The typical Polish refugee is now more likely

---

21 Interview with Jolanta.

to be a widow than a male ex-soldier (see Sword 1988, 28). Polish women are now especially at risk of isolation and loneliness. As this shift in the gender balance has been apparent over the past twenty years, this has also impacted upon the running of the community more generally. Although some men of the second generation have taken up central positions, since the 1980s many of the Committee places previously belonging to men have been filled by women. In general, the gendered spaces of community life have changed dramatically. One of the best examples of this is the Ex-Servicemen's Club; a place which proudly hosted a visit from General Anders in the 1950s, and which acted as an important public focal point for the community, has now been transformed into a private space where elderly Polish men are cared for by women from younger generations, as if they were at home. The caring may still be provided by women, but the male nature of the club is almost unrecognisable from its heyday. Melisa spends some of her spare time cooking there:

> I cook there. Its an Ex-Servicemen's club and a lot are getting elderly and disappearing, there is only a small number which come along to the club but we try and keep up the traditional soldiers' anniversaries, we try and keep it open so that they can come and meet and enjoy each others' company, from time to time we do some sort of gathering, get together, bingo or watching a film, just to get them in. We also do dinners on the Sunday and that is really an event, for some of the old soldiers who don't have a cooked meal during the week.[22]

In fact, the ageing process has diluted much of the community focus on the experiences of the soldiers — most of the refugees who are still alive now came to Britain as children and teenagers, and did not serve in the forces at all.

If gender is still significant in ageing, there is perhaps one aspect of the Polish experience in Britain that has been able to transcend gendered boundaries. Whatever histories the individual refugees have behind them, and however gendered the politicisation of Polish memory in Britain has been, attachment to Polish national identity and the trauma of Second World War have combined to create a powerful cohort identity shared among almost all of the Polish refugees. Men and women alike have spent several decades in Britain struggling to pass down Polish traditions and family wartime memories to the next generations. They have done this in different ways and in different places, but their attempts to build a new life here, to create a Polish community, and to remember the reasons why they came here and what they left behind, have constituted a much bigger, common project.

Conclusions

It is evident that gender has been a hugely significant factor in the experiences of forced migration and settlement among Polish refugees in Leicester. Polish men had well defined expectations of manhood in interwar Poland, and participation in war forced thousands of Polish men to demonstrate their ultimate loyalty to the national

---

22 Melisa was born in Britain to Polish parents in 1951. Interviewed in Leicester, 31 August 1999.

cause. The price paid for this loyalty has had an enormous impact upon the post-war lives of those who survived. All of the male respondents spoke of the loss they have encountered in Britain, and the difficulties they have had in adapting to a new environment carrying the economic, physical and psychological scars of war and refugeedom. The position of the Polish men who did not fight has arguably been even more difficult, as they have not been able to enjoy the same support and status that the ex-servicemen have experienced.

The situation has not been any easier for Polish women. War tore apart the family structures that they were supposed to be guardian of as 'Matka Polka', and in most cases distanced women from public national participation; the histories of female fighters have not been remembered — in Britain at least. In their post-war lives, however, Polish women have found that they have been expected to be strong. They have been charged with the task of passing Polishness down the generations, but also with the more practical needs of economic survival and success.

While the different qualitative experiences of men and women are quite stark, forced migration and settlement have prompted far greater interactions between gendered roles and values than might be expected. Overly idealised notions of gender have been shown to be impractical in forging a new life in Britain. It is important to note too how both men and women have been sidelined in different ways by the more rigid and dominant strictures of community life, whether through moral codes or the centrality of the community's military identity. Over time, furthermore, the gendered balance of power has changed, with women becoming more visible in the public aspects of community activities. All of these factors reinforce the situational, fluid nature of gendered relationships and experiences. There may still be strong beliefs about the different roles of men and women among the post-war Poles, but their actual lives have demonstrated how the reality is often far removed from the prevailing discourse.

References

Abdulrahim, D. (1993), 'Defining Gender in a Second Exile: Palestinian Women in West Berlin', in Buijs, G. (ed.).

Anthias, F. (1992), *Ethnicity, Class, Gender and Migration: Greek-Cypriots in Britain* (Aldershot: Ashgate).

Anthias, F. and Yuval-Davis, N. (1989), 'Introduction', in Anthias, F. and Yuval-Davis, N. (eds).

—— (eds) (1989), *Woman-Nation-State* (London: Macmillan).

Arber, K. et al. (eds) (2003), *Gender and Ageing: Changing Roles and Relationships* (Maidenhead: Open University Press).

British Refugee Council (1988), *Age in Exile: A Report on Elderly Exiles in the United Kingdom*.

Buijs, G. (ed.) (1993), *Migrant Women: Crossing Boundaries and Changing Identities* (Oxford: Berg).

Buijs, G. (1993), 'Introduction' in Buijs, G. (ed.).

Burrell, K. (2006a), *Moving Lives: Narratives of Nation and Migration among Europeans in Post-war Britain* (Aldershot: Ashgate).

—— (2006b), 'Personal, Inherited, Collective: Communicating and Layering Memories of Forced Polish Migration', *Immigrants and Minorities* 24:2, 144-63.

Butler, J. (1990), *Gender Trouble* (New York: Routledge).

Chamberlain, M. and Thompson, P. (eds) (1998), *Narrative and Genre* (London: Routledge).

Daly, M. (1968) *The Church and the Second Sex* (London: Geoffrey Chapman).

Dawson, G. (1994), *Soldier Heroes: British Adventure, Empire and the Imagining of Masculinities* (London: Routledge).

Davies, N. (1981), *God's Playground: A History of Poland Volume II: 1795 to the Present* (Oxford: Oxford University Press).

Donato, M. et al. (2006), 'A Glass Half Full? Gender in Migration Studies', *International Migration Review* 40:1, 3-26.

Eastmond, M. (1993), 'Reconstructing Life: Chilean Refugee Women and the Dilemmas of Exile', in Buijs, G. (ed.).

Forum Polek: Polish Women's Forum (1988) (London: Forum Publication Group).

Giles, W. (1998), 'Gendered Violence in War: Reflections on Transnationalist and Comparative Frameworks in Militarized Conflict Zones', in Indira, D. (ed.).

Glass, R. (ed.) (1964), *London: Aspects of Change* (London: MacGibbon and Kee).

Holmes, C. (1988), *John Bull's Island: Immigration and British Society, 1871-1971* (Basingstoke: Macmillan).

Indira, D. (ed.) (1999), *Engendering Forced Migration: Theory and Practice* (New York: Berghahn Books).

—— (1999), 'Introduction', in Indira, D. (ed.).

Jaworski, R. (1992), 'Polish Women and the Nationality Conflict in the Province of Posen at the Turn of the Century', in Jaworski, R. and Pietrow-Ennker, B. (eds).

Jaworski, R. and Pietrow-Ennker, B. (eds) (1992), *Women in Polish Society* (New York: Columbia University Press).

Kibria, N. (1990), 'Power, Patriarchy, and Gender Conflict in the Vietnamese Immigrant Community', *Gender and Society* 40:1, 9-24.

Lane, T. (2001), 'Victims of Stalin and Hitler: The Polish Community of Bradford', *Immigrants and Minorities* 20:3, 43-58.

—— (2004), *Victims of Stalin and Hitler: The Exodus of Poles and Balts to Britain* (Basingstoke: Palgrave Macmillan).

McDowell, L. (2004), 'Narratives of Family, Community and Waged Work: Latvian European Volunteer Worker Women in Post-war Britain', *Women's History Review* 13:1, 23-55.

—— (2005), *Hard Labour: The Forgotten Voices of Latvian Migrant Volunteer Workers* (London: UCL Press).

McSpadden, L. (1998), 'Negotiating Masculinity in the Reconstruction of Social Place: Eritrean and Ethiopian Refugees in the United States and Sweden', in Indira, D. (ed.).

Mahler, S. and Pessar, P. (2006), 'Gender Matters: Ethnographers Bring Gender from the Periphery Toward the Core of Migration Studies', *International Migration Review* 40:1, 27-63.

Manalansan IV, M. (2006), 'Queer Intersections: Sexuality and Gender in Migration Studies', *International Migration Review* 40:1, 224-49.

Matlou, P. (1998) 'Upsetting the Cart: Forced Migration and Gender Issues, the African Experience', in Indira D. (ed.).

Mayer, T. (ed.) (2000), *Gender Ironies of Nationalism: Sexing the Nation* (London: Routledge).

Mostov, J. (2000), 'Sexing the Nation/Desexing the Body: Politics of National Identity in the Former Yugoslavia', in Mayer, T. (ed.).

Nagel, J. (1998), 'Masculinity and Nationalism: Gender and Sexuality in the Making of Nations', *Ethnic and Racial Studies* 21:2, 242-69.

Nocon, A. (1996), 'A Reluctant Welcome? Poles in Britain in the 1940s', *Oral History* 24:1, 79-87.

Patterson, S. (1964), 'Polish London', in Glass, R. (ed.).

Pietrow-Ennker, B. (1992), 'Women in Polish Society: A Historical Introduction', in Jaworski, R. and Pietrow-Ennker, B. (eds).

Portelli, A. (1998), 'Oral History as Genre', in Chamberlain, M. and Thompson, P. (eds).

Ryan, L. (2007), 'Migrant Women, Social Networks and Motherhood: The Experience of Irish Nurses in Britain', *Sociology* 41:2, 295-312.

Stachura, P. (ed.) (2004), *The Poles in Britain 1940-2000: From Betrayal to Assimilation* (London: Frank Cass).

Sword, K. (1988), '"Émigré Widows" among the Polish Community in the UK', in British Refugee Council.

—— (1996a), *Deportation and Exile: Poles in the Soviet Union, 1939-48* (Basingstoke: Macmillan).

—— (1996b), *Identity in Flux: The Polish Community in Britain* (London: SSEES University of London).

Summerfield, P. (1998), *Reconstructing Women's Wartime Lives: Discourse and Subjectivity in Oral Histories of the Second World War* (Manchester: Manchester University Press).

Tannahill. J.A. (1958), *European Volunteer Workers in Britain* (Manchester: Manchester University Press).

Temple, B. (1994), 'Constructing Polishness: Researching Polish Women's Lives', *Women's Studies International Forum* 17:1, 47-55.

—— (1995), '"Gatherers of Pig-swill and Thinkers": Gender and Community Amongst British Poles', *Journal of Gender Studies* 4:1, 63-72.

—— (1996), 'Time Travels: Time, Oral History and British-Polish Identities', *Time and Society* 5:1, 85-96.

—— (1999), 'Diaspora, Diaspora Space and Polish Women', *Women's Studies International Forum* 22:1, 17-24.

Webster, W. (2000), 'Defining Boundaries: European Volunteer Worker Women in Britain and Narratives of Community', *Women's History Review* 9:2, 257-74.

Winslow, M. (1999), 'Polish Migration to Britain: War, Exile and Mental Health', *Oral History* 27:1, 57-64.

—— (2004), 'Oral History and Polish Émigrés in Britain', in Stachura, P. (ed.).

Wu, J.T.-C. (1997), '"Loveliest Daughter of our Ancient Cathay!" Representations of Ethnic and Gender Identity in the Miss Chinatown USA Beauty Pageant', *Journal of Social History* 31:1, 5-32.

Yuval-Davis, N. (1997), *Gender and Nation* (London: Sage).

Żarnowska, A. (2004), *Workers, Women, and Social Change in Poland 1870-1939* (Aldershot: Ashgate).

Zubrzycki, J. (1956), *Polish Immigrants in Britain: A Study of Adjustment* (The Hague: Martinus Nijhoff).

Chapter 5

Gender, Race and the Ideal Labour Force

Dolly Smith Wilson

This chapter, focusing on the period between 1945 and 1975 explores the impact of the view that women were economically dependent on men in two related areas: firstly, immigration policy and the role of indigenous women in the labour market, and secondly, male and female migrants in the British labour market. During this period when officials, employers and trade union leaders spoke of a worker, they had in mind a very specific type: a skilled white British-born man. They endowed him with characteristics of their ideal labour source: strong, skilled, hard-working — either a professional or, more commonly, skilled manual labourer, not too militant and unencumbered by any personal baggage (such as childcare) that could prevent his long tenure in a job or his working long hours. Nonetheless the labour shortage of over a million workers in 1946 meant that alternate sources of labour beyond this ideal had to be found. However, while the economy needed labour, policymakers did not necessarily want permanent *workers* — which to them meant long-term, skilled, white male labour — but rather a reserve workforce: lower-skilled, lower-paid auxiliaries useful in time of need but easily disposed of in a downturn.

Policymakers generally saw two groups as possible sources of labour: 'women' and 'immigrants'. These were constructed categories. For them, women generally referred to married women, since most other British adults were already in the workforce. While married women's labour had been key during the war, gender ideology meant this source was an anathema to many. Thus eyes turned overseas to migrant labour. As initial supplies of labour in schemes involving Polish soldier refugees and European workers on short-term contracts were quickly exhausted, officials turned to displaced persons in refugee camps and later colonial subjects. Neither source was considered as satisfactory as the permanent UK-born men in the workforce. Nor were the two sources seen as interchangeable. Native white married women were often cited by civil servants as a labour source that could reduce Britain's need for overseas labour, but the reverse was not true. Other officials who debated ways to eliminate the need for native women's labour so that married women would stay at home never spoke of immigration as an alternate source of labour; their preferred solution was automation and increased productivity (Wilson 2005). Most officials were unhappy about the prospect of more married women working, but saw it as vastly preferable to mass immigration.

Native women were rarely considered to be workers, however. Post-war employment and welfare policy characterised women as dependents, giving them an inferior position in Britain's new welfare state, which revolved around employment roles. Even migrant women who entered the country in their own right or were recruited to fill specific jobs were not always identified as workers. At first glance, it might seem odd to argue that policymakers did not see women as workers, given that by the end of the Second World War, they made up a third of the work force, but few saw 'womenpower' as being the same, or as good as, 'manpower'. Policymakers operated on an assumption that a man was naturally a worker, while a woman, even if she worked for pay, was not. As I have argued elsewhere (2006) and Kathy Burrell notes in this volume, because of women's key construction as dependents, they could still be characterised as merely 'supplementing' the family budget even if the main breadwinner. Women existed in an almost entirely separate labour market from men, and traditional 'women's work' — the low paid auxiliary work that allowed the economy to run — did not have the same status as men's 'work'. Even where women did the same work as men (such as teaching or shop assistants) it was rarely considered equal work or rated equal pay. Vacancies for women often outnumbered those for men for the first few decades after the war ended, but policymakers did little about improving the poor conditions and pay that kept many women out of the workforce; they were more interested in what they considered the more important male-employing industries. Inferior wages and conditions for women were justified by their presumed dependence on others — either a father or husband — and the belief that women's employment was temporary as their true work was marriage and motherhood. One of the few developments that drew large numbers of women into the workforce during the period was the opportunity to do part-time work (Wilson 2005; 2006). Native white women were able to do this in far higher numbers than migrant women, as discussed below.

Thus when policymakers spoke about labour and employment policy, they generally meant men. Women disappeared. Similarly, when policymakers discussed 'immigrants', they lumped all migrants together in a category and made policy regarding what they saw as the typical migrant: a lone, sexually-threatening black man (usually Caribbean, but sometimes Pakistani or Sikh). European Volunteer Workers (EVWs) or Irish were mentioned briefly in discussions over legislative regulations on immigration, but the term 'immigrant' or 'migrant' was generally used as a shorthand for race. While the Irish had been negatively racialised in the past, as were the EVWs, their stereotypes did not affect policy in the same way (Kay and Miles 1992; Paul 1997; Hickman 1997). It was such stereotyped classifications (worker as male or migrant as black) that most influenced policy, and those who didn't fit the mould disappeared. This includes white migrants from Ireland, Europe or even the Commonwealth, and migrant women of all ethnicities who suffered the most in the post-war labour market, facing both sexual and racial/ethnic discrimination and the resulting social exclusion (Herbert 2006; Hickman 1998; Carby 1982).

Because of the early post-war labour shortage, both native women and male and female migrants generally obtained jobs, although not always ones with good pay, recognition of their skill, or opportunity for advancement. In many respects they operated as the reserve labour force officials wanted. With a three month lag, the number of immigration entries in the 1950s fluctuated with the numbers of job vacancies. A November 1957 Ministry of Labour memo noted that while 50,000 women workers had left the job market during the 1956 to 1957 recession, nowhere near that amount registered as unemployed (LAB 8/2190). Similarly, in March 1958, the Greater Birmingham Employment Commission reported that while one in three of their registered unemployed were 'coloured', actual numbers out of work were higher since many Indians did not register for unemployment payments (*Birmingham Post*, 14 March 1958). Repeated government investigations in the 1950s and 1960s found little abuse of the system by migrants, whose economic contributions far outweighed what they took out in government services (LAB26/259; LAB 8/2867).

All of those defined as less-than-ideal auxiliary workers shared a similar outsider status and government officials classified them in analogous ways, engaging in behaviour such as marking them on unemployment rolls as unskilled despite qualifications. Government officials also condoned employers' protests that they could not hire such workers in supervisory or managerial roles that would mean having authority over white men or, in the case of migrants, over native white women. Trade union members often complained about outsiders being reluctant to join unions even though they treated them unequally or portrayed labour competition as 'alien' or as 'strangers'. Although the strength of reactions varied by locality, there were similar responses to all rival groups, including EVWs who arrived just after the war's end, migrants from the Commonwealth and Ireland, and the rising numbers of women entering the work force.

Local Interest

Kenneth Lunn (2000) has urged that scholars remember that most migrants were not facing a single national culture but numerous local ones, where varied patterns of pre-war thought or wartime experience affected post-war reactions. Indeed, the nature of prejudice in post-war Britain often seemed to be rather random. Often women (of any colour) or migrants (again of any colour) were considered satisfactory in one job but not in another or even in the same job in different locations — for example the varied acceptability of black porters in train stations in London less than a mile apart. Skin colour, gender, religion and local conditions all factored into such responses but, as recent work on Irish and EVW migrants has made clear, white skin did not prevent discrimination.

With the memory of the widespread unemployment of the interwar period still fresh, many British men were convinced that the economy was a zero sum game and anything given to an outsider, however defined, meant less for those already working. Who was defined as local mattered greatly in the job market. Laura Tabili (1994) has analysed how foreign-born seaman who intermarried or became otherwise tied to local kinship networks in interwar port cities could use those local ties to argue for increased status and rights in the labour market. 'Alien' seaman had far fewer rights than those defined as 'British'. Automatic rejection of non-local labour was not inevitable, but the many historical divisions in the working class of gender, skill or occupational status made it more likely. Workers tended to identify more closely with neighbours or with those in the same industry rather than the working class as a whole, leaving them suspicious of any outsider (Virdee 2000).

A closer examination of several strikes helps illustrate this issue of 'local' interest and skill. In February 1959, 680 workers at a Nuneaton foundry (Sterling Metals) walked off the job to protest at the hiring of migrants. The migrant men had been transferred from the same firm's Coventry plant, where they had been doing skilled work without complaint since 1950. Men at the Nuneaton factory were already on edge due to recent layoffs and disputes about the grading of jobs and resented having workers brought from outside while 'local' men were suffering. Though Coventry was less than 15 miles away, the transferred men were not considered 'local' (*Coventry Evening Telegraph*, 11 and 12 February 1959).

A management spokesman condemned the strikers, most of whom were out for only a day, claiming neither the company nor the men's own union (Transport and General Workers) recognized any colour bar. However, colour *per se* was not the only issue as a representative for the strikers made clear: 'The men complain about Indians working on productive [i.e. skilled] jobs. They do not mind Indians being on non-productive work' (*Coventry Evening Telegraph*, 11 February 1959). Herein lay the biggest complaint, not that the company had hired Punjabis but that they were doing *skilled* work. Overall, South Asians made up about 17 per cent of Sterling Metal's workers, which was close to an unwritten quota operated by most companies in that area of the Midlands since, according to the Ministry of Labour, if more than 20 per cent of workers were of colour then the other men often became 'restive' (LAB 8/2603).

Similarly, in November 1966, 140 men walked out of the Roberts-Arundel textile machinery plant in Stockport. They were protesting at the hiring of women workers to run machines just transferred to the factory from another Roberts plant in Preston, 30 miles northwest. In Preston the machines had been run exclusively by women. However, because similar machines had not been used before in Stockport, they did not have this association for the men there. This allowed men to take what otherwise would have been seen as a 'woman's job' without losing face. When the company began to hire women to run the machines, local unions protested that no women should be hired before Roberts-Arundel had hired back 140 men laid off from different jobs several months earlier. A local labour exchange official reported that shop stewards had complained that 'women should be making shirts, not working in an engineering factory'. Union officials maintained their protest was about seniority and local workers' rights, not sexism. They argued it was Roberts-Arundel's managing director who insisted on having lower-paid women, allegedly saying 'those machines coming back from Preston smell of perfume' (LAB 10/2966).

Trade union officials blacklisted the company and commented that union solidarity would ensure that the company 'may recruit some women and some unskilled and intermediate grade men, but they will not get any skilled labour' (*News and Chronicle*, 7 December 1966). The union officials automatically differentiated men's skill levels, but presumed that women were not skilled. The reaction of the men in both situations to newcomers was a complex mix of defensive tactics to protect skilled status; race and/or gender discrimination; and an insistence on the priority of 'local' men for jobs. In both cases, the real sticking point was that the 'aliens' were taking positions above their expected place as reserve or marginal labour, and eyeing jobs that competed with white British-born men.

Many of these same motives played out in the response to refugee labour immediately after the war's end. At one point in 1948, over 33 local Yorkshire branches of the miner's union were protesting at the hiring of Poles and EVWs, despite a national agreement with the Coal Board that limited the promotion and skill opportunities of EVWs and ensured they would be the first fired in any economic downturn. Miners feared the additional labour would undermine attempts to improve pay and conditions, especially the shift to a five-day week. The miners' and agricultural workers' unions both bitterly opposed EVW labour. Textile unions also demanded similar limits, including quotas on the number of migrants hired. In 1950, a strike was threatened over the promotion of several EVW assistants to the status of full ring spinners in a Lancashire cotton firm. The head office of the union argued that spinning assistants elsewhere in the industry who had previously been spinners on older mule spinners should have the first chance at the jobs, even if they did not work at the same firm. The union made clear its protest was about 'foreign' labour: if the spinners in question had been naturalised, they would have withdrawn the objection (Tanahill 1958).

Skill and Discrimination

As the strike cases demonstrate, a major focus of resentment revolved around skill or the presumed lack of it. Long before the post-war period, notions of skill or non-skill had been tied to characteristics women were believed to possess such as the ability to bear repetitive work or dexterity, better known as 'nimble fingers,' which was defined not as a 'skill' but rather a 'natural trait' (Rose 1992). Similar traits attributed to black men were brute strength and stamina (mostly for those of African descent) or the ability to bear heat. For example, the latter justified limiting Asian men to jobs as ship's firemen or to particularly unpopular hot 'dirty' work in textile factories or foundries. Depending on ethnicity, black men could be depicted as animalistic, effeminate or child-like (Tabili 1994; Sinha 1995). Such interpretations justified the superior place of white men in society and the labour market. A 1963 survey of employers found many still held firmly to such stereotypes, claiming that migrants needed more supervision than whites, Pakistanis had little stamina or West Indian women were 'slow' and had an 'inability to adapt themselves to factory discipline' (LAB 8/2603). Because perceptions of skill are socially constructed, such associations meant any post typically held by minority groups was labelled unskilled or at most semi-skilled, regardless of the tasks performed.

The traits associated with these stereotypes meant that while marginal workers were often *treated* similarly, officials, trade union leaders and employers generally *considered* them to be different sets of 'problem' workers, who created different types of trouble in the labour market and were generally *not* interchangeable — except in a few cases in the textile industry. For example, Asian men stereotyped as smaller, weaker or more fragile than the average man were also associated with the dexterity and quickness — the 'nimble fingers' often associated with women. Few textile mills operated night shifts before the late 1950s as protective regulations prohibited night work for women, but as textile factories shifted to more capital intensive production processes in the 1960s, profitability necessitated keeping factories open 24 hours a day. Pakistani and Bangladeshi men were seen as the perfect solution to do women's work at night (LAB 8/2867; Kalra 1993; Anwar 1979). Despite the effeminisation of such workers, Kalra also notes sexual danger stereotypes prohibited the use of Asian male operatives on dayshifts alongside white women. 'These contradictions of representation and practice highlight how different stereotypes can be utilised in different contexts to justify social control and to legitimate exclusionary practices' (Kalra 1993, 98).

Resistance to workers, as noted earlier, was related to their perceived threat to skilled white male labour. A South Asian man who emigrated to Coventry in 1954 as a boy, later trained as a machinist while on work release from school but men in his factory objected to the employment of 'coloured people' for skilled work. When they threatened a strike, his employer told him and other Asian boys they could only work as cleaners or as unskilled heavy labour (Cheema 2006). Such threats were relatively common. There were also a number of strikes to keep women from taking skilled work (Wilson 2005). In one 1968 case a Great Yarmouth woman gave up a job she had just trained for in bus driving and returned to being a conductor after her male co-workers threatened a strike. The local Transport and General Workers Union district branch secretary (who ironically had failed the same course) argued that 'If this woman was allowed in the floodgates would open and other women would take men's jobs' (*The Sun*, 28 June 1968).

Another sample of exclusionary practices and the arbitrary nature of skill assessment can be seen in a 1961 Ministry of Labour investigation of five London-area Employment Exchanges (EEs) after an analysis of records showed 'the proportion of skilled workers ... was very much higher than we anticipated'. Since close to half of Britain's male manual workers qualified as skilled, the argument that a register in which 17 per cent of men were listed as skilled was 'higher than anticipated' might seem odd unless one knew that the only exchanges questioned were in areas with large numbers of migrants. The investigator claimed: 'It was immediately apparent that a very liberal interpretation of "fully skilled" had been applied at all the EEs visited'. He reassessed the exchanges' data, dividing workers into new categories of skilled and semi-skilled, lowering the number of skilled men listed in the Brixton register, for example, from 126 down to only 20 among the 696 workers listed. He commented:

> City EE had counted as fully skilled a number of Indians who, although very well qualified on paper, had not proved their skill in U.K. employment. Most of the coloured men on this register are Indians and Pakistanis who have not the experience for industrial executive posts and who are not socially acceptable in commercial executive posts (LAB 8/2603).

A similar instance, in this case about the definition of men's and women's work is illustrated by a list given in the early 1950s by a Ministry of Labour civil servant to her male supervisor. The list comprised occupations formerly considered to be 'male' that she thought could easily be done by men or women during the labour shortage. However, he did not know who had held the jobs previously and to her great surprise, he identified over half the jobs on the list, formerly considered to be men's only, as 'women's work, requiring manual dexterity or artistic ability and for that reason, apparently, not interchangeable'! (LAB 8/1902). In both cases, social expectations regarding 'nimble fingers' or 'acceptability' played a larger role than actual skill or qualifications.

Despite Britain's continuing shortage of labour, attempts to make the labour force more flexible by trying to integrate minority workers or especially to combine the highly segregated men's and women's employment markets were fiercely resisted on many levels. The Ministry of Labour and employers both believed it was useless to try to fill 'women's jobs' with anything but women as men would never take on such work, given its low wages and low status (LAB 26/226; LAB 8/1484). The Roberts Arundel case makes clear, however, how much the idea of women's jobs could shift from place to place, regardless of the tasks performed. Nor was the issue always that men would not take such jobs (especially when the pay was raised) but rather the challenge to prevailing gender or racial ideology if they did so. In the 1950s, the Ministry of Health resisted proposals to train male nurses from the colonies, despite numerous applications and requests from hospitals for the labour (LAB 8/1804).

The labour shortage did force employers to hire women for some 'men's jobs' — but generally only the ones which were no longer wanted by men. There was usually no difficulty in recruiting women even for 'labouring work of a heavy and dirty kind' because even low-paid men's work still paid 20 to 40 per cent more than most women's work (LAB 8/1903; LAB 8/2190). This was similar to the recruitment of migrants to fill jobs no longer considered particularly desirable by native-born Britons. The transport system, particularly buses, and the National Health Service depended heavily on migrant labour, with overseas nurses and doctors making up 60 per cent of the staff in a few hospitals (Shaw 2000). With more opportunities in clerical and government service opening up, native white women were often reluctant to take jobs in the sectors that had formally made up most 'women's work': domestic service, laundry or textiles. In January 1953, while women made up 33 per cent of the workforce, 43 per cent of all vacancies were for women, mainly in the traditional women's fields (LAB 8/2190). Incoming migrant women with less ability to freely pick and choose jobs became concentrated in the jobs native women increasingly refused.

When they had specific jobs to fill officials had little hesitation in exploiting the skills migrants could bring, even if they refused to recognize such skill in other circumstances or pushed them into the lowest ranks or most undesirable sectors. Migrant women were concentrated in the ranks of State Enrolled Nurses. This qualification was of a lower standard than that of State Registered Nurse and was not recognized outside of the UK so that the women who studied at this level were tied to jobs in Britain, a fact which many didn't realize until it was too late (Harriot 1992; Chamberlain 1997; Walter 2001). One Irish student who applied for the Registered as opposed to the Enrolled course was turned down during the interview process by a man who asked her 'Who do you think you are? Irish people don't do that, they do enrolled nursing' (Ryan 2007b, 427).

The tendency to recruit skilled workers from the Commonwealth became more pronounced after 1962, when the work vouchers based on skills came into use (LAB 26/259). This made the public belief that most migrants were unskilled all the more ironic. News stories and even sociological treatises on the topic routinely claimed virtually all migrants were unskilled, which perhaps accounts for much of the perception. The Institute of Race Relations found in the late 1960s that only 8 per cent of respondents thought that blacks could be middle-class or skilled. Over 90 per cent classified them as working-class, while 67 per cent defined them as unskilled and 25 per cent semi-skilled (E.B.J. Rose 1969). In reality well over half of Caribbean migrants, especially from the smaller islands, were skilled or professional workers.

Such perceptions meant that migrants, especially women, had difficulty obtaining professional posts (except in nursing). Numerous firms employed large numbers of migrant or female workers but rarely as supervisors or in skilled positions (Rose 1969; PEP 1971; Chamberlain 1997; Walter 2001). Almost all of the subjects in Sharon Daye's study (1994) of middle-class Anglo-Caribbean and African migrants had professional, skilled or semi-skilled positions before leaving the Caribbean but had trouble finding equivalent work in Britain. One man worked as a bus conductor for two years before being able to obtain a job as an architect. Similarly, E.R. Braithwaite wrote that his main problem in finding employment was that he wanted skilled, professional work. On several occasions he was told flatly he could not be hired for a job 'that would mean placing you in a position of authority over a number of our English employees' (Braithwaite 1959, 38). In the 1970s, two graduates in textile engineering from Pakistan approached a mill for technical posts and were told to 'go and work on the factory floor with rest of the "Pakis"' (Kalra 1993, 108). Many European refugee migrants experienced downward mobility — unable to obtain work that utilized their education or skills (Burrell 2006; McDowell 2001; Chamberlain 1997; Tannahill 1958). Employers often claimed they themselves held no bias, it was merely that 'the men' would not stand for it or that their clients would be unhappy.

Even before they arrived in the labour market, most migrants and indigenous women were at a disadvantage in the educational system. Migrant children, especially African-Caribbean boys, were three to four times more likely than average to be declared educationally subnormal and tracked out of the ordinary school system (Rose 1969). From the early 1950s girls tested equally or better to boys until age 16, but far fewer girls continued on to A levels or further education, with some local school systems deliberately upgrading boys' 11+ exam results so that more would be admitted to better secondary schools at the expense of better qualified girls (Sharpe 1976). After leaving school, men outnumbered women 5 to 1 at the university level and 43 per cent of boys went on to apprenticeships, while only 7 per cent of girls did. While 49 per cent of male manual workers were considered 'skilled', only 29 per cent of women were, mostly in the rapidly shrinking textile industry (Hunt 1968). Migrants tended to be blocked from apprenticeships in a similar manner.

Indigenous women professionals in particular often complained they had to be twice as good or have more qualifications than men to even be considered for jobs, as did migrants or their children. For example, nursing students applying from the Caribbean had to have A levels while British-born girls needed only O levels (Harriot 1992; Wilson 1981). One South London man who emigrated from Barbados at age 18 in 1955 remembered visiting the Labour Exchange as a traumatic experience: 'People didn't want to accept my Oxford and Cambridge certificates, even though they were corrected in this country and the system was the same. I had to find manual work, as a kitchen porter at a biscuit factory' (Chamberlain 1997, 184). Employers and officials often argued that migrants overstated their qualifications, an idea echoed by the media. In a January 1955 television programme — *Has Britain a Colour Bar?* — the BBC reported that 'a man from the West Indies might describe himself as a qualified fitter, and believe himself to be one. But Birmingham's industry standards are very high, and he may count himself lucky to hold down a job as a fitter's mate'. However, West Indian men were more likely to be in skilled manual labour than any other ethnic or racial group, again showing the dichotomy between skill and perception.

One area where all men and women have had different responses to discrimination in employment is in self-employment, which reduced the need to compete directly in the general labour market. While women are more likely than men to be underemployed, men are almost three times more likely to be self-employed than women. Of course, many businesses such as the corner shop required the work of unpaid family members, meaning that women's self-employment rates are probably underestimated. Migrant men are even more likely than native white men to open shops, a process that started among many migrants in the 1950s with fish and chips shops or Italian and Indian restaurants and expanded rapidly in the 1970s and 1980s as textile factories and other major sources of employment closed (Kalra 2000). Along with being forced into self-employment by lack of prospects, migrant men also desired autonomy or the ability to aid family. As a South London man whose parents had emigrated from Barbados noted.

> Somewhere along the line I'd like to own my own business. I always feel that a white has always got someone, a dad, a mate, "Get your boy over, we'll find room for him". That's the advantage they've got at the moment, and what black kids haven't got. If I own my own business, if my children can't get their own work, I can turn around and say, "Well come and work for me" (Chamberlain 1997, 197).

Even now many children of migrants, especially boys, forgo additional education in order to help a family business in the short-term (see Ali in this volume) or because they do not view education as a good investment in the belief that discrimination will keep them from getting a good job (Shaw 2005).

As noted earlier, policy and treatment of female workers was commonly based on assumptions of women's dependency or likely workforce participation. Such an assumption belied the trends in indigenous women's employment in this period, and was even less true for migrant women. Minority women are still disproportionately likely to work longer hours, on shift work or insecure temporary assignments or to be unemployed, yet are often stereotyped as being workshy. Most married women migrants worked in higher numbers than British-born white women. The exception was Pakistani and Bangladeshi women but their numbers may be somewhat underestimated as many did not go out to jobs but rather did 'homework' for the textile industry (Anwar 1979; Phizacklea 1990; Anthias 1992 and Ali in this volume). A 1958 study of EVW workers found that while only 20 per cent of the women recruited were still unmarried, about 80 per cent of women who had entered on the scheme were still employed (Tannahill 1958). As Kathy Burrell writes in this volume, while male Polish migrants may have idealised feminine, domestically-focused women, they also accepted that wives and mothers often had to work.

Occupational distribution and workforce participation rates for women have been closer across almost all ethnic or racial groups than men's. Migrant women were disproportionately likely, as with women in general, to be present in a few occupational categories: in this case, domestic service, nursing and medical services, and clothing production. The biggest difference in female work rates was the full and part-time participation rates of ethnic groups and the conditions of their work. By the 1970s, 45 per cent of all women who worked did so part-time. Almost all migrant women used to have higher full-time work rates than native women, but now Asian and other migrant women have similar part-time rates to native women, although Caribbean and African women are still almost twice as likely to work full-time as white women. While this is largely due to economic necessity because of their own low pay, low waged partners or higher levels of lone parenthood (Reynolds 1998), black women also tend to express much higher levels of desire for financial independence and autonomy than other women (Stone 1983).

Wendy Webster has argued that the high part-time work levels and image of native women as 'primarily wives and mothers, centred on domestic and familial life, was facilitated by [the] recruitment of migrant women to Britain as workers' (Webster 1998, xi). Kay and Miles have also argued that one reason that officials were initially determined to recruit only single women in EVW schemes was that it avoided conflict over married women's place, allowing the UK to 'boost number of textile workers whilst minimising the social wage and maintaining the gendered division of labour intact. Put another way, the right to 'family life' was denied to female refugees (as well as to men) in order to ensure that this 'right' could be 'imposed' on a significant proportion of British women' (Kay and Miles 1992, 177-79). Migrant women's identity as mothers was denigrated or subsumed in the need for them to do the work no longer wanted by native women (Webster 1998; Walter 2001). However, I would add that although migrant women's identity as mothers was indeed overlooked and later pathologised, for the reasons outlined earlier they were often denied the status of worker as well, making them even more invisible in the fabric of post-war British society. Schemes to recruit migrant women were primarily for low-status 'women's work' in healthcare, textile factories or domestic service. Officials did not always see this low-paid, subservient work as disrupting women's primary role as domestic and maternal. Even women who worked for pay could still be denied the status of 'workers'.

The ability to take on more flexible or part-time work often increases with skill, but also depends on economic necessity, preference, opportunities or lack of them and problems with childcare, such as cost or aid from a partner. Kathy Burrell's work on Polish migrants shows that many of them worked part-time while Louise Ryan's work on Irish nurses also demonstrates that many echoed the pattern of native white women of part-time work or dropping in and out of work depending on child care. Nurses' skill and social networks allowed them to create flexible or part-time schedules while their children were young, permitting them to keep contacts, skills or find opportunities to retain for positions with more career opportunities (Ryan 2007a and also in this volume).

Gender and Race Together

For many in an era in which the empire was rapidly disappearing, the increasing presence of migrants from the Commonwealth and empire became a focus of resentment and an unacceptable reminder of what had been lost. The image of 'England against empire', as both Wendy Webster and Chris Waters have written, was exacerbated by numerous negative depictions of a threatening empire, ideas which became particularly associated with migrants. These 'dark strangers' menaced the very identity of 'little England' (Waters 1997; Webster 2006).

Such racial stereotypes, combined with gender ideology, affected government immigration and labour policy. Before 1962, officials' view of the typical migrant was that of a black, sexually-threatening, unskilled man. While men did outnumber women, especially in Asian communities, officials acted as if *all* migrants were male. They particularly feared relationships between black men and white women and these sexual fears were a significant factor in shaping post-war immigration policy (Wilson 1997).

This is especially clear in examining the 1962 Commonwealth Immigrants Act. Although many migration histories portray this as simply a blatantly racist policy (Dean 1992; Paul 1997), it had many facets that racism alone cannot explain (Hickman 1998). Why would a government concerned about an influx of migration pass a law which had the effect of forcing an economically-useful migrant labour supply to permanently settle and change the typical migrant from an economically-active adult to a child? Prior to the 1962 legislation the majority of migrants were single males, but thereafter, the majority were part of family units. Officials' fears of interracial relationships meant that they designed the 1962 legislation to encourage the arrival of women as dependents perhaps because they saw them as a force to control migrant men's sexuality. The legislation required entrants to have a work voucher or be the dependent of a worker already in the country, and after its passage 74 per cent of Commonwealth migrants entered as female dependents or children. Women who had previously entered as workers in their own right found entry to the country far easier as a 'dependent'. In 1961, 93 per cent of West Indian and 92 per cent of Asian migrants were of working age, compared with 76 per cent of people born in Britain. In 1971 less than 60 per cent of migrants were of working age. Only the Irish, who had been omitted from the 1962 legislation, were still mainly migrating as single adults.

This policy, encouraging the settlement of wives and children, was premised on false assumptions about gender roles and employment, such as a belief that migrant women would not enter the paid labour force in large numbers because they were dependent on men to support them economically. These types of beliefs persisted in policymaking despite the changing economic and social reality that over half of married women were in paid employment by the mid 1960s, and migrant women worked in even higher numbers. Yet a 1965 telegram to colonial high commissioners discussing the labour impact of migration noted that of the 60,000 Commonwealth migrants admitted in 1964, 70 per cent were 'dependents,' i.e. wives and children, and thus would not be labour market participants (LAB 26/259). In 1985, government attorneys told the European High Court that the UK did not automatically grant entry of husbands of British citizens because they would be economically active, but they could admit wives because they would not be working (Bhabba 1985). Only by ignoring reality in this manner could government officials argue both that married women were non-workers dependent on men *and* that married women were the only suitable source of reserve labour because they found migrant labour so unacceptable. This view of women as dependents — not workers — persisted and shaped tax laws and welfare regulations along with the labour market and government policy generally.

While a negative image of the black male migrant and his sexuality shaped migration regulation to increase the number of women and children, once that happened, officials changed their minds again. As more women and children entered the country, official fears of miscegenation were replaced by an image of an overly-fertile female migrant — a welfare 'queen' living off the system, whose rampant offspring were taking over schools and hospitals, becoming criminal and violent, and threatening Britain's mainstream white culture (Hall 1978; Gilroy 1987). In response, the government moved to limit migration and prevent women and children from joining men already in the country. Ironically, it was migrant women's status as mothers and not workers that made them appear a threat to Britain. As the gender of the assumed typical migrant changed from the sexually-threatening man to the overly-fertile woman or delinquent child, all were constructed as dangerous competitors for shelter, education, medical resources or jobs.

Conclusion

In the post-war labour market, women (both migrants and native) and migrant men often had more in common with each other than with native white men. In many ways it is not surprising that marginal workers faced similar tactics in the job market since the association of 'migrants' or 'women' with reserve labour was so strong. However, there was a continuing belief that the two discursive groups were different kinds of resources and were separate from each other. Migrant men, black and white, existed in a separate market from most native-born men and all women, regardless of colour, just as almost all women existed in a separate labour market from men. In 1970, over 80 per cent of women had jobs in which virtually all their co-workers were female.

It was the assumption of women's dependence that kept the groups separate. Both 'women' and migrant men were constructed as 'problem' workers who belonged in special categories because of expected inherent traits, lack of skill or place in society. While lingering colonial racial ideology often partially feminised migrant men, no matter what — migrant men were still that — men. The irrational obsession and fear officials had regarding sexual relationships between migrant men and indigenous, white women led to the desire to exclude migrant men from British society but ironically helped to underline their masculine status. And because they were men, their status, even if subservient to white men, was inherently independent rather than dependent. Since women's presumed dependence on men was key to their secondary place in the post-war labour market, in this sense gender trumped race. While black men may often have been separated out in a different labour market from white men, the assumption of independence that stemmed from their gender also kept them from being included in the same position as women, despite many similar experiences as marginal employees but not 'workers'.

References

Alexander, P. and Halpern, R. (2000), *Racializing Class, Classifying Race* (London: Macmillan).

Anthias, F. (1992), *Ethnicity, Class, Gender and Migration* (Aldershot: Avebury).

Anwar, M. (1979), *The Myth of Return: Pakistanis in Britain* (London: Heinemann).

Bhabha, J., Klug, F. and Shutter, S. (1985), *Worlds Apart: Women Under Nationality and Immigration Law* (London: Virago).

Braithwaite, E.R. (1959), *To Sir With Love* (Englewood Cliffs, NJ: Prentice-Hall).

Burrell, K. (2006), *Moving Lives: Narratives of Nation and Migration among Europeans in Post-War Britain* (Aldershot: Ashgate).

Burrell, K. and Panayi, P. (eds) (2006), *Histories and Memories: Migrants and their History in Britain* (London: I.B. Tauris).

Carby, H.V. (1982), 'White Woman Listen!', in Centre for Contemporary Cultural Studies, *The Empire Strikes Back* (London: Hutchinson), 212-35.

Chamberlain, M. (1997), *Narratives of Exile and Return* (New York: St. Martin's Press).

Cheema, S.S. (2006), www.coming2coventry.org, accessed 9 September 2006.

Coming2coventry.org (2006), *Coming to Coventry: Stories from the South Asia Pioneers*, Exhibit and Book, The Herbert Museum, Coventry.

Daye, S. (1994), *Middle-Class Blacks in Britain* (New York: St. Martin's Press).

Dean, D.W. (1992), 'Conservative Governments and the Restriction of Commonwealth Immigration in the 1950s', *The Historical Journal* 35:1, 171-94.

Faulkner, S. and Ramamurthy, A. (eds) (2006), *Visual Culture and Decolonisation in Britain* (Aldershot: Ashgate).

Hall, S. (1978), *Policing the Crisis* (London: Macmillan).

Harriot, J. (1992), *Black Women in Britain* (London: B.T. Batsford).

Herbert, J. (2006), 'Migration, Memory and Metaphor: Life Stories of South Asians in Leicester', in Burrell, K. and Panayi, P. (eds), 133-148.

Hickman, M. (1998), 'Reconstructing Deconstructing "Race": British Political Discourses about the Irish in Britain', *Ethnic and Racial Studies* 21:2, 289-307.

Hunt, A. (1968), *A Survey of Women's Employment* (London: HMSO).

Kalra, V.S. (2000), *From Textile Mills to Taxi Ranks* (Aldershot: Ashgate).

Kay D. and Miles, R. (1992), *Refugees or Migrant Workers? European Volunteer Workers in Britain 1946-1951* (London: Routledge).

Kofman, E., Phizacklea A., Raghuram, P. and Sales, R. (2000), *Gender and International Migration in Europe* (London: Routledge).

LAB (Ministry of Labour and Successors) Public Record Office, The National Archives, Kew. The following series were cited LAB 8 – Employment Policy files; LAB 10 – Industrial Relations; LAB 26 – Welfare Department.

Lunn, K. (2000), 'A Racialized Hierarchy of Labour?', in Alexander, P. and Halpern, R. (eds), 104-121.

McDowell, L. (2005), *Hard Labour: The Forgotten Voices of Latvian Migrant 'Volunteer' Workers* (London: UCL).

Paul, K. (1997), *Whitewashing Britain: Race and Citizenship in the Post-war Era* (Ithaca: Cornell University Press).

PEP (Political and Economic Planning) (1971), *Women on Top* (London: Allen & Unwin).

Phizacklea, A. (1990), *Unpacking the Fashion Industry: Gender, Racism and Class in Production* (London: Routledge).

—— (ed.) (1983), *One Way Ticket: Migration and Female Labour* (London: Routledge).

Reynolds, T. (2001), 'Black Mothering, Paid Work and Identity', *Ethnic and Racial Studies* 24:6 (November), 1046-64.

Rose, E.B.J. et al. (1969), *Colour and Citizenship* (London: Oxford University Press for the Institute of Race Relations).

Rose, S. (1992), *Limited Livelihoods: Gender and Class in Nineteenth Century England* (Berkeley: University of California Press).

Ryan, L. (2007a), 'Migrant Women, Social Networks and Motherhood: The Experiences of Irish Nurses in Britain', *Sociology* 4:2, 295-312.

—— (2007b), 'Who Do You Think You Are? Irish nurses Encountering Ethnicity and Constructing Identity in Britain', *Ethnic and Racial Studies* 30:3, 416-438.

Sharpe, S. (1976), *'Just like a Girl!': How Girls Learn to be Women* (Harmondsworth: Penguin).

Shaw, A. (2000), *Kinship and Continuity: Pakistani Families in Britain* (Amsterdam: Harwood Academic Publishing).

Sinha, M. (1997), *Colonial Masculinity: The 'Manly Englishman' and the 'Effeminate Bengali'* (Manchester: Manchester University Press).

Stone, K. (1983), 'Motherhood and Waged Work: West Indian, Asian and White Mothers Compared', in Phizacklea, A. (ed.), 33-52.

Tabili, L. (1994), *'We Ask for British Justice': Workers and Racial Difference in Late Imperial Britain* (Ithaca: Cornell University Press).

Tanahill, J.A. (1958), *European Volunteer Workers in Britain* (Manchester: Manchester University Press).

Virdee, S. (2000), 'Racism and Resistance in British Trade Unions, 1948-1979', in Alexander, P. and Halpern, R. (eds), 122-49.

Walls, P. and Williams, R. (2003), 'Sectarianism at Work', *Ethnic and Racial Studies* 26:4, 632-61.

Walter, B. (2001), *Outsiders Inside: Whiteness, Place and Irish Women* (London: Routledge).

Waters, C. (1997), '"Dark Strangers" in Our Midst: Discourses of Race and Nation in Britain, 1947-1963', *Journal of British Studies* 36:2, 207-238.

Webster, W. (1998), *Imagining Home: Gender, 'Race' and National Identity, 1945-64* (London: UCL).

—— (2006), '"There'll Always be an England": Representations of Colonial Wars and Immigration, 1948-1968', in Faulkner, S. and Ramamurthy, A. (eds), 189-214.

Wilson, A. (1981), *Finding a Voice, Asian Women in Britain* (London: Virago).

Wilson, D.S. (1997), 'True-born English: Gender, Race and Citizenship in Commonwealth Immigration to England, 1945-1972' (MA Thesis, Northeastern University, USA).

—— (2005), '"The True Sphere of Women"?: Gender, Work and Equal Pay in Britain, 1945-1975' (PhD Dissertation, Boston College, USA).

—— (2006), 'A New Look At The Affluent Worker: The Good Working Mother in Post-War Britain', *Twentieth Century British History* 17:2, 206-229.

Chapter 6

Notions of 'Home' and Belonging Among Greeks in the UK

Venetia Evergeti

In his film, *Brides* (*Nyfes* in Greek) Pantelis Voulgaris deals with the massive waves of migration from Greece and Asia Minor to the USA at the turn of the last century.[1] The film follows the journeys of women who, with a photograph in their hands and a wedding dress in their little bags, were making the long boat journey to America where prospective, but unknown grooms were waiting to meet them on Ellis Island. These men were Greek immigrants who wanted to marry women from their own country and often from their own villages or islands back in Greece. The film explores the struggles, the hardships and the risks that these women and men took in order to make a new life for themselves in a new country. In a unique and very delicate way, the film unfolds the issues of migration, war, poverty, family obligations and arranged marriage through the viewpoint of a woman who is forced to choose between love and her obligations towards her family. At the beginning of the film we see hundreds of women waiting in the harbour of Odessa for the boat that will take them away from their homes and families and towards an unknown future. Holding their few belongings, they already look displaced and disoriented, at the beginning of a migration journey with no return that is both 'forced' and voluntary. At the end of the film we see a similar scene — this time another harbour in another country, where hundreds of men are waiting dressed in their best, some holding flowers and the Greek flag, their faces showing similar feelings to the women at the beginning — anticipation and hope but also concern and fear. In this way the film looks at the social reality of human movements and the hopes and anxieties that they involve.

Although this type of Greek and other European migration history has not been fully addressed within migration studies, migrating in order to marry and form a family forms part of family related migration (Kofman 2004, 246). The central theme of the film is beyond the scope of this essay. However, *Brides* captures in a unique way, some of the issues addressed here, namely the experiences of migratory journeys, and the role of family (transnational or not) in forming notions of and attachments to the homeland. In particular, I am interested in the ways in which migrants become 'strangers' and 'home-comers' (Schuetz 1944; 1945) both 'here

---

1   *Brides* (Panteli Voulgaris and Martin Scorsese, 2004).

and there' and in the ways they negotiate their multiple cultural belongings and ethnic 'master statuses' (Hughes 1945). Through two case studies I show how ethnic identity becomes a situated property, a resource, used by members of a particular group to accomplish or resist an ethnic membership (Moerman 1968; Day 1998) or the obligations associated with such a membership. In the same way, the notion of home changes not only according to different individual experiences, but also depending on social situations and circumstances. Furthermore, as Louise Ryan argues in this collection, 'relationships develop in the context of social roles and over time these can change in salience as individuals move in and out of roles'. Therefore, Greekness is 'ethnicised' in a variety of ways and through different memories and practices. It is such 'ethnicisation' processes and transnational family experiences that I wish to explore in this chapter.

Using the life narratives of two Greek women, Miranda and Anna,[2] this chapter explores the interactional order through which they (re)formulate their notions of homeland and manage their achievement of belonging, especially in relation to their transnational family links and contacts. Miranda is in her late 30s and moved to the UK 17 years ago, whereas Anna is in her 60s and has been in the UK for the last 40 years. Both women have 'transnational families' in that they have their own children and husbands in the UK but still retain strong family connections in Greece (parents, siblings and extended kin). Often analyses of migration focus on 'explanations' or the reasons that led to the decision to move. Although such accounts were central in Anna and Miranda's narratives, they did not describe their movement as 'migration' but as a continuous journey. Thus, the symbolism and fluidity of movement and transition were essential in talking about their identities, families and belonging.

I place my discussion within the wider context of this volume: the relationship of gender and ethnicity in migration experiences. Secondly, I analyse parts of the narratives of the two female participants and look at theorizations of Greek communities in the diaspora. By using personal accounts my aim is to explore the migratory experience from the perspectives of the participants themselves and to demonstrate some of the inadequacies of the generalized theorizations of Greekness. In doing so, I emphasize the importance of an interpretive methodological and conceptual stance that is sensitive to the inter-subjective and 'processual' nature of the human lived experience (Blumer 1969; Pruss 1996).

Gender and Family in Migration Studies

Early migration studies focused mainly on labour migrants exploring the lives, economic status and social inequalities of migrant men. Women were seen as simply following the migratory strategies of their families or their husbands. A reaction to this conceptual model and its focus on migrant men came from within feminist studies which showed that migrant women were also active economically and recognising their struggles and hard work as they often looked after their children while taking care of family finances or working in the family business (Phizacklea

---

2   Names have been changed to protect confidentiality.

1983; Morokvasic 1984). Developments within the field of gender and migration theory saw women as independent, self-reliant and active migrants themselves, who played important economic roles both within their family and their migrant communities (Tastsoglou and Maratou-Alipranti 2003; Bauer and Thomson, 2004). Women's experiences were often examined through race, gender and class inequalities (Phizacklea 1982 and 1983; Anthias 1992). This approach has provided invaluable insights. However, through its focus on female labour and the contribution of women to the ethnic economy, it tends to ignore other aspects of family and ethnic relations (Evergeti 2006) whilst also producing a conceptualization of gender as a synonym for women. More recent studies have started looking at the wider social relations and the migration process through the experiences of both men and women (Kofman et al. 2000; Willis and Yeoh 2000).

Until fairly recently, family related migration has not received sufficient academic attention. Eleonore Kofman has identified at least three main categories of family migration in the European context. The first is 'family reunification' relating to processes of bringing in the primary migrant's immediate family members; the second is 'family formation or marriage migration' covering mainly second and third generation migrants who bring in spouses from their parents' places of origin or potential brides from outside the European Union; and the third is 'family migration' and refers to the cases of whole families migrating together (Kofman 2004, 246-247). However, Kofman explains that such categories are not fixed but flexible and changing over time and circumstances. More significantly these cases are not covered by migration statistics, which makes all the more important the usage of a methodology sensitised to the experiences and emotions of migrants, such as family narratives and ethnographic observations (Bauer and Thompson 2004; Christou 2002; Ryan 2002 and 2004). In addition to the above categorization, most migration is related to family in that it often (but not always) entails decisions that involve and have a great impact not just on the migrant but also other members of their families (Nauck and Settles 2001).

Currently there has been a significant shift towards studies that focus on the interactional and inter-subjective reality of migration, exploring the experiences of migrants on a community or household level (rather than the dominant macro-economic one) using mainly qualitative methods such as life stories, participant observation and interviews (Evergeti and Zontini 2006). The focus on transnational relations has also added an important element to our understanding of the migratory experience and the important role of friends and family in maintaining and reproducing ethnic networks across the borders (Vertovec 1999 and 2002; Portes et al. 1999; Zontini 2006). The emphasis here is on social actors and their transnational activities instead of nation-states and their economies. Such studies have unveiled the impact of migration on families both in the country of destination and 'back home' (Agozino 2000). Another area that is currently emerging but was neglected in previous studies relates to women's agency in sustaining transnational cultures and their role in negotiating and reciprocating family responsibilities between the host country and the homeland and across generations (Ryan this collection; Zontini 2006; Evergeti 2006).

Narratives of Greek Migration

The discussion is set within the general context of Greek migration and more specifically Greek diaspora communities. The focus on women's immigrant experiences and narratives does not exclude the importance of masculine identities and their (re)formation through migratory movements, neither does it denote gender as a female property. Rather, it attempts to discover and analyse the perspectives of women and their contributions to the migration process (Anthias and Lazaridis 2000). My exploration of some elements of women's gendered identities in the Greek diaspora also aims to shed light on how men and women negotiate, shape or resist their migrant gendered identities vis-à-vis each other. As shown below, expectations about masculine identities are often revealed or reflected in women's descriptions and orientations.

In their narratives, Miranda and Anna talked about their journeys of migration not as a one-off movement from Greece to the UK but as an ongoing dynamic process of self-searching and identity forming through visits back home and contacts with family and friends both 'here and there'. This continuous movement was even more pertinent in Miranda's case, since she recently moved to Italy with Nick, her Greek husband, and children. Their positions and relationships within their families in Greece seemed to play a very important role in their decisions to stay abroad or return *home*. Their experiences reflect the complexity of living in the *xenitia*[3] (pronounced *ksenetea*) whilst trying to maintain family responsibilities and relations both in the homeland and their adopted country.

Their stories also reflect how migration has been experienced historically in Greece, and to a lesser extent, in Cyprus. At the turn of the century, nearly 7 per cent of the population in Greece had migrated (Laliotou 2004, 53). Although we do not have family narratives that examine the experience of migration from the point of view of the family members that remained behind, it is fair to say that at the time almost the entire population was affected in one or another way by migration (Laliotou 2004). Similarly, by the 1980s it was reported that one in six Greek Cypriots lived abroad and mainly in the UK (Alladina and Edwards 1991). In this respect, in countries like Greece and Cyprus constant emigration (both European and transatlantic) and its cultural representations in the homeland have played an important role in the formation of national histories and identities (Laliotou 2004; Clogg 1999).[4]

---

3   *Xenitia* is a very important concept in the Greek and Greek Cypriot literary tradition and political discourse. It refers to the 'uprooting' or becoming *xenos* (a foreigner or stranger in another country). Many popular songs, national poems and plays have been written on the theme of *xenitia* and its impact on the Greek national identity and the formation of a collective narrative of displacement.

4   Although South Europe has traditionally been a region of emigration, more recently it has been transformed into an important destination for new immigrants. As a result, recent work on the topic of migration in relation to Greece and other South European countries has focused on the new waves of immigrants that have been arriving in these regions during the last 20 years (Fakiolas 2003; Hatziprokopiou 2003; Psimenos and Kassimati 2003; Triandafyllidou and Veikou 2002).

The majority of Greeks and Greek Cypriots arrived in Britain in the post-war period and are part of the wider European, and more specifically Mediterranean, migration to this country. It is difficult to know their exact numbers since they are classified as 'white' in official data, but it has been estimated that their combined numbers in London are approximately 200,000-250,000, making them one of the largest white ethnic minorities in London, with smaller communities in various cities such as Birmingham, Leicester and Manchester (Georgiou 2001; Constantinides 1984). Greeks and Greek Cypriots have, however, been largely ignored within the sociology of ethnic relations in the UK. Alladina and Edwards (1991, 187) have argued that this is a general problem for Mediterranean and other European communities in Britain, who are often invisible and can only be distinguished by their names. Research on other white ethnic groups has, however, revealed the heterogeneity of such groups and the significant cultural and material differences which may divide them from the majority population (Burrell 2006; Zontini 2006).

Greeks and Greek Cypriots are often undifferentiated in the literature on their migration (Constantinides 1984): a practice which neglects the important historical and contextual specificities in their movement to and settlement in the UK. Migrants from mainland Greece have included large numbers of students and professionals, which is also reflected in the stories of Anna and Miranda. Greek Cypriots share more commonalities with other Commonwealth citizens who came to Britain as economic migrants looking for a better life (Burrell 2005; 2006; Anthias 1992). There are some studies of Greek Cypriots in Britain (Anthias 1992; Constantinides 1984; Georgiou 2000; Oakley 1979; 1987; 1989) but research on Greeks from the mainland is more limited. Apart from the pioneering work of Theodore Dowling and Edwin Fletcher (1915) and some historical research exploring the Greek presence in Britain from the early fourteenth century onwards (Harris 2002; Roussou 1992; Carras 1997) there have not been any major studies of mainland Greeks or any studies comparing the two communities. Given this background, the choice of Greek rather than Greek Cypriot women here is intended to cover some of the gaps in the literature on the experiences of mainland-Greeks in the UK. This focus also relates to my own positionality (Willis and Yeoh 2000; Christou 2002) towards the issues and themes addressed in my research. I am a sociologist and ethnographer but also a Greek woman living in the UK and sharing some cultural understandings with the study's participants.

Parental Families and Migrant Voyages

In both interviewees' stories of their movement to the UK, their families (both their parental family in Greece and their own family here) have played an important role in their decisions to stay, settle or return — even for short periods of time. Miranda left Greece when she was 21 in order to join her then partner:

I came to the UK in September 1991, pregnant with my son Alexis who was born in December 1991. Dionisis, his father, was doing his Masters in London and I followed him. I did not want to come to the UK but I wanted to have my child and I loved Dionisis. My mum pushed me a lot to follow him there and pretended as if all was normal, as any married couple. But we were not married and Dionisis was a highly irresponsible father all the way. In May 1991 we went to Zakynthos and Alonisos [two Greek islands] for a year and a half, for his PhD research. After that Dionisis went to the UK in September and I went back to my college to finish my Bachelor in Psychology in Athens. He stopped talking to me from London, he disappeared. My mum saw how deeply sad I was and took me for a trip to India with the 2 year old then Alexis, thus saving me in a way. Dionisis found out how well I was doing in late spring, five months after he abandoned us, came back and begged me to get married. I felt obliged, so I agreed. In September 1994 we three went back to the UK as a family. My mum pretends to her social circle all is normal. She pays a lot and I am to study psychology in London, abandoning my degree in Athens only one semester before the end (Miranda).

At the end Miranda separated from Dionisis because one night he hit both her and their son. However, this time she did not return to Greece but decided to stay in London and raise her son on her own. Both her orientation to how her family in Greece viewed her situation and networks of support in the UK played a significant part in her decision to stay:

My dad said then that I should forgive him, since I chose him. However, for me living with a man that hits is worse than death and I felt betrayed that nobody in Greece asked me to go back, but instead they were all happy for me to be "there", not with them. In the beginning they were living with the shame of having an unmarried daughter pregnant. Then I guess it was far easier for them to have me live in the UK so that they could build the fantasy they wanted about my reality. However they did help a lot, financially and practically. Even the extended family was more or less shameful of me at that time ... Instead in the UK, the police made me feel secure that Dionisis did not even have the right to come within close proximity. The university I was attending in London had a very loving therapist who acted as a mother for me. Dionisis's two Greek female friends who luckily were in our house that night — cannot imagine what would have happened if they were not there to stop him — made it their duty to help and support me out of the horrible phase ... So I stayed in London when I broke up with Dionisis, because I felt, although not explicitly told, that both parents did not want me back there. I also wanted to stay away from all. I wanted to have the space and privacy to see how to proceed, reflect on things. I was clearly a social disgrace for them if living in Greece with my illegitimate son, and I was treated like such whereas I did not feel as such. I was proud of being a great mum, of being me (Miranda).

By attending to the view point of her parents (in relation to herself), Miranda developed her lines of action in order to take into account both her own and her family's version of her situation (Prus 1996).

Although Anna's story is very different from Miranda's, there are some parallels in that her decisions to move and settle in the UK were inter-subjective in nature, her choices reflecting her orientations to her family's perspectives and reality. Anna first came to England in the 1960s in order to study.[5] Her parents initially opposed her decision to leave Greece — at the time she was only 20 years old and they were worried that she would meet and marry someone in the UK. Anna initially wanted to study and then return to Greece but explained that she was always finding excuses in

---

5   For an earlier, preliminary analysis of Anna's narrative see Evergeti 2006.

further courses for staying longer. Once she finished her education as a teacher, she decided that she wanted to stay for a few more years in order to gain work experience in the British educational system. But she explained that her determination to extend her stay in the UK was also a reaction to the constraining norms surrounding women's status in her home town at that time and the social expectations to marry by match making. Because she was opposed to this practice, Anna did not want to get married. In this respect, her interpretation of her social environment and her parents' expectations were important in her decision to remain in the UK.

Other studies of migration have shown how negative aspects of notions of the homeland might influence migrants' choices to settle in the adopted country (Ryan 2002; Georgiou 2001). Earlier studies of Greek Cypriots (rather than mainland Greeks) in the UK have emphasised traditional family structures and their significant role in maintaining a strong ethnic identity (Anthias 1992; Constantinides 1984; Georgiou 2000; Oakley 1979; 1987; 1989). Such studies have highlighted the important role of women not only in relation to familial and community networks but also in facilitating a strong ethnic economy (Anthias 1992; Oakley 1979). However, such studies have failed to address ethnic 'identity-as-context' (Zimmerman 1998) and the interaction order through which Greek women might negotiate different elements of their 'ascribed' ethnic and gender identities. As I mentioned above, focusing on migrant women's gendered identities can also provide an insight into the ways people categorise themselves and, in forming complex identities, often resist (masculine or feminine) categorisations constructed by others (Antaki and Widdicombe 1998). Even when Anna met Jim (her husband) she did not want to get married.

> I didn't want to get married, I just wanted to devote myself to teaching and the truth is I didn't have time for myself. Sometimes even in the weekends I was going to my pupils' houses to visit them. I had chosen to teach in South East London where I had most of my difficulties because it was a rough area and the children had many learning difficulties and other problems. They were orphans or they were from other countries, from Africa, Asia and they used to live in council flats. Sometimes when I was entering their flats I was thinking "hell can't be worse than that". But teaching these children and helping them fulfilled me and I really enjoyed it. And when Jim was telling me to get married and have a family I used to say to him "I have 36 children I don't want anymore" referring to my students (Anna).

Eventually they did get married and now have four grown up children. Marrying Jim brought a strong reaction from her parents and especially her father who initially saw his daughter's marriage outside the Greek Orthodox Church as a betrayal. However, as Anna explained: 'Eventually, my parents came over here and Jim's parents came to Greece and they all met and got on fine. My father loved Jim very much at the end'. Apart from her oldest daughter, who recently spent a year working as a teacher in Greece, none of the other three children speak any Greek. In her narrative Anna was very apologetic about this:

> I tried hard to teach them Greek when they were young but it was very difficult. I did not have any Greek friends or community around me so they did not hear me speak Greek

with others. As they were getting older they started reacting to it and were telling me not to speak to them in that language. Jim was very keen for the children to be bilingual. He would often come in from work and the first thing he would ask would be whether I had taught the children any Greek. That used to make me nervous and only put more pressure on me. Eventually I gave up (Anna).

However, this is an on-going issue for her family and friends in Greece who even now express their disappointment and often reprimand her for not trying harder to teach her mother tongue to her children. They see this as an important element of the children's Greek identity and an important obstacle in their communication with them. For Anna however, this has become an ambiguous issue because as the children have grown up it has become less relevant for them.

Miranda also referred to the changing dynamics of her relationship with her family once she met and married Nick (her husband who is also Greek). She explained that she never had very close relationships with members of the extended family but her status changed once she got married: 'I was a bit of an outcast really. I know that some, more than others, started treating me differently ever since I married Nick. They are proud of me now...' Apart from her first son, Alexis, Miranda has two more children with Nick now. Because of Nick's work with an Italian company they recently moved from the UK to Italy. Although all three children speak Greek she expressed similar issues to Anna's in relation to the importance of language in Greek socialisation but she also expressed her desire for her children to be open to all cultures.

We speak Greek at home, but they do not go to any special school for Greek. I try to respect and learn within limits the Italian culture, or find the common denominators in all cultures. These things that we people have in common and try to perceive and accept in a humoristic way the differences. That is my philosophy to the kids. I am a bit judgemental, in the sense of notifying certain cultural blind spots, for example, British people not enjoying children, Italian people always asking for fashionable dressing at all times or Greek people complaining all the time about their more than average quality of life. I am trying to speak about these things with the kids openly ... (Miranda).

Transnational Roles and Responsibilities

In their narratives, both Miranda and Anna referred to the dual responsibilities that they had towards their own families and their parental families in Greece. They also described how living far away from their parents resulted in not having enough support in caring for their children. This was more pertinent in Anna's case because she had moved to the UK much earlier than Miranda, when traveling back and forth to Greece was not as easy and cheap as it is now. Also, her husband and his parents were English and she did not feel that their sense of providing support was similar to the Greek traditions, where grandparents are often actively involved in bringing up their grandchildren. As she explained:

When the children were young I didn't have anyone close to me to help me. As soon as I had the first child, Jim's parents decided to move to Devon and of course my parents were back in Greece. At that time the trip between Greece and Britain was more difficult to make. But I used to take all four children on extended holidays during the summer months to Greece and we would stay with my mum and dad and it was great to have the help and support then. But I did feel the loneliness and lack of family support when back in the UK (Anna).

Miranda also explained that during the summer months and other important holidays she and Nick try to go for extended periods of time back to Greece where the children can enjoy the extended kin and socialize with other members of both families within their own cultural environment. However, similarly to Anna, she expressed her concern about not having enough support with the children, and the impact on her children of the absence of extended family:

The first impact on my family through living abroad is huge lack of help with the kids especially in the first years … This falls mainly on my shoulders. For the children … they see other kids in extended families and they feel the void. Even more when my parents come over and then leave (Miranda).

She also described how her mother would travel to the UK or more recently to Italy in order to provide help when needed, especially when Miranda is sick.

According to Deborah Bryceson and Ulla Vuorela, transnational families are relational and temporal in nature in that they provide a source of identity through relational ties and are linked to individual life cycles (Bryceson and Vuorela 2002, 3-30). Therefore, such relationships and responsibilities change through the life course and the changing needs of different members of the transnational family (also see Ryan this collection). In this respect, both women expressed their concern about their ageing parents and being able to offer their help and support when needed. As Miranda put it:

I would go if health issues arise. When my grandmother went to hospital and it was serious, I went to Greece with my son while pregnant with my daughter. I was there for three weeks and could not leave to return to Italy. I was waiting and kept postponing my return every weekend. She died a week after and I travelled back less than a month before giving birth (Miranda).

Having been away for longer, and with older parents, this was a very serious and constant concern for Anna. She described how some years ago she had to make a very difficult decision to leave her children with her husband for almost three months and go to Greece to spend time with her dying father. Now that her mother is in her late 80s, Anna travels to Greece every few months to spend some quality time with her. She explained that she always feels bad for leaving behind her own family and, when the time comes to return, she feels guilty for leaving her mother. Both Anna and Miranda described their dual family obligations in relation to their ethnic and cultural belonging and sometimes in contrast to what they perceived as British cultural expectations. In this respect, such dual obligations often became sources of ethnic and gender identification (Evergeti 2006).

Becoming a 'Stranger' and a 'Home-comer'

Anna and Miranda found my questions about belonging the most difficult to address. Interestingly in one or another way they both connected their belonging to their memories of their homeland or particular places and times when growing up. Anna described to me in a nostalgic way her memories of the neighbourhood where she grew up. Her memories of Greece were connected to her childhood community and her notions of homeland and ethnic roots were vividly attached to her locality rather than the country as a whole. As she explained: 'If I don't go to Patra (her birth place, where her mother still lives) when I am in Greece, I don't feel like I have been at home. The sense of neighbourhood and community there is different, much stronger'.

Miranda expressed similar feelings but her situation gave her the extra complexity of interacting with two 'foreign' cultures.

> It is clear to say that I missed Greece far more when I was in England than now in Italy. Is it the weather? The warmth in relationships? ... I do not know where I belong. I do not want to belong to any country. If I imagine Greece without all the people I love there, then I might as well belong to Africa. I love the warm and sunny colours, the sea smell. But that I could find elsewhere I imagine, or not? I know I breathe better when I am there. Why, I do not know. But it's as if I come more alive. When I was little, I remember feeling that I was coming alive when we went to the patriko (family) house in Nafplio, the house of my grandmother. I felt alive there and when we went back to Athens it was like a dark cloud on my shoulders. It is a bit similar now... (Miranda).

What Anna and Miranda described to me about their position in relation to their homeland is very similar to Schuetz's portrayal of the 'stranger' and the 'home comer'. Schuetz has differentiated these two social categories (Schuetz 1944 and 1945). He states that:

> To the home-comer, home shows — at least in the beginning — an unaccustomed face. He believes himself to be in a strange country, a stranger among strangers ... But the home-comer's attitude differs from that of the stranger. The latter is about to join in a group which is not and never has been his own ... The home-comer, however, expects to return to an environment of which he always had and — so he thinks — still has intimate knowledge and which he has just to take for granted in order to find his bearings within it (1945, 369).

However, these are not static conditions and depending on the interactional context Anna and Miranda found themselves becoming strangers and home-comers both in Greece and in their adopted countries. Such experiences were often connected to interactions with family members and friends. As Anna put it:

> In Greece my friends and family often tell me that I have become Anglicized. My accent, my mannerisms even the way I dress, is often seen as different as a result of living in Britain. Sometimes I feel like a *xeni* (foreigner, stranger) in my own country. But here (in the UK) I am always seen as foreign (Anna).

Although she goes to Greece three to four times a year, for at least ten days at a time, in order to spend time with her older mother, Anna still sometimes feels unaccustomed to the every day practices and home environment of her mother. She attributes this to the fact that her mother does not like change and she finds Anna's acts of caring (for example, cooking or doing the shopping for her) as interfering with her usual routine. Often the home-comer's every day interactions and interpretations are different from those of her family. The intimate knowledge she thought she had of her home environment is not there any more. Similarly her family's intimate knowledge of her and 'the way she used to be' is not relevant any more because it does not reflect her current status.

In Miranda's case, her experience of being a *xeni* is often rooted in her sense of rejection from her parental family. She explained that there are times when she, as well as Nick, feel isolated and in some ways cut off from their families in Greece.

> We used to go to a therapist in Milan. One day he said to us that our parental families did not want us in Greece, both of us. If I look objectively at the situation, they all four (hers and Nick's parents in Greece) have never made a single move, symbolic or not, to have us or to keep us close ... I am definitely not a victim type, but I do feel in my body the loss or the rejection of the family in a very subtle level and not only. Now after 16 years, I have consciously decided to let go. So we are now looking towards creating our own roots in Greece, meaning buying property independently of where our families live (Miranda).

However, ethnic identification techniques are intrinsically connected to resisting the status of the 'stranger'. For example, recent research has highlighted the importance of managing and maintaining transnational family links with the homeland and the diverse notions of Greekness that these facilitate (Evergeti 2006). Political participation and activism, return migration and extended visits are all important transnational activities through which national and local conceptions of the homeland are reproduced and maintained (Burrell 2006). Although Miranda felt her family's rejection she explained that she and her children would spend the best part of the summer months 'back home' and that the children enjoyed the family and extended kin connections of both hers and Nick's Greek families (especially with her mother's side of the family which was big). Thus, families are often brought together to share special occasions and important life-cycle events such as births, christenings, weddings and funerals. These family connections across borders reinforce caring responsibilities both 'here' and 'there' but also a sense of ethnic belonging (Bryceson and Vuorela 2002).

Some studies have shown that ethnic solidarity and associations provide an important platform for formulating and reinforcing ethnic values, practices and identities within a multicultural environment (Anthias 1992; Rex and Josephides 1987; Georgiou 2000). Community clubs, satellite media, the church and other formal and informal institutions facilitate a connection with one's ethnic community in Britain (Georgiou 2000; Burrell 2006). In different degrees this was true for both my research participants. For Anna, religion and her social connections with the community of the Orthodox Church she attends every Sunday were of paramount importance in keeping in touch with her ethnic and cultural roots. Their importance was described to me not only in terms of religion (which plays a significant role in

Anna's life) but also in terms of the friendships and networks of support shared with
the other Greek and Greek Cypriot women in her parish. Although religion was not
as important for Miranda and she did not try to socialize her children in the Greek
Orthodox Church, she explained that she wanted them to be comfortable with their
religion's rituals and customs. She explained that during Christmas and Greek Easter
she would observe some of the rituals associated with the holidays. As she put it:

> I am not trying to socialize the children in the Greek religion, but I do want them to feel
> comfortable with its rituals as well as those of other religions. I burn incense and I do have
> some Greek icons at home. If we stay at home for Easter I would paint red some eggs, or
> make *vasilopita* (a Greek cake made for new year's eve) for new year. I definitely do not
> feel like going home when I go to church, and I only go once or twice a year maximum.
> However, I love it when I go and sit alone in the church, it stirs emotions in me and
> thoughts or childhood memories like when I used to act the ceremonies with my cousin in
> the little *eklisaki* (church) near my grandmother's house ... (Miranda).

Conclusion

Using selections from the narratives of two research participants, this chapter has
explored the inter-subjective nature of migration and movement and the on-going
negotiation of roles and responsibilities within transnational families. As shown in
both Miranda's and Anna's life stories their choices and decisions about staying
abroad or returning home were highly influenced by their orientations towards
their families. In this respect, both women had difficulties with their families
back in Greece around issues of autonomy, career and their gender roles. Miranda
encountered her family's disapproval because of splitting up with her first partner
and initially becoming a single mother, whereas Anna felt that she disappointed
her parents because she married a 'foreigner' outside the Greek Orthodox Church
and did not manage to teach her children the Greek language. As mentioned in the
beginning, migrants' orientations to different members of their transnational families
are important in negotiating their different roles and responsibilities and in forming
their decisions about staying abroad.

Other studies of Greek immigrant communities (mainly in America and Australia)
have also shown the diversity of Greek experience outside the homeland (Kourvetaris
1997; Orfanos 2002). Being 'Greek' is expressed in a variety of ways and manifests
itself concurrently with other forms of identity depending on the social, cultural or
situational specificities. As Brubaker argues, diaspora, and I would add ethnic identity,
is not a 'bounded entity', but a 'category of practice' (Brubaker 2005, 12) which
acquires practical and symbolic significance in particular circumstances. In Anna's
narrative this was expressed in her description of the church services she attended
every Sunday. Miranda on the other hand, mentioned that she and her husband tried
to bring up their children within some of the Greek customs and cultural rituals.
Furthermore, Anna's and Miranda's stories show that ethnic belonging is a dynamic
and flexible property that social actors achieve through multiple interactions both
'here and there'. The family, the community of origin and memories of the past
become significant ethnic identification tools in describing experiences of movement.

In this respect (Greek) ethnic and gender roles are expressed, acquired, interpreted or in some cases resisted through different relations, experiences and appreciation of a given situation.

What becomes apparent in Anna's and Miranda's narratives is the complexity of transnational family ties and responsibilities and the way these change over time and with the shifting needs of different members of the family. As shown throughout the chapter using detailed qualitative evidence is of immense importance in drawing attention to the complex ways in which such relationships can be related to movement and migration. The sense of becoming a 'stranger' in both cultures was strong for both women but this was often resisted by the reiteration of family links back in Greece and the family's mutual involvement in caring obligations. Regardless of the periodic disapproval that Anna and Miranda encountered from their parental families, they still considered it important not only to socialize their own children within their extended Greek families but also viewed their own involvement in transnational caring as a significant component of their ethnic culture.

References

Agozino, B. (ed.) (2000), *Theoretical and Methodological Issues in Migration Research: Interdisciplinary, Intergenerational and International Perspectives* (Aldershot: Ashgate).

Alladina, S. and Edwards, V. (eds) (1991), *Multilingualism in the British Isles: The Older Mother Tongues and Europe* (London: Longman).

Antaki, C. and Widdicombe, S. (eds) (1998), *Identities in Talk* (London: Sage Publications).

Anthias, F. (1992), *Ethnicity, Class, Gender and Migration: Greek Cypriots in Britain* (Aldershot: Avebury).

—— (1998), 'Evaluating 'Diaspora': Beyond Ethnicity?', *Sociology* 32:3, 557-580.

Anthias, F. and Lazaridis, G. (2000), 'Introduction: Women on the Move in Southern Europe', in Anthias, F. and Lazaridis, G. (eds), *Gender and Migration in Southern Europe* (Oxford: Berg).

Bauer, E. and Thompson, P. (2004), '"She's Always the Person with a Very Global Vision": The Gender Dynamics of Migration, Narrative Interpretation and the Case of Jamaican Transnational Families', *Gender and History* 16:2, 334-375.

Blumer, H. (1969), *Symbolic Interactionism: Perspective and Method* (Berkeley: University of California Press).

Brubaker, R. (2005), 'The "Diaspora" Diaspora', *Ethnic and Racial Studies* 28:1, 1-19.

Bryceson, D. and Vuorela, U.V. (eds) (2002), *The Transnational Family: New European Frontiers and Global Networks* (Oxford: Berg).

Burrell, K. (2005), 'Urban Narratives: Italian and Greek-Cypriot Representations of Community in Post-war Leicester', *Urban History* 32:3, 481-501.

—— (2006), *Moving Lives: Narratives of Nation and Migration among Europeans in Post-War Britain* (London: Ashgate).

Carras, C. (1997), 'Hellenism, Orthodoxy and the Greek Community in Britain', in Ioannides, C.P. (ed.), *Greeks in English-Speaking Countries: Culture, Identity, Politics* (New York: Melissa Media Associates Inc.).

Christou, A. (2002), 'Greek American Return Migration: Constructions of Identity and Re-constructions of Place', *International Journal of Migration Studies* XXXIX:145, 201-229.

Clogg, R. (1999), *A Concise History of Greece* (Cambridge: Cambridge University Press).

Constantinides, P. (1984), 'The Greek Cypriots: Factors in the Maintenance of Ethnic Identity', in Watson, J.L. (ed.), *Between Two Cultures: Migrants and Minorities in Britain* (Oxford: Basil Blackwell).

Cylwik, H. (2002), 'Expectations of Inter-generational Reciprocity Among Older Greek Cypriot Migrants in London', *Ageing and Society* 22, 599-613.

Day, D. (1998), 'Being Ascribed and Resisting, Membership of an Ethnic Group', in Antaki, C. and Widdicombe, S. (eds), *Identities in Talk* (London: Sage Publications).

Demos, V. (1989), 'Maintenance and Loss of Traditional Gender Boundaries in Two Greek Orthodox Communities', *Journal of the Hellenic Diaspora* XVI, 1-4.

Dowling, T. and Fletcher, E. (1915), *Hellenism in England* (London: The Faith Press).

Evergeti, V. (2006), 'Living and Caring Between Two Cultures: Narratives of Greek Women in Britain', *Community, Work and Family* 9:3, 347-366.

Evergeti, V. and Zontini, E. (2006), 'Introduction: Some Critical Reflections on Social Capital, Migration and Transnational Families', *Ethnic and Racial Studies* 29:6, 1025-1039.

Fakiolas, R. (2003), 'Regularising Undocumented Immigrants in Greece: Procedures and Effects', *Journal of Ethnic and Migration Studies* 29:3, 535-561.

Georgiou, M. (2000), 'Beyond the Domestic: Constructing Ethnic Identities and Media Consumption in the Public Ethnic Space: The Case of the Cypriot Community Centre in North London', at www.photoinsight.org.uk.

—— (2001), 'Crossing the Boundaries of the Ethnic Home: Media Consumption and Ethnic Identity Construction in the Public Space: The Case of the Cypriot Community Centre in North London', *Gazette* 63:4.

Harris, J. (2002), 'London's Greek Community', in *Treasured Offerings: The Legacy of the Greek Orthodox Cathedral of St. Sophia London* (Athens: Byzantine and Christian Museum, Exhibition Catalogue).

Hatziprokopiou, P. (2003), 'Albanian Immigrants in Thessaloniki, Greece: Processes of Economic and Social Incorporation', *Journal of Ethnic and Migration Studies* 29:6, 1033-1057.

Hughes, E.C. (1945), 'Dilemmas and Contradictions of Status', *The American Journal of Sociology* L, 352-359.

Kofman, E. (2004), 'Family-Related Migration: A Critical Review of European Studies', *Journal of Ethnic and Migration Studies* 30:2, 243-262.

Kofman, E., Phizacklea, A., Raghuran, P. and Sales, R. (2000), *Gender and International Migration in Europe* (London and New York: Routledge).

Kourvetaris, G. (1997), *Studies on Greek Americans* (New York: Columbia University Press).

—— (2002), 'The Futuristics of Greek America', in Orfanos, S. (ed.), *Reading Greek America: Studies in the Experience of Greeks in the United States* (New York: Pella).

Laliotou, I. (2004), *Transatlantic Subjects: Acts of Migration and Cultures of Transnationalism Between Greece and America* (London and Chicago: The University of Chicago Press).

Moerman, M. (1968), 'Accomplishing Ethnicity', in Helm, J. (ed.), *Essays in the Problem of Tribe* (Washington: University of Washington Press).

Morokvasic, M. (1984), 'Birds of Passage are also Women...', *International Migration Review* xviii, 886-907.

Nauck, B. and Settles, B. (2001), 'Immigrant and Ethnic Minority Families: An Introduction', *Journal of Comparative Family Studies* 32:4, 461-463.

Oakley, R. (1979), 'Family, Kinship and Patronage: The Cypriot Migration to Britain', in Saifullah Khan, V. (ed.), *Minority Families in Britain: Support and Stress* (London: Macmillan Press).

—— (1987), 'The Control of Cypriot Migration to Britain Between the Wars', *Immigrants and Minorities* 6:1, 30-43.

—— (1989), 'Cypriot Migration to Britain Prior to World War II', *New Community* 15:4, 509-525.

Orfanos, S. (ed.) (2002), *Reading Greek-American: Studies in the Experience of Greeks in the United States* (New York: Pella Publishing Company).

Phizacklea, A. (ed.) (1982), *One Way Ticket: Migration and the Female Labour* (London: Routledge & Kegan Paul).

—— (1983), 'Migrant Women and Wage Labour: The Case of West Indian Women in Britain', in West, J. (ed.), *Women, Work and the Labour Market* (London: Routledge & Kegan Paul).

Portes, A., Guarnizo, L.E. and Landolt, P. (1999), 'The Study of Transnationalism: Pitfalls and Promise of an Emergent Research Field', *Ethnic and Racial Studies* 22:2, 217-237.

Pruss, R. (1996), *Symbolic Interaction and Ethnographic Research: Intersubjectivity and the Study of Human Lived Experience* (New York: State University of New York Press).

Psimenos, I. and Kassimati, K. (2003), 'Immigration and Control Pathways: Organisational Culture and Work Values of Greek Welfare Officers', *Journal of Ethnic and Migration Studies* 29:2, 337-371.

Rex, J. and Josephides, S. (1987), 'Asian and Greek Cypriot Associations and Identity', in Rex, J., Joly, D. and Wilpert, C. (eds), *Immigrant Associations in Europe* (Aldershot: Gower).

Roussou, M. (1992), 'Ethnicity, Language, and Gender: Greek Women in the United Kingdom from the 1900s to the 1990s', in Ioannides, C.P. (ed.), *Greeks in English-speaking Countries: Culture, Identity, Politics* (New York: Melissa Media Associates Inc.).

Ryan, L. (2002), '"I'm Going to England": Irish Women's Stories of Migration in the 1930s', *Oral History* 30, 42-53.

—— (2004), 'Family Matters: (E)migration, Familial Networks and Irish Women in Britain', *Sociological Review* 52:3, 351-370.

Schuetz, A. (1944), 'The Stranger: An Essay in Social Psychology', *American Journal of Sociology* 49:6, 499-507.

—— (1945), 'The Homecomer', *American Journal of Sociology* 50:5, 369-376.

Tastsoglou, E. and Maratou-Alipranti, L. (2003), 'Gender and International Migration: Conceptual, Substantive and Methodological Issues', *The Greek Review of Social Research* 110:A, 5-22.

Triandafyllidou, A. and Veikou, M. (2002), 'The Hierarchy of Greekness: Ethnic and National Identity Considerations in Greek Immigration Policy', *Ethnicities* 2:2, 189-208.

Tsemberis, S., Psomiades, H. and Karpathakis, A. (eds) (1999), *Greek American Families: Traditions and Transformations* (New York: Pella Publishers).

Vertovec, S. (1999), 'Conceiving and Researching Transnationalism', *Ethnic and Racial Studies* 22:2, 447-461.

—— (2002), *Transnational Networks and Skilled Labour Migration* (Oxford: Oxford University Press, Transnational Communities Working Paper WPTC-02-02).

Willis, K. and Yeoh, B. (eds) (2000), *Gender and Migration* (Cheltenham, UK: An Elgar Reference Collection).

Zontini, E. (2006), 'Italian Families and Social Capital: Care Provision in a Transnational World', *Community, Work and Family* 9:3, 325-345.

Chapter 7

Becoming Nurses:
Irish Women, Migration and Identity
Through the Life Course

Louise Ryan

Introduction

Contrary to the predominantly male image of Irish migrants, embodied in the Paddy
and Mick stereotypes, the majority of Irish migrants to Britain in the twentieth century
have in fact been female (O'Sullivan 1997). Irish workers, both male and female,
have long been a reserve pool of labour for the British economy (Hickman 1998).[1]
Unlike many other flows of migrant women into Britain in the post-war period, Irish
women arrived not as part of family groups but predominantly as young, single
migrant workers (Travers 1997). Along with migrants from other regions such as
the Caribbean, Irish workers were actively recruited to fill specific vacancies in the
British labour market after World War II. For example, during the 1940s and 1950s
large numbers of young Irish women were recruited to Britain as student nurses
(Walter 2001). Even into the 1960s, more than one in every ten nurses recruited to
hospitals in the south east of England was born in the Irish republic (Walter 1989).
After decades of recruitment of Irish student nurses, by the early 1970s there were
31,000 Irish-born nurses in Britain, constituting 12 per cent of all nursing staff
(Daniels 1993, 5-6). Although there is a growing awareness of the contribution made
to British society by women migrants, Irish women are often forgotten or neglected
in studies of female migration.[2]

This chapter draws upon in-depth, oral history interviews with 25 Irish nurses,
most of who came to Britain in the 1940s-1960s. All the women were recruited into
nursing as young, single childless economic migrants (Ryan 2007a). Most of these
women are now retired from nursing but are still living in Britain. This paper maps
their on-going negotiations of identity and changing attachments to place through
their life course. These women were not just economic actors they were also members
of families, local and transnational, and active participants in friendship groups and
neighbourhood support systems. Applying a life course perspective, this chapter

---

1   For a discussion of the reasons behind the high levels of female migration from Ireland
see O'Sullivan 1997 and Walter 2001.

2   I discuss this point in more detail in 'I Had a Sister in England' (forthcoming) in
Journal of Ethnic and Migration Studies, 2008.

examines how the women constructed and negotiated their various interconnected and interchanging identities over time, for example, as nurses, as migrants and as mothers. The chapter also explores how these women navigate their attachment to place through various dynamic relationships.

Methods

This study grew out of my previous work on older Irish women in Britain (Ryan 2003; 2004). I developed a particular interest in Irish women who were recruited to Britain in the post-war period of whom nurses represented a significant but under-researched group. I recruited the participants through advertisements in Irish newspapers in Britain, the *Irish Post* and *Irish World*, through Irish organisations such as the Federation of Irish Societies and I also used snow balling. Because I am interested in how migrants' needs and experiences change over time, I sought participants who migrated as single, childless women and who subsequently became mothers in Britain.[3] Most of the 25 women were interviewed in their own homes, although two were interviewed in cafés. With the exception of one woman in Birmingham and one in Coventry, all the others were based in the south-east of England, including Kent, Essex, Sussex and Hertfordshire, and 15 in London.

In studying the employment patterns, family relationships, social networks and identity formations of migrants, it is important to consider how these may change over time. Rather than taking a snap shot of a particular period in the migrant's life, it is useful to take a more long-term perspective and examine the changes that have occurred with passing time. The sociological orientation of a life course perspective emphasises the dynamism of social roles and relationships over time. 'Life course events and transitions usually involve a change in social roles and situations, often altering the basis for the social relationships that were formed in the context of the role' (Larner in Cochan et al. 1990, 182).

Relationships develop in the context of social roles and over time these can change in salience as individuals move in and out of roles, for example changing jobs, starting a family, moving house (Cochan 1990). Oral history is a useful method of doing research with older migrants. As they look back over their lifetime, participants can discuss the changing nature of their relationships with other people, such as friends and family, and with particular places such as the 'host' society and their attitudes about returning to their 'homeland'. Of course, doing oral history research inevitably raises questions about memory and how the past, particularly the distant past, is remembered and reconstructed. Mary Chamberlain argues that remembering is not random or neutral but is constructed through our experiences. Memory not only recounts, it also seeks to explain the past (Chamberlain 1997). As Alastair Thomson points out 'we compose our memories to make sense of our past and present lives' (1998, 301). As I have previously argued in an oral history study involving a different group of participants, migrants tend to 'compose' their past, in particular their migration, in a way that feels comfortable and makes sense of the

---

3   The interviews were carried out between October 2004 and August 2005.

many years they have spent in Britain (Ryan 2006). My interest is not in the veracity or reliability of these women's memories of past events but rather with how they describe and construct the stories of their lives.

Social Construction of Gendered Identities

This chapter analyses the experiences of Irish nurses in Britain through a framework of social construction. An analysis of the social construction of gender allows one to uncover the expectations and values underpinning masculinity or femininity in any given society.

> It is in understanding how men and women are socially constructed, and how those constructions define and redefine social activities, that the value of a symbolic analysis of gender becomes apparent (Moore 1994, 16).

However, gender constructions do not simply operate on a symbolic level or indeed at the generalised societal level. Theories of gender have tended 'to focus either on one-to-one relationships between people or on the society as a whole' (Connell 1994, 29). However, as Connell suggests 'we live most of our daily lives in settings like the household, the workplace and the bus queue' (1994, 29). Elsewhere I have applied Lacy's concept of 'construction sites' to examine how migrant identities are constructed in particular sites such as the workplace (Ryan 2007b). Whether one uses Lacy's concept of 'sites' or Connell's notion of 'settings', these are arenas in which identity is constructed in particular ways according to specific rules and norms. Connell uses the concept of 'gender regime' to mean the rules, regulations and social practices that serve to define appropriate gender behaviour within a particular setting (Connell 1994, 30). In defining particular types of gendered behaviour within specific arenas, these regimes begin to impact on identity formation through processes of internalisation. However, while it is important to analyse how gender norms are constructed and how rules of behaviour are imposed, it is also important to consider the ways in which people may actively engage with and negotiate these social processes.

Following the influence of postmodern theories, there has been growing interest in multiple identities and performativity, in other words the ways in which social actors display and perform different facets of identity in different settings. Thus, far from being fixed, identities may be negotiated in diverse ways through a range of social roles, locations and relationships. In the area of race and ethnic studies, there has been increased awareness of the situatedness of identity (Hall 1996). This is particularly relevant for migrants whose geographical relocation may result in a repositioning and reframing of their ethnic identity (Eriksen 1993). The extent to which migration is a gendered experience is a key theme of this book. As I will argue in this chapter, migration may result in reframing of both ethnic and gender identity within a series of new social settings but also in reconfiguring ethnicised gendered identities.

'Performing a Role': Irish Women Becoming Nurses

Almost all the women in my study had been directly recruited from Ireland to train in British hospitals. Many had responded to advertisements placed in Irish newspapers such as the *Irish Independent* and *Irish Press*. The average age of the women at the time of migration was 18 years and most had never been away from home before. They were conscious of the distance and how far away they were from home: 'there was no Ryanair[4] ... Ireland was a long way from here then, whereas now it's just an hour, isn't it' (Maeve).[5] The sense of distance and the time taken to travel from the rural west of Ireland to the south-east of England was also vividly recalled by Eileen: 'I remember it was a January morning, I remember it was awfully cold, and you know that time when you came on the boat, you were so tired'. England was a new and very different environment from anything they had previously experienced.

> oh coming here was very different, very, very, different. Just for instance, even the cockney accent, it was very difficult to understand and they didn't understand us. It was really, really hard (Maeve migrated 1966).

But these young women encountered England not just as migrants but also through their new role as student nurses. Their routine and timetable were strictly mapped out for them. All the women I interviewed lived in nurses' homes during their student years. Thus, nurse training was a full time, all encompassing experience. They worked long hours and lived on-the-job. From the moment they arrived their new identity was being constructed. Eileen recalled arriving at the hospital where she was to spend the next three years: 'I remember you were sent straight away to be measured for a uniform before you even had anything to eat'.

Becoming a nurse meant conforming to particular norms or 'gender regime' to use Connell's (1994) concept, not just in the workplace, the wards, but also when off duty, in the 'home' as well. All the women spoke about the matron and the rules and regulations governing their behaviour, not just while on duty, but during their leisure time as well. Emer arrived at a hospital in Surrey:

> of course it was all new, we were living in the nurses' home, you had to live in the nurses home, we had no choice, the matron was more or less the mother hen looking after us, she was always responsible for us, so we had to be in by half past ten, we missed all the ends of all the movies, believe me, because the pictures didn't finish until half past ten, so we would be running down the road (Emer migrated 1955).

Despite the initial homesickness felt by these teenage Irish migrants, living in the nurses' home appears to have been an effective antidote to any feelings of loneliness or isolation. I asked Eileen who migrated in 1951, at the age of 17, if she had been homesick and she replied: 'I suppose I was, yeah, but not for long, because you got into the routine, and in the nurses' home we were all in and out of each others rooms'.

---

4   Ryanair is the low cost Irish-owned airline that now operates regular flights from most Irish airports. Before low cost airlines, most migrants from Ireland travelled by boat and train.

5   The names of all participants have been changed to protect confidentiality.

Because of the recruitment patterns at that time, it was not unusual for these newly arrived migrants to find themselves surrounded by groups of other Irish student nurses. Eileen said that most students in her set were Irish. This experience was shared by Clodagh who migrated in 1958: 'I can't say I was desperately unhappy, I did miss home like anything but there was a great crowd of Irish there and we are still friends [and] this is a wonderful thing' (Clodagh). The importance of having a group of friends in the nurses' home was emphasised by Emer:

> I think the reason we survived was that there was a great mateship, when we went off night duty we all converged in one room, somebody made a pot of tea and somebody had a packet of biscuits, that was what made us survive … I am sure I would not have survived if I was on my own (Emer).

Like many of the women in my study, Roisin trained in a hospital where many in her set were also young Irish migrants: 'there were quite a few Irish … And I started to go out with them of an evening … When we were on night duty, we would get up on Sunday afternoon and go to a dance at the Blarney, like a tea dance and be back to go on night duty. It was good, it was all community spirit'. For these young women being in a group gave them a feeling of security and confidence about going out and exploring new environments. The sense of 'community spirit' among the students in the nurses' homes also appears to have been a key factor in helping them to settle into their new roles as nurses. As well as providing a ready-made circle of female friends, living in the nurses' home had another advantage for these migrants. It enabled them to live cheaply and survive on quite meagre wages: 'the salary was just unbelievable, I think we got £6 a month and we lived in so we got all our food and everything. But I used to send money home and my mother recently produced a letter that I sent when I sent home about £2 or something, which was a lot of money to them' (Clodagh). This story was echoed closely by several of the women. As a young student Eileen had sent money home to her parents every month: 'You were paid monthly of course you didn't have to worry because you had your meals and didn't have to pay any rent. I remember we used to send home £2 every month'.

For these young migrant women, the process of becoming a nurse was mediated through ethnic identity. Within the narratives ethnicised gender identities were described in different ways. On the one hand, several women remarked that being Irish was a positive advantage in the nursing profession. For example, Siobhan observed: 'You have to be very caring … some people shouldn't be there [because] they are not caring. I found that Irish nurses were very good' (Siobhan migrated 1968). Eileen said, 'the Irish were very good workers'. Most women emphasised that nursing was hard work. 'I was a very hard worker' (Grainne); 'It was hard work, we worked very hard' (Cliona); 'It was extremely hard work' (Clodagh). Emer told me: 'the hours were ridiculous, of course, you started at half past seven in the morning and then you had this nonsense of the split duty where you had a couple of hours off in the middle of the day, God knows what you were supposed to do with that, and then you didn't finish until half past nine at night'.

In addition to being hard workers, Irish women had other qualities that made them good nurses. Clodagh highlighted the communication skills of the Irish: 'I think the Irish have a great way of communicating and they are very supportive' (Clodagh). Similarly, Grainne said:

> I feel that when people put a uniform on they perform a role, but I think that Irish nurses were able to break through that mask of the uniform. I also think that accent, ... and the way Irish people speak is different and it is more of a conversational speech, and listening, it gives people an opportunity to engage in a conversation rather than just a nicety I think that is something about the way Irish people structure language (Grainne migrated 1974).

In this quote Grainne is suggesting that Irish nurses were not simply 'performing a role' but were genuinely interested in the patients and had meaningful conversations with them. Several women also said that patients appreciated the kindness and dedication of Irish nurses. As Bronwen Walter points out Irish nurses had a 'positive stereotype in strong contrast to almost all other Irish people' in Britain especially in the 1950s-1970s (1989, 71). Niamh observed that: 'I was aware the way people looked at Irish people here, I didn't come across any myself, I think I was quite well respected as a nurse'. Niamh's status as a nurse seems to have protected her from being looked down on as Irish. Thus for some women their relationship to their professional status was positively mediated through their gender and ethnic identity. However, as Niamh suggests in the quote above, Irish people in general were looked down in Britain and some narratives highlight how such negative images impacted on their nursing experiences.

In talking about becoming nurses, these women identified a range of ways in which the mediation of their experiences through Irishness was negative and up setting. Roisin said 'We had quite a strict matron, English, and they said of course that she wasn't very keen on the Irish but then her hospital was staffed entirely by Irish nurses' (Roisin migrated 1950). This irony of matrons relying on Irish nurses but at the same time harbouring anti-Irish attitudes was something commented on by several women. Kathleen was recruited to a hospital in South London in 1949. Speaking about the matron, Kathleen recalled: 'she didn't have a lot of time for Irish people, you could tell, you just knew the feeling, you were like something that came off the sole of her shoe'. Emer told me that Irish nurses were highly regarded by 'the patients, not by the staff':

> I can remember, they used to teach us all this stuff about hygiene, cleaning baths and all this, the sister tutor holding up a box of Vim and then she would say "of course you Irish girls wouldn't know about this". The knife sticking in all the time, you know (Emer).

Sheila was recruited to a prestigious London hospital in the early 1950s. She found that there were few if any Irish nurses on the staff and that there was open hostility towards the Irish based on stereotypes of dirtiness, fecklessness and backwardness:

> The sisters were really snappy with the Irish ... "oh, there's the Irish again, I'll show you this is how you clean a thing". As if we weren't clean. The English would say "didn't your mother teach you better than that" (Sheila migrated 1952).

Sheila and Emer are describing virtually identical incidents based on presumptions about Irishness, dirty and poor upbringing. In the racialised discourses of the British popular press the dirty Irish were depicted as having a 'notorious apathy to soap and water' (Douglas 2002, 46). In addition, stereotypes of the Irish as poor, ignorant and backward were augmented by gendered images of Irish women as lacking domestic skills (Walter 2001). Connell argues that 'gender relations are present' in all institutions such as workplaces, however, he adds that 'they may not be the most important structure in a particular case' (1994, 30) for example, in the case of Irish nurses gender relations intersected with powerful ethnic relations. But that is not to imply that relations between Irish and English nurses were always fraught or tense: 'People used to say that we didn't get on with English people but I remember it was an English ward sister [who] on my 21st birthday, had a surprise party and took us out for a meal' (Eileen migrated 1951).

Another issue through which identity is experienced, constructed and ascribed is religion. Religious labels are used to denote social boundaries as religious identity constructs a symbolic divide between in-group and out-group (Lacy 2004). For the Irish in Britain, religion is often constructed as a key marker of identity and difference (Hickman 1998). All the respondents mentioned religion as a site on which they confronted and negotiated their identity but once again it is important to acknowledge that experiences were diverse. Sheila said that although there was a Catholic church 'across the road' from the hospital, it was very difficult for the Catholic students to get time off to attend mass as the matron said 'we were wasting time' (Sheila). In their study of Irish Catholics in Scotland, Walls and Williams interviewed a Protestant nurse, now retired, who complained that Catholic nurses always wanted extra time off to attend church (Walls and Williams 2003, 642).

In addition, it is also apparent that particular aspects of religion were ascribed to these young women, for example through assumptions about how Catholicism would influence their professional and private lives. Roisin left a small town in the Irish midlands in 1950 when she was 17 years old. In those days student nurses were put to work on the wards at a very early stage in their training, thus, although they also attended classes, to a large extent they learned on-the-job. One of Roisin's first patients was a woman who had tried to induce an abortion. Roisin described her shock and sense of disbelief: 'I was so immature, I wasn't a bit street wise'. Roisin's reaction to the self-induced abortion was one of surprise rather than a strong religious objection. However, several women commented that senior staff often interpreted their behaviour as driven by religious ideology. This observation was also made by Cliona:

> early on in my training there was a big thing made about the Irish Catholic nurses and you don't have to have anything to do with anybody having a termination, and I said "I'm not there judging and I don't know why they ended up in that bed having to have an abortion, it is not by place to judge them". I said "you don't have to worry about me" (Cliona migrated 1978).

Thus, Cliona resented being pigeon-holed as a stereotypical Irish Catholic and argued that in her capacity as a nurse she was non-judgemental and professional.

Assumptions about how Irish women's religious beliefs might impact on their work as nurses were also manifested in other ways. At a job interview Siobhan was asked if she planned to have any more children because 'obviously you are a Catholic so you won't be using contraceptives' (Siobhan migrated 1968).

Thus, Irish nurses constructed their identities and asserted their professional competence through varied and dynamic relationships with colleagues as well as through complicated negotiations of gender, racial and religious stereotypes (Ryan 2007b). So far this chapter has concentrated on the women's experiences of training and employment as nurses. To examine the changes that occurred through the life course it is necessary to move on to discuss their later experiences in particular around motherhood and child rearing as migrants in Britain.

Becoming Mothers and Friends in New Neighbourhoods

After she married and had her first child Maeve, like many of the other women, combined part time nursing and motherhood. However, when her second child was born she decided to become a full time mother. Having always had a busy working life in Britain, she now found herself at home with two young children.

> It was difficult because I am quite an active person. But you soon get into the routine of being a full time mother. And then obviously when William went to nursery, I met different people, coffee mornings here and there … when your child starts school you make a lot of new friends (Maeve).

In this quote Maeve describes the process of adjusting to a new gender identity, from full time professional to full time mother. Clearly accessing a local network of female friends was crucial to that process of adjustment. Maeve has lived in the same area in Essex for many years and she has established a wide social circle many of whom are also Irish. 'I suppose I am lucky, I do have a good social life, I have a lot of friends' (Maeve). Bell and Ribbens argue that the social sciences have been slow to theorise 'the significance of networks operating informally between women … many mothers of young children … are actively and regularly involved in informal contacts with other women like themselves, especially in localised settings' (1994, 229). This was certainly the case for most of the women I interviewed. But, as several other chapters in this volume also demonstrate (see Ahmad, Weber-Newth and Burrell), it is important to consider the local environments within which migrant women adapt to marriage and motherhood and attempt to forge new networks.

Cliona had a very different and much more difficult experience of trying to adjust to full time motherhood. After marrying, she and her husband moved to a new town in Hertfordshire. She had two children in quick succession: 'I was drained, I was here on my own, it was horrific … I felt displaced, it was a huge jump from living in a nurses' home, to live in a house cos I was actually living in society and we had horrible neighbours, it was a council estate and I was really unhappy'. For Cliona ethnicity was an important factor in this process: 'I am not English and I still have that problem relating to people … they didn't have the same way of life as we do'. Being Irish in a predominantly English housing estate led Cliona to feel like an outsider who did not belong or fit into the local community. She coped with this situation by returning to work as a way of preserving her 'sanity'.

Having lived in the nurses' homes for many years, most of the women only moved out 'into society' for the first time when they got married. This was often a time of loneliness and isolation but, depending on the ethnic composition of the locality, it could also result in feelings of being an outsider who does not fit in. Eithne gave up nursing in Birmingham and moved to a village in Yorkshire where her husband had got a teaching post. There were no other Irish people in the village and she found the local people quite unfriendly towards her as an outsider. In this close-knit community, Eithne struggled to fit in. Like Cliona, her experiences indicate how some communities can prove exclusive and impenetrable for newly arrived migrants. Thus, ethnic composition may be a factor in one's feelings of attachment to a particular locality (Kadushin and Jones 1992). Although Irish migrants are mostly white and English-speaking, they can also experience being 'outsiders' in Britain (Walter 2001). For Eithne, like Cliona, returning to paid work was a means to escape the confines of this dense knit but unwelcoming community.

Becoming Working Mothers

After several years as a full time mother, Kathleen felt that she was being 'taken for granted' by her family. 'I thought there must be something more in life than children, school, mothers, whatever'. When her youngest child started school she returned to nursing as a staff nurse. One of the oldest women in my study, Una (migrated in 1948) went back to work when her children started school and developed her career attaining a senior managerial position, she continued nursing until the age of 65. She says 'I did have a long career ... I loved it'.

When their children were young, most women combined motherhood and paid employment by going on the night shifts. Night working meant that women could leave their children at home to be looked after by their husbands and so save on child care costs: 'My husband was always here at nights so I never had to get anyone to do baby minding' (Siobhan). This kind of arrangement was common among the women I interviewed. Work sequencing is a recognised strategy that can overcome childcare problems but requires the cooperation and commitment of both partners (Preston et al. 2000). Black migrant women were also congregated in professions such as nursing as well as manufacturing which operated in shift systems. 'Working on a shift system meant that Black mothers could arrange to work different shifts to their partner, leaving someone available to care for their children at different times of the day and night' (Reynolds 2001, 1056). This arrangement partly reflected the dearth of childcare alternatives in the post-war era and, for migrants in particular, the absence of extended family networks who could look after the children (see Ryan 2007a; Burrell, this volume). 'There was no childcare, and I had no parental input' (Roisin). However, it is clear that this type of arrangement meant partners spent little time together: 'it was hard, he'd come in and I'd just walk out the door' (Siobhan).

But work sequencing does not necessarily imply an equal division of labour between partners. Like a lot of other women, Roisin acknowledged the support of her husband who looked after the children while she went on night duty: 'I couldn't have done it without him but I did a lot of preparation in the week for the weekend, like I'd make a casserole on the Friday for lunch and I'd get the children ready for bed before I went to work and then I would be back the next morning about half past eight'. Thus although her husband minded the children, most of the preparation, cooking and organising of the household was done by Roisin.

It is important to locate these arrangements and experiences within the specific historical context. As Wendy Webster has written, during the post-war period 'there were a range of anxieties about the ways in which the 'working wife' deprived children of a 'good home', and she was blamed for a wide variety of social ills' (1998, 130). These dominant discourses about working mothers were reflected in a strong sense that women should not leave their children with childminders. Like most of the other women, Mairead switched to night work after the birth of her two daughters: 'But in them days, children were never given out to carers' (Mairead). This social and historical context, and the associated gender regimes, forms the backdrop to many of my interviewees' stories. They were working mothers at a time when 'stay at home mothers' were idealised. Women's decisions about returning to nursing and how many shifts to work were not made in isolation from a wide array of social, economic and personal factors. The dearth of childcare, the option of flexible working hours, the attitude and level of support provided by their partners were all important (Ryan 2007a).

Maintaining Family Ties in Ireland

There is growing interest in the ways in which women are implicated in transnational families (Ehrenreich and Hochschild 2003; Zontini 2004; Yeates 2004). This has led to a consideration of global care chains which may be defined as 'a series of personal links between people across the globe based on the paid or unpaid work of caring' (Hochschild 2000, 131). This concept provides a useful tool for understanding the shifting relationships and caring roles within transnational networks. In the early stages of their migration, most of the women I spoke to returned to Ireland at least once a year for a two-week holiday. When they married and had children they usually had family holidays with relatives in Ireland and in several cases sent their children to be looked after by grandparents for the entire school holidays. For example, while her mother was alive, Nuala used to send her two daughters back to the family farm in the Irish midlands for the entire school holidays and then she and her husband joined them for the last two weeks. Her children benefited from the fresh air and freedom of life on the farm: 'you could let them run where they liked, the freedom, you know'. But these family holidays often involved reciprocal care arrangements as free childcare was exchanged for helping out on family farms. Eileen, her husband and their three children, spent their summer holidays in Ireland every year and helped on the farm: 'you always wanted to help your parents, so when I'd go back we'd be bringing in hay and turf and everything, and I would help decorate or things like that'.

In addition, some relatives came to England for brief periods to provide help and support, for example, after the birth of a baby. Fiona's mother came to London for an extended trip to help look after her baby. When her children were young, Cliona's sister travelled to Hertfordshire from Dublin every summer to help out with childcare during the school holidays. Through chain migration, much of which was family-related, many of the women in my study had joined or were joined by relatives. As I have discussed at length elsewhere (Ryan forthcoming), because of the high levels of female migration, many of these relatives in Britain were women, in particular sisters, aunts or female cousins. The relative proximity between Ireland and England, the relative affordability of ferry tickets, in the days before cheap airlines, plus the lack of immigration restrictions facilitated this mobility back and forth.

It is important to track the changing nature of these movements and relationships through the life course. As Breda Gray (2004) has noted, Irish women migrants are often expected to continue playing daughterly caring roles long after they have left home. Although middle-aged themselves, many of the women I interviewed were regularly visiting Ireland to care for aged relatives, especially mothers. In addition, several women had brought aged relatives to live with them in Britain. For example, Fiona brought her mother to live with her, while Noreen and Emer brought both of their parents to join them in London. Thus, as women and perhaps especially as nurses, these women were expected to play highly gendered caring roles, in particular providing care to their aged parents.

However, while many of the women in my study had maintained regular contact with Ireland throughout their lives, visiting every year, phoning and writing letters to relatives back home, this was not the case for all the women. In some cases relations with family back home could become fractured and this tended to impact on attitudes to returning to Ireland. For example, after the break up of her marriage, Grainne encountered disapproval from her family: 'I didn't go home that often … So in terms of Ireland, I wasn't writing much, we weren't phoning, I wasn't in contact that much'. Hence, good relations with family in Ireland may be predicated upon women playing highly gendered and socially approved roles (Ryan 2004). Women who deviated from these roles could find that transnational relationships become strained or social support is withheld.

Returning to Live in Ireland

In following through the life course perspective, it is necessary to come full circle in the migration process. Having begun with the women's youthful arrival in Britain, as they approach retirement age or have already retired, the question of whether or not to return to Ireland becomes inevitable. If you are recruited to Britain to do a job of work, when that job is completed do you remain in Britain or go back home? But of course all migrants are more than simply economic actors. They are social actors, embedded in various relationships with people and places. Unsurprisingly, the women in my study had varying attitudes about returning to live permanently in Ireland.

Many of the women said they felt settled in England, or more specifically in their local neighbourhoods. Eileen had always resisted pressure from her family in Ireland to return permanently: 'my family wanted me to come back to Roscommon, to the farm, but no I wouldn't … really it wasn't practical'. While some of the women told me that they might like to return to live in Ireland at some future time, it was also acknowledged that return was not without its complications. Having lived in Britain for over 30 years, Grainne has started to regard it as 'home': 'when I used to go away on holidays and come back to England I never felt like I was coming home … It is only now I feel I am home' (Grainne). Having divorced many years ago, Grainne now has a new partner and enjoys a close relationship with her grown up son. Siobhan said that it would be hard to go back to Ireland now because 'we've got grandchildren'. These relationships can help to root migrants. Thus, returning to Ireland would not only mean separation from friends and adult children but also grandchildren.

As other chapters in this volume demonstrate, after a working lifetime spent in Britain, the 'homeland' can seem unfamiliar and strange (Burrell; Weber-Newth, this volume). Upon retirement, two nurses in my study had returned to Ireland permanently but in both cases these women found it impossible to settle back into Irish society and decided to re-migrate. Both women spoke about how Ireland had changed. Roisin described a sense of 'culture shock' being back in Irish society again. Emer said: 'I don't like all the new roads, the fly-overs, but it is necessary, so much traffic, the violence and the drugs … Cos I was always praising Ireland, "there's no drugs in Ireland" you know. But there is a lot of drugs in Ireland'. As Skrbis has written, return home for migrants is about an immersion in the familiar, not the familiar of the present but often a 'familiar that belongs to the past' (2007, 322).

Both women had visited Ireland on a regular basis for many years but each said that holidays had not prepared them for what it would be like to live there: 'of course you never know a place by visiting it, but when you live in a place you get to know it very, very quickly' (Emer). Similarly, Roisin said: 'It is different when you go on holiday, people put themselves out to entertain you, but it is different when you go to live there'. However, upon return to Ireland, these women had to reconstruct their relationships with people and places. Far from feeling at home in Ireland, Emer described feeling like 'a fish out of water': 'I think it is the isolation, you see, my age group they have their own families, grandchildren, that is their whole lives, and they are very nice to me, but they have their own [families]'. For Emer, it is apparent, that attachment to a place and her ability to settle into a location is mediated largely through friendship and social contacts. A lifetime of migration made her feel like 'a fish out of water' in her homeland, so much so that at the age of 68 she left again. The decision to sell up and return to Kent was not an easy one for Roisin and her husband: 'It cost us a lot to go and come back again … oh yes, it nearly killed me, I was only 7 stone coming back'. As Skrbis has noted, for migrants homecoming may be associated with a sense of 'disorientation, disappointment, and realisation that memories no longer correspond with reality' (2007, 322).

Concluding Thoughts

This chapter has focused on the experiences of Irish nurses in Britain drawing upon a social construction approach to examine the ways in which gendered roles and identities are constructed, experienced and negotiated. I have also sought to contextualise these construction processes both spatially and temporally by tracing the ways roles change through the life course and in different social settings such as the workplace and nurses' home, but also in local communities and neighbourhoods. Roles and identities were never simple or one-dimensional but involved various intersections of gender, ethnicity and religion. Within the post-war period it is apparent that British hospitals needed migrant nurses but upon arrival these women were confronted by negative stereotypes based on racialised images and religious prejudice. The process of becoming a nurse involved defining ones professionalism in opposition to these negative images. Some people used positive ethnic stereotypes about 'caring' and 'hard working' Irish women to counter negative labels.

The 'gender regime', or dominant discourses of a particular period, defined the roles that women were expected to play as mothers. However, these nurses illustrate how women adapted to and negotiated around these roles. The role of husbands in supporting women was important but did not necessarily challenge a strongly gendered division of labour. Women's efforts to juggle career and children could be eased by a support network of friends and family. In addition, as migrants, these women had complex and changing relationships with transnational families. Across the life course these relationships proved to be highly dynamic. The close geographical proximity between Ireland and Britain, the relative affordability of travel and the absence of immigration restrictions may actually increase expectations about migrants' on-going involvement in caring relationships.

As is becoming apparent from studies of a range of post-war migrants, the extent to which migrants return home is varied and uncertain (Ganga 2006; Warnes and Williams 2006). Despite regular visits, there is an almost inevitable weakening of relationships and connections with people and places in the homeland. Obviously, interviewing migrants in Britain, I have not spoken to those who have successfully returned and re-settled in Ireland. Nonetheless, it is apparent that none of the women I spoke to felt that going home would be easy or straightforward. While all 25 women strongly identified as Irish, despite having lived in Britain for 40 or 50 years, nonetheless, it is clear that their relationship to Ireland had shifted over time. Their sense of Irishness had been defined and shaped by decades of living and working in Britain. Now, many felt disconnected from the culture, lifestyle and values of twenty-first century Irish society. The sense of dislocation from their homeland is part of the price of migration. Nonetheless, looking back over their lives the women were proud of having been nurses. It is a key facet of their identities and for many it is a source of lasting memories of hard work but tremendous job satisfaction. To conclude with Una's words:

"I did have a long career ... I loved it".

References

Bell, L. and Ribbens, J. (1994), 'Isolated Housewives and Complex Maternal Worlds: The Significance of Social Contacts Between Women with Young Children', *Sociological Review* 42:2, 227-262.

Chamberlain, M. (1997), 'Gender and the Narratives of Migration', *History Workshop Journal* 43, 87-110.

Cochan, M., Larner, M., Riley, D., Gunnarsson, L. and Henderson, C. (1990), *Extending Families: The Social Networks of Parents and their Children* (Cambridge: Cambridge University Press).

Connell, R.W. (1994), 'Gender Regimes and the Gender Order', in *The Polity Reader in Gender Studies* (Cambridge: Polity Press), 29-40.

Daniels, M. (1993), *Exile or Opportunity? Irish Nurses and Midwives in Britain* (Liverpool: Institute of Irish Studies).

Douglas, R. (2002), 'Anglo-Saxons and Attacotti: The Racialisation of Irishness in Britain Between the World Wars', *Ethnic and Racial Studies* 25:1, 40-63.

Ehrenreich, B. and Hochschild, A. (eds) (2003), *Global Woman: Nannies, Maids and Sex Workers* (New York: Metropolitan Books).

Eriksen, T. (1993), *Ethnicity and Nationalism* (London: Pluto Press).

Ganga, D. (2006), 'From Potential Returnees to Settlers: Nottingham's Older Italians', *Journal of Ethnic and Migration Studies* 32:8, 1395-1413.

Gray, B. (2004), *Women and the Irish Diaspora* (London: Routledge).

Hall, S. (1996), 'The New Ethnicities', in Hutchinson, J. and Smith, A.D. (eds), *Ethnicity* (Oxford: Oxford University Press), 161-163.

Hickman, M. (1998), 'Reconstructing Deconstructing "Race": British Political Discourses About the Irish in Britain', *Ethnic and Racial Studies* 21:2, 289-307.

Hochschild, A. (2000), 'Global Care Chains and Emotional Surplus Value', in Hutton, W. and Giddens, A. (eds), *On the Edge: Living with Global Capitalism* (London: Jonathan Cape), 130-146.

Kadushin, C. and Jones, D. (1992), 'Social Networks and Urban Neighbours', reprinted in Scott, J. (ed.) (2002), *Social Networks* (New York: Routledge), 108-127.

Lacy, K. (2004), 'Black Spaces, Black Places: Strategic Assimilation and Identity Construction in Middle-class Suburbia', *Ethnic and Racial Studies* 27:6, 908-930.

Moore, H. (1994), 'The Cultural Construction of Gender', in *The Polity Reader in Gender Studies* (Cambridge: Polity Press), 14-21.

O'Sullivan, P. (ed.) (1997), *Irish Women and Irish Migration* (Leicester: Leicester University Press).

Preston, V., Rose, D., Norcliffe, G. and Holmes, J. (2000), 'Shift Work, Childcare and Domestic Work', *Gender, Place and Culture* 7:1, 5-29.

Reynolds, T. (2001), 'Black Mothering, Paid Work and Identity', *Ethnic and Racial Studies* 24:6, 1046-1064.

Ryan, L. (2003), 'Moving Spaces and Changing Places: Irish Women's Memories of Emigration to Britain in the 1930s', *Journal of Ethnic and Migration Studies* 29:1, 67-82.

—— (2004), 'Family Matters: (E)migration, Familial Networks and Irish Women in Britain', *Sociological Review* 52:3, 351-70.

—— (2006), 'Memories of Migration: Irish Women's Oral History Interviews', in Burrell, K. and Panayi, P. (eds), *Histories and Memories: Immigrants in Britain Since 1800* (Aldershot: Ashgate), 191-209.

—— (2007a), 'Migrant Women, Social Networks and Motherhood: The Experiences of Irish Nurses in Britain', *Sociology* 41:2, 295-312.

—— (2007b), 'Who Do You Think You Are?: Irish Nurses Encountering Ethnicity and Constructing Identity in Britain', *Ethnic and Racial Studies* 30:3, 416-438.

—— (forthcoming), 'I Had a Sister in England: Family-led Migration and Irish Nurses in Britain', *Journal of Ethnic and Migration Studies*.

Skrbis, Z. (2007), 'From Migrants to Pilgrim Tourists: Diasporic Imaging and Visits to Medjugorje', *Journal of Ethnic and Migration Studies* 33:2, 313-329.

Thomson, A. (1998), 'Anzac Memories', in Perks, R. and Thomson, A. (eds), *The Oral History Reader* (London: Routledge), 300-310.

Travers, P. (1997), 'There was Nothing There for Me: Irish Female Emigration, 1922-72', in O'Sullivan, P. (ed.), *Irish Women and Irish Migration* (Leicester: Leicester University Press), 146-167.

Walls, P. and Williams, R. (2003), 'Sectarianism at Work: Accounts of Employment Discrimination against Irish Catholics in Scotland', *Ethnic and Racial Studies* 26:4, 632-662.

Warnes, A. and Williams, A. (2006), 'Older Migrants in Europe: A New Focus for Migration Studies', *Journal of Ethnic and Migration Studies* 32:8, 1257-1281.

Walter, B. (1989), *Irish Women in London: The Ealing Dimension* (London: Ealing Women's Unit).

—— (2001), *Outsiders Inside: Whiteness, Place and Irish Women* (London: Routledge).

Webster, W. (1998), *Imagining Home: Gender, Race and National Identity, 1945-64* (London: UCL Press).

Yeates, N. (2004), 'A Dialogue with Global are Chain Analysis: Nurse Migration in the Irish Context', *Feminist Review* 77, 79-95.

Zontini, E. (2004), 'Immigrant Women in Barcelona: Coping with the Consequences of Transnational Lives', *Journal of Ethnic and Migration Studies* 30:6, 1113-1144.

Chapter 8

Spaniards in the UK — A Successful Female Post-industrial Migration

Tony Morgan

There are very few published studies of Spanish migrants in Britain — a small part of an overview of Spanish migration to Europe (De Miguel 1986), a largely anecdotal narrative of Spaniards in the UK (Luis Botín 1988) and an in-depth study of a small group of Spanish women in London (Bravo Moreno 2006). However, in 2003 the Spanish Government commissioned a socioeconomic survey of the Spanish emigrant population worldwide, to assess the post-1950s progress of its diasporic community. This chapter reflects some of the findings of the UK part of that survey (Morgan 2004). Its principal aim is to profile Spanish migrants in Britain in the late twentieth and early twenty first centuries, focusing on the diverging evolution of male and female experiences. Predictable elements of socioeconomic disadvantage are revealed; however, much progress is displayed, especially in the headway made by women in various respects. Improved employment status, rising living standards, higher educational qualifications and enhanced personal autonomy are the main features which distinguish the current generation from those who preceded them to the UK, while issues of cultural integration, linguistic confidence and uncertainty about return complicate their identities.

The chapter is based largely on analysis of published and commissioned unpublished data from the UK censuses, together with data from the Office for National Statistics Longitudinal Study. It is reinforced by responses given by 602 respondents to a postal survey conducted from Anglia Ruskin University (ARUS) in September 2003-February 2004.

An Historical Overview

Until recently, the numbers of Spanish-born in the UK were low. Spaniards emigrated in large numbers, mostly to the Americas in the nineteenth and early twentieth centuries, but few of their substantial emigrant numbers to Europe in the 1950s and 1960s reached Britain, compared with those migrating to France, Germany and Switzerland (Straubhaar 1988, 97). However, latterly the pattern has altered, as Spaniards, like their European counterparts, have increasingly sought employment in the UK, via the free-moving European Union Single Market, to reach their highest recorded total in the 2001 UK Census (54,482) — known considerably to understate the likely actual number. Of that total, 59 per cent were female and 41 per cent male, a predominance of females only reached once before during 140 years of recorded migration — in 1961. In the earliest recorded analysis, the 1861 Census of England and Wales reported a mere 324 Spanish females in a total community of 1,437. These figures rose slowly over a century, with females rarely amounting to a third of the total. The pattern confirmed early observations that 'the sex and age distribution of the European foreigners sojourning in this country differed very widely from that of the total population. The men largely outnumbered the women, as was the case also with the Scotch and Irish colonies. The men come to England in search of work, leaving their wives and families at home ...' (1881 and 1891 Censuses of England and Wales General Report 1891, 66). Such observations on the sex ratio of migratory patterns still informed late twentieth century analyses (Salt 2002, 142), especially those analysing migration from developing countries, such as the 1994 United Nations' conclusion that 'women, as spouses or daughters, are traditionally assumed to have primarily non-economic roles, under the assumption that their husbands or fathers are responsible for satisfying the family's economic needs' (Kelson and DeLaet 1999, 4). However, Ravenstein's perceptive early caveat that 'woman is a greater migrant than man' (Ravenstein 1885) and that women 'not only migrate autonomously but also ... do so for a variety of reasons' (Kelson and DeLaet 1999, 3) is illustrated by several chapters in this collection including this study of Spanish female migrants to Britain in the post-war period.

Post-war Trends

A gendered analysis of the statistical evidence on Spanish migration to Britain reveals interesting migration patterns. For example, in 1945-1962 the profile of Spanish female migrants to Britain mirrored changing international economic and cultural circumstances, in which the UK experienced for the first time a wave of immigration almost entirely economically motivated (Panayi 1999, 13). In 1963-1972 nearly half of immigrants to Britain with work permits originating outside the Commonwealth were female (Bhaba and Shutter 1994, 168), contesting traditional assumptions about the dominance of male migrant bread-winners; 'depending on economic circumstances, either males or females may be more migratory ... a particular job or profession may influence' (Ogden 1984, 5). This trend was reasserted in the 1990s as Yugoslav, French, German and Spanish immigrant women again outnumbered men. Four European countries in that decade imported more females than males — the UK, Italy, Greece and Spain — and immigration to the UK was female-dominant from all countries except Italy, Greece and Holland (Ackers 1998, 149-150). This was part of a scenario in which women outnumbered men in migrant flows to Britain for most of the last two decades of the twentieth century, a phenomenon attributed '... partly to the increased employment of spouses/females partners moving with employed males and to a larger volume of independent movement by working women' (Dobson et al. 2001, 106). It is Dobson's last observation which is especially pertinent to Spanish women.

Spanish Female Migrants in the Boom Years of the 1950s and 1960s

In the post-war reconstruction and industrial expansion of the 1960s, Irish, Spanish and other European immigrant groups reported an excess of women in the British workforce, while New Commonwealth immigrant workers were predominantly male. In 1966, for example, while women amounted to 60 per cent of Spanish and German migrant workers and 52 per cent of the Irish, Pakistani women workers accounted for only 20 per cent of their ethnic total (Castles and Kosack 1985, 53). In Europe in general at this point, migration was still largely male-dominated. Women who migrated '… often used emigration as a way of negotiating difficult marital relations or overcoming gendered hierarchies in their own country' (Kofman et al. 2000, 5). This observation reflects the rapid internal socio-cultural changes taking place in Spain through urbanization, industrialization, democratization and rising tourist influence during Spain's 'Economic Miracle' of 1960-1975. It offers, too, an alternative reading of the conventional view that females dominated the Spanish population in Britain at this point merely because of their suitability for hotel, catering and domestic service employment (Vilar and Vilar 1999, 74). Increasingly, the presence of women in these migrant populations was a consequence of 'crises in the country of origin, where roles and relations are changing fast, and produce reasons for their emigration, often associated with a 'wish to become emancipated', to gain autonomy and independence, to follow the model of Western women' (Cohen 1995, 547). In the European Economic Community, women rose from 30 per cent to 45 per cent of the migrant population in the period 1960-1980, and averaged 50 per cent in the European Union in 2001. The perception was consolidated that countries such as the UK offered a space that encouraged personal growth and independence for women from more traditional societies in southern and central Europe; 'I love my family in Madrid, but you can't imagine how good it feels to be able to pay your own rent' (María José, 24, ARUS 2003). There was indeed good reason to depart from the militarised and repressive patriarchy of Franco's Spain in the 1950s and 1960s, as has been observed: 'Learning English was a pretext … to go abroad and escape from parental policing' (Bravo Moreno 2006, 215-216). For middle-class women especially, this could in effect be 'resistance within hegemony, resistance shaped by patriarchy and material factors' (Bravo Moreno 2006, 215-216). This echoes the attitudes of the Greek migrant women discussed by Evergeti (in this volume).

Geographical Origins of Migrants

There has also been a significant shift in the geographical origins and cultural backgrounds of these migrants in recent times. Spanish female migrants in the 1950s and 1960s were overwhelmingly from poor peripheral rural areas — a profile still dominant in the mid-1980s when most were from the traditional communities of the depressed northwest and southwest regions (De Miguel 1986). Chain migration was clearly dominant: 80 per cent of the Andalusian migrants came from the small town of La Línea, and 70 per cent of the Galician migrants were from La Coruña and Lugo, areas where educational levels were also low. However, in 2003 whilst

17 per cent were still from Galicia, Spain's other regions were producing migrants in approximate proportion to their populations, with many from developed urban locations with metropolitan and even cosmopolitan outlooks, such as Madrid (16 per cent) and Catalonia (13 per cent), with Andalusia only accounting for 11 per cent (Morgan 2004, 160). Many are young and educated, such as those contemporary Galicians who are almost as comfortable speaking English as they are Spanish or Galician, and identify as much with Santiago, Madrid or London (Rivas 1997, 14). They are part of the spectrum of female migrants from across the European Union who ' ... today ... originate increasingly from an urban environment ... less marked by patriarchal structures ... more likely to engage in autonomous moves and look for job opportunities which leave them more independence and flexibility in decision-making' (Kofman et al. 2000, 5). A 1995 survey underlined this new independence and mobility represented by female migrants to the UK, of whom no less than 70 per cent were unmarried — with many having varied periods of marriage, divorce, being single or cohabiting (Ackers 1998, 157).

Marital Status

This latter point was well illustrated in the 2001 UK Census report on the marital status of the Spanish-born.

Table 8.1   Marital status of Spanish immigrants to the United Kingdom, 1981-2001 (per cent)

		Males	Females
Single	1981	27.8	27.7
	2001	54.9	48.3
Married	1981	69.4	63.0
	2001	34.4	40.1
Divorced	1981	1.8	2.9
	2001	4.0	5.6
Widowed	1981	1.0	6.3
	2001	1.6	6.0

Source: Census Office Reports for United Kingdom 1981 and 2001.

As Table 8.1 indicates, there was a steep rise in the proportion of single males and females in two decades, with a corresponding decline in the married total. Large numbers of single women entered in the 1950s, seeking employment (66.3 per cent in the 1961 UK Census were single); many married in the next decade and many more came to join migrant spouses. In 1971 the actual number of married women was more than a quarter greater than it was thirty years later, even though the total number of women rose 12.9 per cent in that time. Rates of divorce, while still far below the UK average, approximately doubled for both sexes, with the female rate consistently higher — increasing by nearly a third for women in the 1990s — almost twice the rate of the increase for males, as a pattern of greater female independence was established. The consistently higher widowed figures for women reflect their longer life expectancy. While the pattern for marital status hardly varies across England and Wales, the very high proportion of unmarried Spanish women in Scotland — almost three quarters — is a good indication of the new mobility that has taken young students and job-seekers to fashionable Edinburgh and Glasgow — locations not previously associated with Spanish migration (Commissioned Data General Register Office for Scotland 2003).

The Evolving Family Unit

Just as the clichéd large family has dwindled in Spain during recent decades, with falling birth rates well below population-renewal levels for a generation, so the Spanish migrant community in the UK has formed ever smaller family units. 65.3 per cent of the Spanish-born population in the 2001 UK Census inhabited households of no more than three persons. A mere 10.8 per cent inhabit households of four to ten persons (2001 Census Commissioned Data). Yet the accommodation they inhabited had consistently improved. More than half in 1971 were renting in the private sector, almost a quarter shared a bathroom and lavatory, and nearly a third lived in only one or two rooms. By 1991, however, only a fifth were renting in the private sector, almost none shared a bathroom and lavatory, and less than a tenth lived in one or two rooms. Moreover, 58.8 per cent were owner-occupiers, and the largest proportion (39.2 per cent) occupied six or more rooms (Office for National Statistics Longitudinal Study 2004). In 2001, despite the influx of the single young people in the 1990s, still more than half of their homes were owner-occupied — with the figure in the more populated South East 58.1 per cent, only 10 per cent below the UK total population average (2001 Census Commissioned Data). Car ownership is taken by the Office for National Statistics to be a reliable guide to disposable income in Britain. From 1971 to 2001 the proportion of Spanish-born owning one car or more rose from under half to over two thirds — only a small percentage below the UK total figure. These trends of housing type and car ownership suggest substantially higher living standards for the community in the space of one generation. This is true for the population at large, but also reflects rising educational standards of more recent Spanish migrants, and consequent improved employment prospects, as indicated below.

Evolving Employment Patterns

Nineteenth century European urbanisation provided employment for the few Spanish women who did migrate 'as marriage markets extended and women became urban servants and seamstresses' (Cohen 1995, 128). Indeed, in the 1901 Census of England and Wales the only Spanish employee groups deemed worthy of official comment were 1,464 male sailors and 96 female domestic servants (Census of England and Wales General Report 1901, 145). There was little growth up to the Second World

War. However, from 1950 the employment patterns of Spanish migrants evolved significantly. In the 1950s their employment profile resembled those of other migrant groups in the great post-war population shifts in Europe in which ' ... since 1945 the main flows have been between the countries of the Mediterranean basin and the industrial economies of Northwest Europe ... a northward flow of migrants, many of rural origin, to seek a temporary or permanent livelihood in the advanced urban economies ... exchanges with the Mediterranean lands ... comprised ... mainly of unskilled workers and their families' (Salt 1981, 133-137). Of the 11,540 Spanish-born employed in the UK in 1961, 71.5 per cent worked in hotels and catering or health care and domestic service (Census for England and Wales 1961). Many of the single women who migrated in the 1950s worked as low-paid cleaners, nannies, kitchen staff and hotel maids: 'For Spaniards (as for several other nationalities), the female surplus is due to the large portion of domestic servants and au pair girls' (Castles and Kosack 1985, 59). They were part of 'European groups, such as Germans and Spaniards ... dominated by women ... Irish women in domestic work were joined by Italian, Spanish and Portuguese women — on work permits' (Kofman et al. 2000, 52-108). Work permits were instituted in 1953 to regulate the inflow of 'selected economic migrants from West and South Europe ... more recently from Spain ... to fill jobs in the undermanned industries and services (particularly domestic) ... ' (Patterson 1969, 2). Over half the Spanish women were in service jobs, three quarters of them in domestic service (Bhaba and Shutter 1994). 'Spanish women came here to jobs purely in domestic service; they were needed in hospitals, in public schools to do the cleaning. Most of the service in the boarding schools was Spanish ... in the restaurants, in the hotels. The natives didn't want to work in that kind of job' (Tania cited in Bravo Moreno 2006, 145). Unhindered at first by the Spanish authorities and the Home Office, they often found work in the grey economy and via dubious employment agencies (Luis Botín 1988).

In these respects, Spanish migrants followed the established pattern of European migration to Britain, finding themselves 'at the lower end of the social scale, but with some social mobility' (Panayi 1999, 8). After a decade or so, these low-paid, hard-working Spaniards began to be noticed, though not as a prominent group among the new immigrant workforce: 'In the late 1960s ... people could observe that some hospitals had a largely Spanish staff ... but this integration remained curiously invisible and un-regarded' (Dummett 1995, 100). There was a visible European labour hierarchy, in which 'French and Germans were more likely to be highly skilled and in the non-manual occupations. In contrast, workers from the Southern tier of EU countries (Spain, Portugal, Italy, Greece) are over-represented in manual employment' (Dummett 1995, 143). Assumptions that they were largely unskilled persisted, perhaps unfairly, for some time: 'It was frequently argued that these were the jobs for which migrant workers were well suited because of their poor educational backgrounds and the limited opportunities for skill acquisition in their own countries. This argument was far from always the case' (King 1993, 23).

This profile shifted markedly during the next quarter century. The data revealed in the special census of 1966 challenged some of the stereotypical assumptions. Over half of the employed Spanish women were still in 'miscellaneous services', but 4,100 were employed in 'professional and scientific services', mostly in education and healthcare, 1,350 worked in various branches of manufacturing, 590 in wholesale and retail, and 320 in financial services and public administration (Sample Census 1966, table 24). More than a quarter of these women were classified in the top three of the six categories of 'social grade' — professional, intermediate and skilled, substantiating the assertions made by Panayi and King above. The figure in those top three categories for Spanish-born males was 37.2 per cent. For the Spanish migrant population as a whole, in the following decades the community evolved from a blue-collar, semi-skilled group to an increasingly white-collar and professional group. The women interviewed for the ARUS discuss these changes: 'British society doesn't know what really to expect of us. But with time, comes change. Opportunities arrive in the end.' (Susana, 26, mental health support worker); 'Spanish women who have been here a long time are independent and organised, and all have struggled but have known how to triumph in their own way' (María Isabel, 42 years residence).

Data from the Office for National Statistics Longitudinal Study reveals proportions of Spanish-born professional, intermediate and skilled non-manual employees more than doubling in two decades, from 19.0 per cent in 1971 to 44.2 per cent in 1991. Similarly, the proportions classed as managers, professionals, non-manual supervisors, junior non-manual staff and self-employed almost trebled from 19.5 per cent to 50.6 per cent (Office for National Statistics Longitudinal Study 2004), in a period in which the numbers of Spanish-born and Spanish employed in the UK stagnated.

Recent Socioeconomic Advances of Spanish Immigrants

Through the decade of the 1990s and beyond, the situation of the Spanish-born in the UK has been transformed by a number of factors. The creation of the Single European Market, the rise of budget airlines, an educational revolution in Spain, together with the buoyancy of the British labour market, continuing high levels of unemployment in Spain, and the rise of English as almost the lingua franca of the business world conspired to boost the numbers of Spaniards in the UK to historic highs. The UK, Ireland and Luxembourg ' ... gain more benefit in terms of skills of their foreign populations, who are more likely to come from high income countries ... while the reverse is true for Germany, Italy, France and Finland' (Dobson 2001, 34). Spanish immigrants have increasingly shared in the positive experiences of other migrants from 'white' ethnic backgrounds who tend to perform as well as, or better than, the existing population — in terms of their employment and participation rates and wage levels (Haque 2002, 5). The following observations were fairly widespread in the ARUS: ' ... in general, the reception of the Spanish population in the UK has been excellent. Employment opportunities are the same as for the host population' (Flora, 43, laboratory project manager).

Rising Spanish migration to Britain is part of the broader movement of skilled people, especially younger professionals, from several European countries, principally into London and the South East of England. In the intercensal period 1991-2001, besides the rise in the Spanish population, the number of Italian-born rose 17 per cent, the German 21 per cent, the Dutch 35 per cent and the French by no less than 80 per cent. Sectors where Spaniards have been prominent include education: there are now over 200 Spanish-born university lecturers (many female) in the UK. In healthcare, although there are still unqualified Spanish hospital cleaners in National Health Service and private hospitals, there has been an unprecedented drive to recruit doctors, nurses, specialists, dentists and veterinary surgeons from Spain. As one medical professional told the ARUS 'I have a high standard of living, I daresay higher than in Spain, as the UK offers better salaries' (Ana, 35, National Health Service psychiatrist). Similarly, a doctor said: 'The general feeling is that we are very happy from the professional point of view, and we are well-placed financially' (Monica, 38, hospital A & E staff doctor).

In marked contrast to the limited employment opportunities of the generation of the 1960s revealed in the ARUS, well-qualified women show an individual confidence and range of focused ambitions. 'There are better job prospects here and a higher standard of living' (Cristina, 39, university lecturer). Many in the survey contrasted the range of opportunities, openness of the labour market, chance of personal development particularly for women and fairness of promotion procedures with the more personalised and often clientelist culture back home. 'There are more professional opportunities and better salaries, and more chance of getting a first job related to your qualifications, or retraining, than in Spain' (Alexandra, 29, university secretary).

Despite the well-chronicled limitations of the National Health Service (NHS), responses from Spanish recruits suggested they felt that their skills could be better exploited and developed in Britain. A young female orthopaedic surgeon from Madrid commented on her experience in the North East 'In England there is much more opportunity. I believe it is more of a meritocracy … ' (Belén cited in Hall 2001). Spanish nurses comparing the experience of working in intensive care units in Spain and the UK commented that the career development support available to them in the UK helped avoid the 'burnout syndrome … very common among Spanish nursing staff' in Spain (Martínez and Martínez 2002, 59). They appreciated the probability of promotion: 'It's also much easier to go up a grade from being a staff nurse to managing and supervising other nurses — the NHS Trust encourages you to train up to E grade, which is good experience and advances your career' (María de Zaragoza in Department of Health 2002, 1).

The Contemporary Female Employment Profile

The 2001 Census illustrates the new profile of the Spanish female immigrant workforce.

Table 8.2 Sector of employment of the Spanish-born in England and Wales by gender, 2001 (per cent)

	Males	Females	Total population
Agriculture	0.8	0.2	1.5
Fishing	0.04	0	-
Mining and quarrying	0.2	0.07	0.2
Manufacturing	11.2	6.4	15.0
Utilities	0.4	0.3	0.7
Construction	3.9	0.8	6.8
Wholesale and retail	11.1	12.2	16.8
Hotels and catering	22.2	14.0	4.8
Transport, communications	7.9	6.5	7.0
Finance	5.4	5.6	4.7
Business, property	15.0	15.1	12.9
Public admin.	2.0	2.6	5.7
Education	6.1	15.0	7.7
Health and care	8.0	14.7	10.8
Other	5.6	6.4	5.2
	12,962	16,042	23,627,751

Source: Commissioned Census Data England and Wales 2001, Census 2001 *National Report* Table SO39.

Spanish women are now a presence across a spectrum of sectors. There are small proportions in manufacturing, transport and communications, and finance (where they are relatively more numerous than Spanish males and than the England and Wales total workforce). Larger groupings are in wholesale and retail, hotels and catering, health and care, and education, but the largest single proportion is now in business and property (15.1 per cent, rising to 18.1 per cent in London). Similarly, they exceed the proportion of Spanish males in business and property, health and care and education, and also substantially exceed the UK total average in these sectors. In hotels and catering, both sexes greatly exceed the UK total average, and for the 22 per cent of Spanish in this sector — generally low-paid bar and restaurant work — this activity is easily the most significant concentration of their employment. One female hotel worker told the ARUS 'the wages, although low, allow us to live a life, not like in Spain where we can never leave home because of the cost of mortgages and rents' (33, hotel receptionist). The ghost of Manuel lives on still in 'Fawlty Towers'.[1] Nonetheless, this Spanish female employment profile is unrecognisably more diverse and higher-skilled than the position of a generation earlier. 'The probability of promotion and work in areas connected with your training are much higher here ... I've decided to 'sacrifice' the 'good social life' of Spain for the 'good

---

1 Manuel was the bumbling Spanish waiter in the popular British comedy series of the 1970s, *Fawlty Towers*.

working life' of England' (Mercedes, 30, assistant hotel financial controller, ARUS). The success is widely spread geographically too. Outside of London and the South East, Spanish females are even more dominantly represented in education and health and care.

Accordingly, the occupational status of many of the Spanish-born women in the UK has risen markedly. In the 2001 Census, while the largest concentration of women (18.6 per cent) was in the lowest of the nine categories (elementary occupations), this was somewhat lower than the male figure of 21.9 per cent. A higher proportion of males (15.7 per cent) than females (9.5 per cent) was unsurprisingly placed in the highest category (managers and senior officials). However, the 45.5 per cent of women placed in categories two, three and four (professional occupations, associate professionals and technical staff, and administrative and secretarial) not only significantly exceeded the male figure of 32.9 per cent, but also the total England and Wales figure of 38.1 per cent. Clearly, well-educated Spanish female professionals have been succeeding in the employment market, significantly more so than their male compatriots. The profile, then, is of a Spanish-born population ranged between unskilled low status occupation at one end, and a high-performing, professional skilled class at the other. They are not alone: in 1992-2000 the proportion of immigrants from Southern Europe (Spain, Portugal, Italy, Greece) classed as 'professionals' rose from 19.4 per cent to 26.6 per cent, while the proportion classed as 'manual' fell from 62.5 per cent to 45.0 per cent. Moreover, if London alone is considered, where the Spanish-born female population is heavily concentrated, then the performance is even better. They total 11.5 per cent of category one, and 56.5 per cent of categories one to four — exceeding the total population average of 52.8 per cent.

When applying the definition 'social grade' in the 2001 Census, which links social class to employment status, Spanish women (29.7 per cent) outscore their male compatriots (27.7 per cent) both in the highest of the five grades (AB: higher and intermediate managerial/administrative/professional) and also in the second (C1: supervisory, clerical, junior managerial/administrative/professional), with 30.5 per cent against 29.2 per cent of Spanish men, indicating a generally superior socioeconomic weight. A study of highly-skilled Spanish female employees in Cambridge identifies 'dynamic new forms of mobility ... an intertwining of different aspects of professional progression, familial loyalties, and a novel Hispano-European cultural and professional frame of reference. This could herald the advent of a dynamic, educated 'avant-garde' ... borne out of the congruence of specific challenges: dual-career with care responsibilities, non-embeddedness into an elusive and post-migration social environment, and unsatisfactory opportunities within the conventional labour market in Spain' (Salje 2007, 18). However, the challenges facing such women have also been observed: 'While women scientists continue to engage with the labour market at quite a high level, life course events and in particular partnering and parenting, present serious challenges to their career decision-making' (Ackers 2004, 38).

The Role of Education in the Improved Migrant Status

Education (along with greater mobility and motivation) is at the heart of the progress illustrated above. In Spain, educational opportunities for all were greatly expanded in the 1980s. This especially affected females, who were energetically encouraged by the Socialist government of that decade to maximize their opportunities. Accordingly, the educational achievements of females at all levels, but especially in higher education, greatly improved, to outstrip males. By the end of the century, females accounted for 53.1 per cent of the state university sector, against 46.8 per cent males. This rise in educational opportunity for Spanish girls in the decades of the 1980s and 1990s is acutely reflected in analysis of UK Census data. In 1971 only 3.4 per cent of the Spanish-born population in the UK had tertiary educational qualifications, a figure which rose slowly to 12.2 per cent in 1991. However, in 2001 this leapt to 41.8 per cent for the UK as a whole (reaching even 51.1 per cent in Scotland and 64.6 per cent in Northern Ireland), against the total population average of 19.7 per cent. For Spanish-born men the figure is 37.2 per cent, while for Spanish-born women the percentage with tertiary education is 42.9 per cent — more than twice the total England and Wales population rate. This pattern may well apply to other European immigrant groups. 'In contrast to Germany, the UK has a tradition of attracting not only educated people, but also highly skilled workers' (Buchel and Frick 2001, 2). Since the teaching of English has mushroomed in Spain in the last generation, linguistic barriers in the UK are much less daunting than they were for Spanish migrants. It has also been observed that both Commonwealth and European Union migrants to Britain enjoy 'substantially higher incomes than the native-born white population'. European Union immigrants, in particular, in the period under study (1995-1998) had 11 per cent higher income than the natives, while an earlier study in 1972 found little difference between the two groups. White immigrants — which would include these Spanish migrants — were also less dependent on 'non-market incomes' (i.e. welfare benefits) (Shields and Wheatley Price 1996).

Motives for Migrating

As part of the study of the Spanish immigrant community commissioned by the Spanish Government in 2003, the ARUS consulted 602 respondents to establish other socioeconomic parameters to complement Census and other data. Information sought included place of origin, reason for migrating, length of residence in the UK, dependants in the UK, levels of English language competence, gross family income, and intentions towards returning to Spain.

Table 8.3 Reasons for migrating from Spain to the United Kingdom (per cent)

Reason for migrating	Male	Female
Employment	67.7	51.0
Family	8.4	11.4
Romance	7.6	12.5
Study, language-learning	7.6	16.1
Other	8.7	9

Source: Anglia Ruskin University Survey (2003).

As indicated in Table 8.3, Spanish women have been significantly more willing than Spanish males to migrate for reasons other than employment: almost half of them gave a motive unconnected to employment. They cited language learning, romance and adventure as fairly common drivers. The high proportion of single Spanish women in the 2001 Census has been underlined: it is a commonplace that in Spain women have seized autonomy for themselves and increasingly challenged patriarchal assumptions during the past quarter century, to the point where women have even been characterised as the 'motor of social change' (Graham and Labanyi 1995, 387). They share similarities with women from the former East Germany, where in 2005 it was reported that 'the exodus of young females (400,000 in the age range 18-29 since 1991) is believed to have more to do with the fact that they are better educated than men and set on improved opportunities away from the rather depressed climate at home'[2] (Kroehnert et al. 2006, 7). It is a mark of the risen status of females in Spain that the current government of Zapatero deliberately instituted female parity of numbers in the cabinet in 2004.

One migrant's personal account of her relocation from Catalonia to London in the mid-1970s explores this issue when analysing her compatriots' reactions to the news of her marriage to a British man. While Spanish males of her acquaintance bridled at the news, one opining that she was marrying into a 'barbarous clan', and reminding her that nowhere else in the world would she find the Spanish mother-in-law or the Spanish family — 'which is exactly what I was escaping from' — her Spanish female friends 'reacted with a mixture of envy and solidarity, as if I was a jail-mate about to go over the wall ... Until that moment, I was unaware of how little ordinary Spanish females valued the Spanish male, whom they described as emotionally disabled, a demanding and immature grump who had not learned how to return all the attention that had been lavished upon him' (Isla 2002, 107).

While the ARUS revealed a wide range in duration of stay, levels of qualification, employment levels, income and linguistic fluency, there were certain well-established patterns. Those of long duration in the UK were generally satisfied, valuing the ability of their children to do well and prosper. Typical responses included: 'The children have university education and good jobs which they may not have found

---

2   Thirty-one per cent of them are graduates, compared with 20 per cent of men (Kroehnert et al. 2006, 7).

in Spain' (América, 42 years residence). A similar point was made by María del Carmen, who has also been resident in the UK for 42 years: 'We feel proud of what we have achieved through work and the education we have been able to give our children, most of whom have been to university'. As other studies have found, for working-class women educating their children was of paramount importance, for example, Marta, a cleaner, said 'I want them to be more than me, because anybody can be what I am' (Bravo Moreno 2006, 201).

The Key Role of English Language Competence

For some women, the opportunity to migrate primarily to learn English was an important factor. For example, Madalena 'trained as a nurse for the sole reason of separating herself from the 'other' Spanish and foreign care workers that inhabited her living and working spaces so that she could learn English, which was the reason that had brought her to the UK in the first place' (Pozo Gutiérrez 2007, 210). Indeed, twice the proportion of females as males in the ARUS cited education or language-learning as their motive for migration. However, for many of the recently arrived, good qualifications insufficiently compensated for poor levels of English. For example, Emma (29, biology graduate, bar-worker): 'The language is the barrier to getting a job related to your qualifications'. Similarly, Isabel a 26 year old law graduate currently working as shoe-shop assistant said: 'I'm doing a job way below my qualifications, until I reach the right level of English' and Sonia (29, nurse): 'They don't rate you if you haven't got perfect English'. The issue of linguistic inadequacy has been highlighted and it is central to the degree to which these migrants feel integrated or not.

Inadequate English is one of the factors contributing to a persistent sense of 'foreignness', a point that will be discussed in more detail below. Limited language skills also contributed to being 'disadvantaged economic and social capital gained in Spain ... working conditions in the English labour market, and ... their position as foreigners as perceived by English nationals' (Bravo Moreno 2006, 198).

Table 8.4 Reported level of English language competence (per cent)

Level of English	Male	Female
Good	61.0	74.5
Intermediate	26.2	18.0
Basic	12.2	6.8

Source: Anglia Ruskin University Survey (2003).

Table 8.4 confirms the superior linguistic competence of the Spanish females compared with Spanish males, a feature of other European immigrant groups too. It is also in line with better records of girls in the Spanish school system and the much higher proportions of females in the languages training programmes at secondary and tertiary levels in Spain. Table 8.5 and Table 8.6 demonstrate the earnings advantage this has helped give more linguistically able females of the recent generation of immigrants. While males are more likely to feature in the highest earnings bracket (£100,000 +) — some as footballers — 30.6 per cent of females were represented in the next two brackets, spanning £35,000 to £100,000, against 22.3 per cent of males. In many cases this represents marriage to a non-Spanish male, which in itself usually raises linguistic competence levels.

Table 8.5 Gross family income and sex of Spanish immigrants (per cent)

Gross family income	Male	Female
-£10,000	18.3	16.7
£10,001-£20,000	24.5	24.2
£20,001-£35,000	29.4	26.0
£35,001-£50,000	11.6	15.6
£50,001-£100,000	10.7	15.0
£100,000+	5.3	2.3

Source: Anglia Ruskin University Survey (2003).

Table 8.6 Gross family income and level of English language competence (per cent)

	Good English	Intermediate English	Basic English
-£10,000	5.9	6.4	3.8
£10,001-£20,000	14.6	6.3	1.9
£20,001-£35,000	20.4	3.3	2.1
£35,001-£50,000	11.6	1.1	0.4
£50,001-£100,000	11.9	0.4	0.1
£100,00 +	2.9	0.3	0

Source: Anglia Ruskin University Survey (2003).

Integration and Perception of Role

It may well be that the surviving generation of the 1960s are so well-integrated that 'they now don't identify much with Spain' (ARUS respondent Josefina). However, there are also other issues related to cultural expectations and value systems which mark differences. Working-class women may define 'being Spanish' in terms of being 'a good mother and wife', while middle class Spanish women describe their Spanish characteristics as 'being friendly, upfront and spontaneous' (Bravo Moreno 2006,

216). ARUS respondents registered predictable nostalgic yearning for the climate, food and social life of Spain. Few valued these features of British life. In Bravo Moreno's study of women in London, 'food is the meeting point for both sexes; it is the mediating device to trigger memories of familiarity of their past in Spain in a present foreign context' (Bravo Moreno 2006, 180). Lala Isla's personal account identified other ways in which, despite 25 years duration and married to a Briton, she felt separate values: arriving in London in 1974, she recounted the cultural challenges typically faced by Spanish females adapting to life in the UK. Her observations reflect widespread anecdotal evidence of similar dilemmas faced by her compatriots. On becoming a mother, she mourned the help of an extended family that she would have had in Spain. The lack of positive admiration for children disappointed her, though she was impressed by how much more parents were engaged in amusing their children, playing with them in the park, for example, than is the case in Spain. By contrast, she valued the lack of social or religious pressure to raise her son in any particular fashion, and felt this to be liberating. The much more distant relationships between members of her husband's family, and the greater sense of autonomy of each member she found difficult to come to terms with; indeed, she even had to reconsider her definition of 'family', as her British friends seemed to understand the term as embracing only parents and siblings — while for her it included nephews, uncles and aunts and cousins. 'I think that in Great Britain children see themselves as the product uniquely of their parents, and not as descendants of a group identity, as is the case in other societies' (Isla 2002, 301).

Many respondents to the ARUS commented on the notable absence of a 'community spirit' amongst the new Spanish immigrant community — unlike the generation of the 1950s-1960s who maintained ethnic ties through local societies, religious ceremonies and annual picnics (Luis Botin 1988, 173-186). This type of community spirit was also described by Irish nurses from that era (see Ryan, this volume).

It is clear that many of the female respondents in the ARUS valued more than anything else the sense of individual freedom and personal autonomy that life in the UK gave them. 'The UK has given me the chance to prosper in my career, and consequently in my personal development' (Pilar, 29, accounts administrator). Raquel, a 30 year old sales account manager referred to the freedom of life in London: 'One thing which attracts lots of Spaniards is the cultural diversity ... the freedom of thought and expression combined with a great respect for the individual' (Raquel, 30, sales account manager, London).

Finally, as Table 8.7 illustrates, Spanish women, however content with their situation, share with their male compatriots a strong attachment to Spain and a desire to return home one day: 'I'm very happy in England, though I'll never forget my beloved Galicia' (Dolores, 43 years residence). This is not the mindset of the committed permanent settler, rather the rift between head and heart of the contemporary transnational migrant. This dilemma about staying or returning home is discussed elsewhere in this volume (see Ryan and Evergeti, this volume).

Table 8.7 Intentions of returning to live in Spain (per cent)

Probability of returning to live in Spain	Male	Female
High	45.7	42.7
Medium	27.3	30.1
Low	21.7	23.6
Zero	5.1	3.4

Source: Anglia Ruskin University Survey (2003).

Conclusion

Using census data, complemented where possible by some survey data from ARUS, this chapter illustrates the usefulness of statistical data in illustrating changing migration patterns and trends over a long historical period. The evidence indicates a transformation in the fortunes of most Spanish migrants in the UK during the past generation, but especially in the case of the younger generation of women. Education and skills acquired either in Spain or elsewhere has granted them opportunities for a professional career their mothers could only have dreamed about. This has combined with independent attitudes and a new sense of mobility. Their social profile is vastly more variegated than that of the earlier generation and they enjoy the absence of stereotyping the environment of the UK affords them.

References

Unpublished Primary Sources

Office for National Statistics, *Commissioned Datasets on the Spanish-born in England and Wales in the 2001 Census.*
Northern Ireland Statistics and Research Agency, *Commissioned Datasets on the Spanish-born in Northern Ireland in the 2001 Census.*
General Register Office for Scotland, *Commissioned Datasets on the Spanish-born in the 2001 Census.*
Office for National Statistics Longitudinal Study, *Commissioned Datasets on the Spanish-born in England and Wales 1971-1991.*
Salje, L. (2007), *Between Culture and Career: 'Coping Strategies' of Highly-skilled Spanish Migrants in Cambridge* (Cambridge: Anglia Ruskin University, unpublished paper).

Published Primary Sources

Published Reports of the Census Offices of England and Wales, Scotland and Northern Ireland 1861 to 2001.

Secondary Sources

Ackers, L. (1998), *Shifting Spaces: Women, Citizenship and Migration in the European Union* (Bristol: Polity Press).

—— (2004), *Managing Work and Family Life in Peripatetic Careers: The Experience of Mobile Women Scientists in the EU* (Leeds: University of Leeds Centre for the Study of Law and Policy in Europe Research Report No. 1).

Bhabha, J. and Shutter, S. (1994), *Women's Movement: Women Under Immigration, Nationality and Law* (London: Trentham).

Bravo Moreno, A. (2006), *Migration, Gender and National Identity* (Bern: Peter Lang).

Buchel, F. and Frick, J. (2001), *Immigrants in the UK and West Germany – Relative Income, Positions, Income Portfolio and Redistributive Effects* (Colchester: University of Essex Institute for Social and Economic Research).

Castles, S. and Kosack, G. (1985), *Immigrant Workers and Class Structure in Western Europe* (Oxford: Oxford University Press).

Cohen, R. (1995), *The Cambridge Survey of World Migration* (Cambridge: Cambridge University Press).

Department of Health (2002), 'Maria from Zaragoza, Spain, Began Nursing in Epsom in February 2002', *Nursing UK*, December, www.nursinguk.nhs.uk/maria.asp, accessed 19 December 2003.

De Miguel, A. (1986), *Panorama de La Emigración Española en Europa* (Madrid: Ministerio de Trabajo y Seguridad Social).

Dobson, J. et al. (2001), *International Migration and the United Kingdom: Recent Patterns and Trends* (London: Home Office Occasional Papers No. 75).

Dummett, A. (1995), 'British Immigration Policy in the Twentieth Century', in Lowe, D. et al. (eds), *Immigration and Integration* (London: Institute of Commonwealth Studies).

Graham, H. and Labanyi, J. (1995), *Spanish Cultural Studies* (Oxford: Oxford University Press).

Hall, C. (2001), 'The NHS Looks for 1,000 Foreign Doctors', *Daily Telegraph*, 7 November 2001.

Haque, R. (2002), *Migrants in the UK: Their Characteristics and Labour Market Outcomes and Impacts* (London: Home Office RDS Occasional Paper No. 82).

Isla, L. (2002), *Londres, Pastel Sin Receta: La Vida Londinense Vista Por Una Española* (Barcelona: Plaza & Janes).

Kelson, G. and DeLaet, D. (1999), *Gender and Immigration* (Basingstoke: Macmillan).

King, R. (1993), *Mass Migration in Europe* (Chichester: John Wiley & Sons).

Kofman, E. et al. (2000), *Gender and International Migration in Europe: Employment, Welfare and Politics* (London: Routledge).

Kroehnert, S., Medicus, F. and Klingholz, R. (2006), *The Demographic State of the Nation: How Sustainable are Germany's Regions? Study Summary* (Berlin: Berlin Institute for Population and Development).

Luis Botín, M. (1988), *Españoles en el Reino Unido: Breve Reseña 1810-1988* (Madrid: Dirección General del Instituto Español de Emigración).

Martinez, A. and Martinez, C. (2002), 'Working in Spanish ICUs Compared with UK ICUs', *Critical Care Nursing in Europe* 2:2, 59-60.

Morgan, T. (2004), *The Spanish Migrant Community in the United Kingdom* (Cambridge: Anglia Ruskin University and Ministerio de Trabajo y Asuntos Sociales).

Ogden, P. (1984), *Migration and Geographical Change* (Cambridge: Cambridge University Press).

Panayi, P. (1999), *The Impact of Immigration: A Documentary History of the Effects and Experiences of Immigrants in Britain Since 1945* (Manchester: Manchester University Press).

Patterson, S. (1969), *Immigration and Race Relations in Britain 1960-1967* (Oxford: Oxford University Press).

Pozo Gutiérrez, A. (2007), 'From Neglect to Re-discovery: Language and Identity amongst Spanish Migrants in the United Kingdom', *International Journal of Iberian Studies* 19:3, 205-230.

Ravenstein, E.G. (1885), 'The Laws of Migration', *Journal of the Royal Statistical Society* 48:2, 167-235.

Rivas, M. (1997), 'La Galicia Emergente', *El País Domingo*, 26 October, 14.

Salt, J. (1981), 'International Labour Migration in Western Europe: A Geographical Review', in Kritz, M. et al. (eds), *Global Trends in Migration* (New York: Center for Migration Studies).

—— (2002), *European International Migration: Evaluation of the Current Situation* (Strasbourg: Council of Europe).

Shields, M. and Wheatley Price, S. (1996), *The Earnings of First and Second Generation Immigrants in England* (Leicester: University of Leicester Press).

Straubhaar, T. (1988), *On the Economics of International Labour Migration* (Stuttgart: Haupt).

Vilar, J. and Vilar, M. (1999), *La Emigración Española a Europa en el Siglo XX* (Cuenca: Universidad de Castilla la Mancha).

Chapter 9

Gender and Generation in Pakistani Migration: A Critical Study of Masculinity

Ali Nobil Ahmad

Introduction

A veritable explosion of academic work on gender in recent years has argued that the study of women should be a central part of the history of migration. The scarcity of research that deals with masculinity in the migration process, however, is testament to the fact that gender often gets conflated with the study of women in isolation rather than the migratory processes that produce and reflect social and power relations between and among men and women. Moreover, whilst attentiveness to the specificities of *new independent* female labour migration is surely welcome, a historical myopia tends to pervade sociological literature, as Ryan and Webster argue in the introduction to this volume, and threatens to overlook the economic activities of previous waves of female migrants, including those who migrated secondarily but did waged work nonetheless.

This chapter examines Pakistani migration to the West in an analysis of the economic activity (defined, somewhat narrowly, as waged labour) of successive waves of Pakistani migrants in East London. The objective is to show how change at the structural level within a given locality has shaped and reconfigured gender relations over time through and in relation to a series of different labour regimes. Whilst particular attention is paid to the question of masculinity, men's experiences are placed in comparative context rather than taken in isolation, with a view to shedding light on the experiences of women and other groups. This is done to combat the 'internalist' tendencies which threaten to turn 'men's history' into a field that, perversely, occludes women, and obscures the dominant relations of men over them (Ditz 2004, 17). This dominance is explored not only in structural terms, but also through the functioning of patriarchal ideology, which renders it largely 'doxic' in Bourdieu's sense — invisible to those implicated in its reproduction. As will be seen, this is especially evident in the way women's work is subjectively remembered by relevant actors.

However, a study such as this, which details patterns of gendered privilege involving men of the global South must take into account what Brah (1996) has termed the 'politics of intersectionality', or multiple axes of difference along which subjectivity is constituted — in this context, the specific set of constraints that position

Pakistani males as economically and politically marginalised and racialised subjects in British society, as well as beneficiaries of their power over women. Furthermore, it is shown that despite the overall patriarchal patterns that shape Pakistani migration, the extent and form of gender domination that women experience in East London varies considerably in accordance with a number of factors, above all, historical circumstances but also at the individual point at which it is measured in the course of migrants' lifecycles.

The empirical material presented on migration is based on 53 interviews conducted with Pakistani migrants in East London in 2003-4, spread over 'first generation' male migrants who came to Britain in the early postwar decades, referred to in the text as *Babas*, following Kalra (2000); their spouses who followed through family reunification (referred to as *Valdas*); their young male and female dependents — *Chachas* and *Bajis* respectively, and 'new' Pakistani migrants, including a mix of *mangeters* (marriage migrants), students and visit visa holders, and individuals who entered the UK illegally.

Men's Work, Masculinity the Politics of Production

The rag trade in and around Aldgate, in London's East End, had been an immigrant-dominated industry since at least the eighteenth century when the Huguenots transformed the area around Spitalfields market into a dynamic centre of the silk-weaving industry, which was gradually replaced and reinvigorated by Jewish tailoring towards the end of the 1800s. The latter was in turn succeeded by Pakistani (and Bangladeshi) leather-making and textile production from the late 1960s (Kershen 1997, 74-5). The local labour regime, which remained in place even after the departure of the Jews, is classifiable as 'paternalistic' (Burawoy 1985, 94-98, 111-116), in that it left workers dependent upon a single employer in a neo-feudal bargain which gave their bosses benevolent responsibilities in exchange for 'loyalty' in highly personalised settings involving close supervision and control in what were small garment and textile factories.

As processes of South Asian settlement spread further East to Newham and Walthamstow, however, factories as diverse as steel and rubber production plants, engineering firms and flour mills absorbed the labour power of subsequent arrivals. Most of these were more ostensibly 'modern' than those in and around Aldgate, with migrants less attached to a single employer, moving from job to job, and routinely subjected to a more antagonistic regime that, following Burawoy (1985, 40) is referred to here as 'despotic' since it entailed the arbitrary and willful imposition of discipline and control over the workforce. Baba Anwar, who migrated in 1964, recalls being treated 'like a slave' by employers of medium sized factories who colluded with hostile, racist white workers to single-out Asian workers for harsh treatment, an atmosphere that culminated in his being summarily sacked following a dispute with a white co-worker that was itself a product of the latter's blatant racism. Pakistani masculinity, in this context, was subordinate and vulnerable, the object of a racialised capitalism that dished up systematic discrimination and abuse. The position of South Asians at the bottom of the racial ladder ensured their designation to the most unpleasant, physically taxing jobs that involved heavy lifting and other gruelling tasks. Compulsory union membership appears to have been meaningless. Accidents and sackings were frequent and uncompensated.

More generally, factory work was characterised by many features that are today strongly associated with poor health and safety. Whilst this regime applied to all workers, the lower status of 'coloured' immigrant newcomers compounded the natural tendency of most employers to assign novices to high-risk jobs rather than jeopardise the investments already made in their experienced workforce (Robinson and Smallman 2006, 92). These hardships in the labour process were compounded by poor and unsanitary housing arrangements. Several men recalled 'horrible' conditions, with four people sleeping in each room and beds being used in shifts.

However, most of these difficulties were specific to a period of time and were overcome as the 1960s came to an end. Baba Anwar remembers improvements in health and safety towards the beginning of the new decade ('regulations were coming in'). An impressive series of victories by labour over capital at the national level ensured that the paternalistic and despotic regimes prevalent in East London factories gave way to a new era of stability, security and prosperity together with an improvement in working and living conditions for migrants. In small increments, Ford Dagenham established itself as the largest single employer for Asians in the East London area. The older participants in my study remember this, the relatively protected epoch of Fordism, fondly. Baba Rashid, who started working at Ford in 1972 and stayed there up until his retirement says: 'It was good working at Ford'; 'Ford's wages were the best of all'. Baba Sheikh was similarly positive: 'I think that was a time when we all had difficulty getting decent jobs, decent wages. Ford was a safe haven for Asians'. Baba Shabir, who worked in quality control for 16 years having migrated in the 1970s, was unambiguous: 'Those were nice times'. 'My job was to inspect those parts fitted properly'. 'It was light'. He even recalled a relative leniency in the way the regime was administered, with an industrial jurisprudence system on the shop floor that was favourable to workers.

All this runs counter to the popular impression of Ford based on highly publicised legal cases brought against the company alleging racial discrimination: 'Plum' jobs, we now know, were reserved for whites; a disproportionate number of non-whites were confined to the 'dirty line' jobs on the North Estate of the factory, which operated as a ghetto for some twenty years (Manning 2003). Yet this discrimination does not figure in the narratives of the men I interviewed. For them, it was a privilege to be protected by a bastion of stability in an otherwise perennially insecure environment, and much preferable to working for 'apne' ('one's own kind'). The Babas' only regret is that this golden age was short-lived. Having been based on a 'Faustian bargain', Fordism was rapidly dismantled in the early 1980s. Reduced to a 'redundant colonial/racialised labour force' in much the same way as colonial immigrants across the West in what proved to be a global economic downturn (Grosfugel and Georas 2000, 108), many Babas were effectively left stranded. Thousands lost jobs and though some turned to self-employment, unemployment became widespread. Most coped on a combination of savings, welfare benefits and pensions. A number had already purchased second and even third rental homes which continue to generate income. This perhaps explains why many Babas refuse to see themselves as victims, and remember the period as one in which they were properly rewarded for their toil, boasting material acquisitions and achievements: 'It was okay because the money was good', remembers Baba Rashid. They preferred to talk about the rewards they reaped and what they spent it on (above all, property) than to dwell on what they had endured in the factory.

Nobody regarded factory work in this period as a picnic: the 1960s especially is recalled as a time of extremely hard graft and sacrifice. The men I interviewed feel a fierce sense of entitlement to the material gains they made in this period (Baba Sarwar: 'we gave our blood to this country'). Indeed, the physical toll of the 1960s and psychological impact of unemployment in the 1980s are not to be underestimated. However, today, these silver-bearded patriarchs clearly enjoy their status as respected elders within the community and household heads. I met former Union activists, religious leaders and councillors who had achieved a considerable degree of institutional, 'structural incorporation' (Portes and Sensenbrenner 1993). Their extensive involvement with the local public sphere appears to have allowed them to recover much of the dignity and self-esteem that may have been lost in the early years, and the value of their achievements appear self-evident, allowing them to narrate their life stories with pride and enthusiasm.

Women's Work and the Gendered Visibility of Waged Labour

The Commonwealth Immigration Act began the trend of family reunification that rapidly transformed an almost exclusively male community in 1961 to one that, by 1974, was 35 per cent female. By 1982, the predominance of men dropped to just 58 per cent and by 1991 it had virtually disappeared altogether (Ansari 2004, 253-4). The consequences of family reunification for gender relations and the labour process were profound. Rather than trigger the adoption of a more balanced life-style, it ushered in an intensification and diversification of economic activity. If the household had previously been a place of respite where migrants slept in between shifts, it was now absorbed into the textile industry with the family itself becoming integrated into the production process. At the exact moment at which the Babas began to experience better working conditions at the Dagenham Ford plant, they forged a new set of connections with the leather and textile businesses in inner London through their imported brides and elder male and female children who migrated as young dependents. The latter were put to work by the Babas, who facilitated their incorporation within the sectors they were leaving, thereby ensuring that Aldgate's enduring appetite for sweated labour was met by the newcomers.

Asian women's work thus played an important role in meeting the needs of demand for cheap labour that was instrumental in the formation of small enterprises for which the 1980s under Prime Minister Margaret Thatcher is so well remembered. As Abdul Bari explains, the transformation of some 'homes' into factory or work/ sweat shops ensured that production continued to operate beyond official hours on weekends, holidays and during evenings. The arrival of women (though he omits to mention them) spelt the end of the 'working day' as it had been known in Aldgate:

Before you worked from seven or eight in the morning until 5.30pm. Then you did overtime. That was from 1963 until 1970. After 1970, men worked until 11pm — when they started opening their own leather businesses. The working day then extended (Abdul Bari).

Research by Joanna Herbert reveals that South Asian women working outside the home tended to present patriarchy with a more direct challenge (see Herbert in this volume). However, while a minority of Pakistani women worked in such factories outside their homes, most were confined to the private sphere, doing homework. This held the advantage for materially struggling families of allowing households to draw upon the labour power of women without challenging the patriarchal ideological norms of 'purdah', allowing men to control and govern their sexuality and mobility in social space (Ansari 2004, 271-2). For the Valdas, childrearing duties, together with other household chores related to maintenance of the workforce (including making clothes for their children) were blended together with commercial sewing in the course of each working day, blurring the lines between the two, despite being analytically divisible, and rendering problematic any notion of the 'home' as a purely domestic sphere and site of reproductive labour.

Most women faced an altogether different set of challenges to men, which raises the controversial question long posed by feminist scholars, of whether men and women within the same household might have different class positions (Oakley and Oakley 1979). In some cases, the chains of production that connected women in the East London borough of Newham to their indirect employers and the host society's economy were mediated through their husbands, who often brought home cloths, fabrics and unfinished garments for them to sew by hand. Having sourced the work for them from Aldgate, men such as Baba Rashid appear (and present themselves) as their wives' direct employers:

I got the wife working — sewing, at home. That helped a little.

And you found that work for her?

Yes … I would take the sewing work home, and they would come and collect it.

Who would come?

The factory people, *apne* — Pakistanis — and white people too. They would send work to homes … at that time the factories were in Aldgate (Baba Rashid).

In other cases, work was delivered and collected directly by their real employers — subcontractors who did drop-offs to homes in what were clearly informal, untaxed transactions, outside the sphere of anything resembling a regulated labour market. Baji Sayed's mother worked in accordance with such an arrangement:

Some people used to come around and drop the clothes, and then they'd say after so many days, "I'll come around and collect it". They worked for factories. They'd go around in their van with all these clothes.

And who were they, white? Asian?

Well the one who used to supply to mum was Jewish.

So they would pay them cash in hand?

Yeah, cash in hand (Baji Sayed).

The factory representatives appear as anonymous figures in the narratives of women and children, in whose recollections the association of masculinity with public space is unmistakeable; women's confinement to the home was such that vans brought and collected the work to and from the threshold of the feminised domestic domain. The latter's subordinate position within a male-dominated wage economy is reflected in the appalling levels of compensation she received for this labour: 'Most of these factories were in Aldgate. The money was really bad. Wages were seven or eight pounds a week – sometimes ten pounds a week'. This is in stark contrast to the wages of the Babas, for whom pay, even at the worst of times in the 1960s (over a decade earlier) had ranged from between nine pounds a week to twelve pounds for the nightshift, and was limited to twelve hours a day. For Valdas, who were paid by the piece, neither compensation nor hours of work were fixed. In addition, their waged working day was structured around the intense pressures of child-rearing and domestic work.

However, the objective reality of a class difference within households is in fact difficult to posit. Some Babas wilfully exaggerate their own elevated status over their wives for ideological reasons; the gendering of labour in garment industries was as much related to the demands of employers as it was to any inherent patriarchal features of supply. As Brah (1996, 137) has pointed out: 'Asian patriarchal discourses and practices in Britain are not exogenous to Britain; they are very much an internal dynamic of the British social formation'. Indeed, homework was also a product of ethno-racial geo-spatial logics of 1970s and 1980s Britain, an era in which it was often unsafe for Black and Asian women to leave their homes due to the realities of 'Paki-bashing' and racial terror (Mitter 1985, 130). Confinement to the home produced a kind of paradox in which many Asian women experienced both invisibility at home and hyper-visibility in public spaces simultaneously (Pettman 1996, 186). The privileged position retained by Pakistani men (and to some extent, boys) as guardians of public space was not without its responsibilities and risks, as is clear when contextualised within the well-known history of racial terror that culminated in series of brutal attacks and murders across East London in the 1980s, including, perhaps most famously, that of Aftab Ali, after whom a park in Aldgate is commemoratively named. It should also be remembered that women did not endure quite the unsanitary living conditions and overcrowding that were typical of male migration in the 1960s. Nor were they at risk from industrial accidents and ill health associated with despotic labour regimes in this last period. Patriarchal dominance, for the Babas, was something of a poisoned chalice.

It was also negotiated. Extreme seclusion and claustrophobic consignment to the home upon arrival, though not uncommon amongst Pakistani women in the 1970s, is often 'only a phase' (Werbner 1990, 148). Viewed over time, the experiences of the Valdas reflect increases in agential room for manoeuvre as they become surer of their positions within the household and community. Like Werbner's respondents in Manchester, who built up their own social networks with neighbours and swapped notes on homeworking (1990, 7, 124), the women I encountered had engineered a kind of informal unionisation by making friendships, pooling childcare resources and altering the terms of the patriarchal bargain. Drawing upon Bourdieu again, this demonstrates how 'the impact of femaleness as negative capital may be assumed to decline in direct proportion to the amount of other forms of symbolic capital amassed' (Moi 1991, 1038-40). Whether women in East London managed to deploy income from homework to build up an independent economic base, as Werbner's informants did, remains unclear (1990, 129, 132-3). Forthcoming research conducted by Kaveri Harris on Pakistanis in East London suggests that, when it came to the pooling of household income, control of the purse strings was subjected to increasingly complex arrangements that do not always bear out the general pattern of male control often associated with Asians in East London (Bhopal 1999). My own findings suggest that the extent to which women were able to negotiate and challenge the terms of the patriarchal bargain, as the 1980s wore on, tended to reflect the educational backgrounds of their husbands: generally, the higher a man's own educational and social capital, the greater his openness towards drawing upon the creative and intellectual energies of his wife in the sphere of business, for example. The opportunity for a woman to amass and utilise social capital, in other words, was shaped by the particular masculinity she found herself in negotiation with.

Gender, Generation and Representations of Women's Work

Virtually without exception, Pakistani women engaged in wage labour of some sort in addition to their household duties, confirming what most accounts of the labour process for South Asian women who migrated to Britain in this period have long held: the extent of their economic activity has been underestimated (Ansari 2004, 268). This underestimation is a product of what Sen (1990) has classed the 'perceived contribution response': that is, the subjective perception of its value by men and women alike, both of whom tend to underestimate its importance due to ideological distortions.

The Babas, perhaps inevitably, were especially dismissive of their wives' contributions to household income. Often, when respondents referred to women doing wage-labour, they did so parenthetically, making constant reference to its insignificance. Baba Rashid was similarly blasé when I suggested that the work regimes for women were 'tough'. He replied, shrugging, 'Well, women do sewing work anyway — that's what they do'. Though he admits the hours she worked were not unsubstantial, he refuses to concede the net contribution could have been more than a 'little'. Even where women's labour played a material role in the very transformation of rental properties into workshops, its role is downplayed. It was only as an aside that Baba Bari pointed out his 'missus' used to cut in his Aldgate factory. Yet later, when I asked about specifics, he remarked: 'No no, she was just a housewife'. 'But you said she used to help?', I pointed out. 'Well, she did a bit of help', he grudgingly conceded, before moving on to discuss other matters. The compatibility of women's paid employment with patriarchy is premised precisely on the fact that its value remains invisible because of its *perceived* insignificance. Its low pay and low status are what allow it to take place.

By comparison, the offspring of migrants are less forgetful of the role their mothers played in the development of the textile business in Aldgate. Most grew up observing their mothers sewing at close quarters. Their testimonies too, however, are subject to distortions:

> *So how many dresses would your mother make in a week?*
>
> Not many ...
>
> *How long would she have to work ... ?*
>
> I'd say about three or four hours a day. Evenings mostly (Baji Sayed).

For Baji Sayed, who went on to concede that her mother made 12 dresses a week, the response 'not many' was automatic, despite the fact that the amount of time daily spent by her mother ('only three or four hours') adds up, according to her own calculations, to a 28 hour working week. On the basis that the work was done from home and not full-time, she went on to suggest that it was somehow, not 'real' work in the course of our interview quoted below:

> I find from my experience, a lot of Muslim women don't work. The younger generation, or people from my period, they're working, but my mum's age, they didn't work.
>
> *But this sewing, it was work!*
>
> But it isn't full time. I mean, *go out* to work (Baji Sayed).

Imran was under no illusions that women played an important role that was not merely adjunctive, but instrumental in the achievements of the first generation. Despite acknowledging their labour, however, he tended to romanticise their heroics by assuming an absence of power relations, and recalls the period with nostalgia for a lost age in which women knew and performed their 'authentic' and true roles dutifully, without being obliged or coerced to in any way. Pakistani women today, it is suggested, are of a lower calibre for their rejection of their predecessors' willingness to make extra sacrifices:

> The women worked very hard — very, very hard. Now they don't make them like they used to. The old women stuck by their families, by their husbands, arm in arm — did whatever they had to do to make just that little bit extra happen, for their home. Nowadays it's not like that. The new generation, they don't need to be (Imran).

This intuitive observation of generational difference is backed up by academic accounts which have demonstrated definitively that young Muslim women born in Britain have a thoroughly different set of life expectations than their mothers (Dale et al. 2002). For Imran, the old schools' stoicism was borne of lack of expectations:

'I don't think they ever complained ... They were happy because they were better off than where they were before, weren't they'.

In reality, the absence of protest ought not to be taken as an absence of inequality (Sen 1990, 126), and the absence of overt protest does not constitute willing compliance. The apparent acquiescence of women, rather, in such scenarios, is more often recognition of the fact that they have no other options (Agarwal 1997, 23-5). According to most of the women I interviewed, who were of middle- and lower middle-class families and backgrounds, they were anything but 'better off' during these early years in East London than they had been as privileged youngsters in Pakistan. Some were of lower middle-class backgrounds and had lived in large, spacious and lively family homes alongside siblings and cousins with servants to help with domestic work, and were ill prepared for their heavy workloads. The transition to living in small, dreary terraced houses in which they were expected to sweat away at piece work in between rearing several children, often in the complete absence of family and friendship networks, triggered feelings of isolation and depression, often reflected in the high rates of mental illness (Ansari 2004, 259). The notion that these women were happy with their lot is thus highly questionable.

Some communicated opposition to the circumstances they had faced in the UK in the 1970s and 1980s, though they did so, as it were, retrospectively. The Valdas seem well aware of the difference in opportunities their British-born offspring enjoy, and are far more ambivalent about its implications for their own place in history than Imran's nostalgia suggests. His assessment accords little with the frustration some women communicated to me at the total lack of recognition of the sacrifices they made. Parveen was one of several women who spoke of their frustration at the erasure from history of their contribution:

> When we found out that here, we would have to work. It was a surprise. The ones these days, they don't have to do this. We paid for houses with hard work. We went [to Pakistan] only every ten years. The ones today do less work (Parveen).

Just as Baji Sayed described her mother's generation as one which did not work, Valda Parveen returns the compliment, rendering visible once more the generational cleavages that cloud any notion of a singular feminine, or indeed singular masculine, experience. It is to these inter-generational tensions to which we now turn in a more detailed account of the testimonies of Bajis and Chachas.

The complexities of gender and migration are such that, as the testimonies reveal, it was not uncommon for the burdens of household labour — both waged and unwaged, to fall upon eldest daughters in particular. The latter bore some of the brunt of the high volumes of work their mothers were expected to do. Baba Rashid told me that the female children would help their mother in completing the piecework he brought home to her for some seven to eight years whilst he worked at Ford. Baji Sayed explains the division of domestic tasks between her and her sisters:

> Before going to school, me and my younger sister, we had to clean the house — she had to do half I would clean half. Getting up at seven o'clock. That's how we shared our work. And in the evening we'd have to help mum — when you would come back from school you'd have to do your schoolwork and help her (Baji Sayed).

This situation was common amongst many Asian families in Britain according to other studies (Wade and Souter 1992). For Baji Sayed, it impacted heavily upon her life trajectory by reducing her opportunities for education and recreation. Removed from school at the age of sixteen, the option of a white collar or professional career was beyond her grasp. Werbner (1990, 72) suggests that a sense of pride in helping family overcomes bitterness amongst such individuals, even if they are exploited. Yet Baji Sayed seems to speak only of the cost of her own personal sacrifice when she refers to this past, and implies awareness of its injustice. Her British-born siblings, she feels, did better:

> Me being the eldest daughter, they didn't let me do further studies, mum having eight kids altogether. Back home you can have a servant. Mum used to say you have to help me in the house ... So my younger brothers and sisters did quite well. One of my sisters is a lawyer. The other one is a secretary, and one of my brothers is a mechanical engineer. Another works for Newham Council. He's gotten quite high up — he's a surveyor for the council and his position is quite high (Baji Sayed).

Valdas, then, were not uniquely oppressed, and women do not form a homogenous gender group. A set of restrictions equivalent to those which retarded the development of some of their eldest daughters, had similarly negative consequences for the life chances of many of their eldest sons, a fact which complicates once more any notion that oppression can be divided neatly along gender lines. Male dependents (chachas), some of whom arrived before their mothers to join fathers and uncles and work in factories, were victims in their own way of the hierarchical, patriarchal positioning of individuals within the migrant household, complicating any notion of a homogenous, all-dominating masculinity.

Several respondents confirmed that it was not unusual for men to claim children who were in fact not their own as their dependents before controls were introduced by the British immigration authorities to stamp out the practice. Having migrated as boys, they would then be compelled to attend school for a short period as a formality to satisfy the authorities, and begin work disguised as young adults. The changing of birth dates on passports appears to have been widespread in this period, and a number of these men would have been below the legal age limit to work. Imran's father, who worked in Aldgate, was a case in point:

> When he came, he went to school for two years. Obviously they put the date of birth forward about two or three years so he could work quickly. He had to get out of school and start working to get an income. There was no messing about. We've got it easy. In those days, they wanted to avoid school and work (Imran).

Rabeena's husband was another such case:

> My husband came here at 12-13 but his passport said 15, as he wanted to work. He didn't go to school but after two or three years (he went to English classes), he just started working in the Ford factory (Rabeena).

If East London's Pakistani households were hierarchically structured production units with the patriarch positioned firmly at the top — enjoying the privileges of optimum protection under Fordist labour conditions, and his wife and daughters at the bottom, doing household work and sweated home-sewing, his sons appear to have been somewhere in between these two poles. Rashid, for instance, put his 18 and 19-year-old sons to work in Aldgate, manufacturing blouses and shirts in a Pakistani owned enterprise. Whilst they tended to work in factories and received weekly wages accordingly, Chachas were far more likely to end up in smaller operations in Aldgate, where pre-Fordist regimes prevailed. Like their mothers and sisters, they did not benefit from the improvements in labour conditions at Ford unless they were lucky enough to benefit from contacts. 'You were only getting the job at that time', Baba Sheikh remembers, 'with a reference — if you know the foreman or friend who works there'. As with the Bajis, the consequence of being put to work so young work for the long-term careers of the eldest Chachas are clearly visible when their trajectories are compared with those of their younger, British-born siblings, most of whom were schooled for longer and thus able to achieve more prestigious and well paid jobs.

Gender and Masculinity in New Migration

The augmentation in volume and proportion of Pakistani immigration since the 1990s is unmistakeable: The International Passenger Survey reveals that total international immigration from Pakistan to the UK from 1995 to 2004 was 29,100, up considerably from the figure of 17,600 over the previous corresponding period of 1992-2001 (ONS, table 2.3, 6). The vast majority of this latest wave of arrivals, however, is made up of single men. Independent female international migration from Pakistan is almost non-existent, and although 7,590 of the 212,000 Pakistani nationals admitted into the UK in 2004 were 'mangeters', a greater number (12,600) were students and around half were visitors (Home Office 2004, table 2.2, 34-5). Indeed, outflows from Pakistan remain profoundly gendered, and because of illegal migration, have become, if anything, more male-dominated. Of the estimated 430,000 illegally resident migrants that populate the UK (Woodbridge 2005), Pakistanis are one of several nationalities that figure prominently in Home Office asylum and immigration statistics, which give a rough indication as to which groups and genders make up the 'illegal' population: the vast majority are men (Home Office 2004, table 3.2, 43). In an obvious sense, then, the Pakistani migration system has remained, in Bourdieusian terminology, one that appears largely 'doxic' in gender terms. That is to say, the patriarchal norms that compose the established order remain largely naturalised to those who live them and unchallenged (Moi 1991, 1026, 1033).

However, upon arrival, few of these men have become patriarchs. Where family reunification became an option for 'old' migrants within a few years of their incorporation, it is far more complicated for those who enter as students and visitors to marry and virtually impossible for those who enter illegally. For those Pakistani men who migrate as spouses to wed British-born Pakistani women, the household scenario that awaits them often poses enormous challenges to their traditional roles and status, as anthropological research on masculinity has shown (Charsley 2005). Today's 'mangeters' cannot impose the regimes of patriarchal dominance that the Babas did when they imported young brides in the 1970s. Indeed, in stark contrast to the free reign enjoyed by their predecessors, they experience a complex set of gendered power relations within the household and face challenges to their authority. Many feel bitter and disempowered by the limits of their dominance in a society that permits women to stand up to rigid forms of patriarchy. Their higher level of education to the previous waves of migrants makes the downward mobility experienced in migration more psychologically demoralising and comparable to that experienced by East African migrants (see Herbert, this volume): Thirty-five year-old degree educated Ilyas from Karachi was separated from his wife when I first interviewed him in 2003 (they are now divorced):

> Whenever there's a problem she keeps talking about "solicitors", "domestic violence", "lone parent benefit". Even for small problems she keeps bringing the English system and English law into the situation … The problem here with this system is that women now have more rights than men. Look at what this lone parent benefit has done to me. Look at me! I have no life. My son is all I had … Now I can't see him … I've even become homeless. A Pakistani girl would say lone parent benefit is haram. She would never take it. She would only want to live off her husband's money (Ilyas).

Nadir, a 31-year-old Punjabi with three children, was also going through a divorce when I interviewed him. He too was adamant that women in Britain have excessive rights and autonomy. Like Ilyas, he saw himself as a victim and emphasised his vulnerability in a scenario that pit him as an outsider against his supposedly cruel in-laws, a long settled family that he perceived as seeking to dominate and undermine him at every opportunity. He does *not* distinguish between men and women, but views these in-laws as a unitary power block whose position of strength is premised upon their greater 'structural' and 'relational' incorporation (Portes and Sensenbrenner 1993).

> I was alone. I had no elders. I spoke bad English. They had 40 to 50 families to back them up. They said, "Become British, forget your family!" I didn't stand a chance. Their whole family had council flats — the mother and father were on disability benefits, income support. They weren't working. They wouldn't let me meet anyone. They wouldn't let me build friendships … They didn't want me to understand how things work here. I found out myself about how to get a council flat that I'm entitled to … they tried to stop me (Nadir).

My data confirms what others, including Samad and Eade (2003, 59-60) and to some extent, Charsley (2005), have found before me: many such unions are fraught with tension that can lead to marital problems, divorce and separation.

State controls with respect to immigration are likely to become even more restrictive. With a growing sense amongst even Britain's liberals that migrant families are a costly burden on the welfare state (Dench et al. 2006) and the perceived 'problems' surrounding illegal work and trafficking (together with a general atmosphere of dismay with 'multiculturalism'), a tightening of internal controls is on the agenda, to go with the ever-stricter entry restrictions. These are likely to include sterner measures to restrict welfare benefits and laws which make it more difficult for irregular entrants to legalise their status and crackdowns on illegal work. The defining characteristics of the new migrant generation are thus its predominantly male and single makeup, along with its increasingly precarious legal status.

Most new migrants are incorporated within the businesses and rental homes of settled Pakistanis, since they prefer to remain near to residential areas populated heavily by co-ethnics for the obvious material, practical and psychological advantages that familiarity brings: above all jobs in South Asian businesses; cheap and informal accommodation arrangements; anonymity (and therefore amnesty) if they are 'illegal'. An important consequence of this fact is that they frequently live alongside, work for and pay rents to 'old' families, living in the very dwellings that once housed the Babas during their early years in East London factories. This proximity throws into stark relief the difference between the lived experiences of these respective constellations of migrants, and further complicates the dynamics of gender and generation within the community: a vast power discrepancy exists between the old migrant family and the new, lone, male 'breadwinning' migrant individual, reflected above all in capital assets such as property and businesses. Apart from not having families, newcomers are unlikely to be able to afford property even in the medium and long-term given the rise in prices over the last two decades. Few ever manage to raise the start-up capital to launch their own businesses and having been educated in Pakistan, they are at a disadvantage within the mainstream labour market when compared with their British-born (male *and female*) counterparts, who are conspicuous by their absence within the Pakistani businesses where these new migrants work.[1]

There also exist important differences within the labour process as migrants in East London's post-industrial economy experience it today. In Fords the Babas' working hours were restricted; weekends and holidays were contractually fixed, as were their rates of pay and redundancy packages. The contemporary service sector, and in particular the ethnic enclave economy, on the other hand, is made up of takeaways, grocers, halal butchers and other enterprises that provide few such guarantees. The now staggering costs of migration for smuggled migrants (and students who must pay fees) mean that many of those receiving the lowest rates of pay and working the longest hours have considerable debts to eradicate before they can accumulate any capital at all. The service sector employment performed by new migrants, moreover, is predominantly composed of catering work and poses an unprecedented challenge to constructions of masculinity (see Keeler's chapter in this volume). Nor do new migrants have wives and children that can be integrated into the production process in order to ease their burden and supplement household income. Unlike the Babas, the existence they know is that of a lone, single (uninvited) guest worker which, in all its material (and emotional) deprivation, entails few of the powers and privileges that were once associated with Pakistani masculinity in East London.

1　The handful of Chachas I encountered who worked within these ethnic enclaves are now the employers, their status merely reinforcing the class distinction between these British-born and the newly arrived Pakistani migrants.

Conclusion

Although they experienced racism, poor housing and difficult working conditions in the 1960s, Babas enjoyed relatively decent labour regimes under Fordism in the 1970s, which represented an improvement over the paternalism and despotism that reigned in inner East London's smaller and medium-sized factories. Moreover, first generation migrant families and households in Britain were economically incorporated in the 1970s and 1980s along segmented lines of gender and generation in ways that allowed men to share (and in some cases pass on) low-status labour to their families whilst maintaining patriarchal dominance, actually and ideologically. Close examination, however, reveals local variation, complexity and contestation as time wore on. The agency of women was contingent upon the juncture of their life at which it was examined, and the specific masculinity they found themselves in negotiation with.

The variable nature of masculinity is particularly clear when we turn to new migration, where it has been challenged by historical change in the economic climate, the price of housing, the structure of demand for labour, state-legislation on migrants' residential legal rights and protection as workers in destination societies such as Britain. The legitimacy and material base of the patriarchal migrant family as a resource for male migrants seeking economic incorporation within host countries is being eroded, and post-Fordist 'new' migration since the 1990s has rendered many recently migrated men particularly vulnerable in ways that their predecessors were not. Their status as lone breadwinners in a vastly transformed context of reception, together with their relations to previous waves of migrant families which are often imbued in relations of power and economic exploitation reveal the highly contingent, variable nature of masculinity and masculine power in different times and places, underlining the merits of an historical approach to the study of gender.

Acknowledgements

A sizeable part of the research presented here was completed as part of the Leverhulme Project on smuggling and trafficking (2003-04), based at the Migration Research Unit at UCL. Many thanks go to Pnina Werbner and Kaveri Harris for invaluable feedback on an earlier draft of this paper.

References

Agarwal, B. (1997), 'Bargaining and Gender Relations: Within and Beyond the Household', *Feminist Economics* 3:1, 1-51.

Ansari, H. (2004), *'The Infidel Within': Muslims in Britain Since 1800* (London: Hurst & Company).

Bhopal, K. (1999), 'Domestic Finance in South Asian Households in East London', *Journal of Ethnic and Migration Studies* 25:1, 81-93.

Brah, A. (1996), *Cartographies of Diaspora: Contesting Identities* (London: Routledge).

Burawoy, M. (1985), *The Politics of Production* (London: Verso).

Charsley, K. (2005), 'Unhappy Husbands: Masculinity and Migration in Transnational Pakistani Marriages', *The Journal of the Royal Anthropological Institute* 11:1, 85-105.

Dale, A., Shaheen, N., Fieldhouse, E. (2002), 'The Labour Market Prospects for Pakistani and Bangladeshi Women', *Work, Employment & Society* 16:1, 5-25.

Dench, G., Gavron, K., Young, M. (2006), *The New East End: Race, Kinship and Conflict* (London: Profile Books).

Ditz, T.L. (2004), 'The New Men's History and the Peculiar Absence of Gendered Power: Some Remedies from Early American Gender History', *Gender & History* 16:1, 1-35.

Grosfugel, R. and Georas, C. (2000), 'Coloniality of Power and Racial Dynamics: Notes Toward a Reinterpretation of Latino Caribbeans in New York City', *Identities* 7:1, 85-125.

Harris, K. (forthcoming), Unpublished Doctoral Thesis.

Home Office (2004), *Control of Immigration Statistics* (CM6690).

Kalra, V.S. (2000), *From Textile Mills to Taxi Ranks* (Ashgate: Aldershot).

Kershen, A. (1997), 'Huguenots, Jews and Bangladeshis in Spitalfields and the Spirit of Capitalism', in Kershen, A. (ed.), *London: the Promised Land?* (Aldershot: Avebury), 66-90.

Manning, C. (2003), 'The Ford Ghetto', *Daily Mirror*, 28 March 2003.

Mitter, S. (1985), *Common Fate; Common Bond: Women in the Global Economy* (London: Pluto Press).

Moi, T. (1990), 'Appropriating Bourdieu: Feminist Theory and Pierre Bourdieu's Sociology of Culture', *New Literary History* 22, 1017-1049.

Oakley, A. and Oakley, R. (1979), 'Sexism in Official Statistics', in Miles, I. and Evans, J. (eds), *Demystifying Official Statistics* (London: Pluto Press), 172-189.

Pettman, J. (1996), *Worlding Women* (London and New York: Routledge).

Portes, A. and Sensenbrenner, J. (1993), 'Embeddedness and Immigration: Notes on the Social Determinants of Economic Action', *American Journal of Sociology* 6, 1320-50.

Robinson, A. and Smallman, C. (2006), 'The Contemporary British Workplace: A Safer and Healthier Place?', *Work, Employment and Society* 20:1, 87-107.

Samad, Y. and Eade, J. (2003), *Community Perceptions of Forced Marriage* (A Report for the Foreign and Commonwealth Office: London: Community Liaison Unit).

Sen, A. (1990), 'Gender and Cooperative Conflicts', in Tinker, I (ed.), *Persistent Inequalities* (New York: Oxford University Press), 123-149.

Wade, B. and Souter, P. (1992), *Continuing to Think: The British Asian Girl* (London: Clevedon).

Werbner, P. (1990), *The Migration Process: Capital, Gifts and Offerings among British Pakistanis* (Oxford: Berg).

Woodbridge, J. (2001), 'Sizing the Unauthorised (illegal) Migrant Population in the UK', online report 29/05, Home Office.

Chapter 10

'No Job for a Grown Man': Transformations in Labour and Masculinity among Kurdish Migrants in London

Sarah J. Keeler

Introduction

The interstices of gender and migration are now being more thoroughly mined for analyses which can shed light on the reformation of identities and inequalities in the twenty-first century global economy (Piper 2007; Tastsoglou and Dobrowolsky 2006; Willis and Yeoh 2000). However, such work tends to equate gender with female migration, often obscuring the presence of men. As both Joanna Herbert and Ali Ahmad argue in this volume, the cultural and economic (re)construction of masculinities, as migrants and refugees become enmeshed within new localities and transnational systems, remains neglected: part of a wider neglect of masculinity as a domain of analysis within social science (Gutman 1997). Transnational migration has generally created conditions in which identities — those of gender, ethnicity, class, nation, religion — are destabilised, rendering locatedness problematic (Appadurai 1996; Hall 1996). In what follows, I outline the complexity of such interstices using a case study to highlight the changing ways in which certain identity markers (those of gender) are foregrounded as a kind of response to the simultaneous invisibility of others (those of ethnicity and 'nation').

The case study looks at Kurdish migrants from Turkey, many of whom arrived in London as refugees in the early 1990s, during the height of conflict between members of the Kurdistan Workers Party (PKK) and the Turkish state. It focuses on self-perceptions of masculinity and their relation to labour trends which research participants have seen as diminishing their ethnic identity as they experience a process of being subsumed into the local 'Turkish speaking' economy and into productive roles traditionally attributed to women — namely those of sewing and food preparation. The research is based on my more than three years of close contacts with Kurdish diasporans in London and elsewhere. This chapter also draws on interviews with six men, varying in age from 27 to 46, about their experiences and ideas of migration, gender, identity, labour and the challenges they face as Kurdish men engaged with these issues, on informal group discussions with people in the community, and on participant observation which took place during and since the time of my fieldwork in 2004-2005. I draw on the experience of my PhD research into transformations in identity discourse within the Kurdish diaspora, much of which centred upon narratives that situate differences of gender, political ideology, age, and social class as constitutive elements in the shaping of 'authentic' Kurdishness. Because this particular Kurdish population is not yet well-established relative to other UK immigrant populations, and remains largely invisible in terms of the ethnic monitoring and overall demographic delineations prevalent in contemporary Britain (Griffiths 2002), it represents a particularly pertinent example of how such complex realities play out, drawing on both transnational and local realities.

A conversation I had near the outset of my PhD fieldwork was the initial impetus for this piece. I was speaking with Hasan,[1] a 39 year old community worker who has lived in London for the last seventeen years, and has thus witnessed the many transitions which have taken place in identity formations — ethnic, gendered, political, social — at the community level within this relatively 'new' Kurdish migrant population in London. Seeking to understand the relationship between the growing commodification of 'ethnic' identity in the global cityscape of London, the development and uses of ethnic nationalist discourses transnationally, and their implications for the placement of Kurdish migrants within local political economy, I wanted to know about labour practices. Hasan told me:

> The important thing is, most men, when they came from Kurdistan — at first they came alone, as young single men, like me ... even if they went back and married or brought family later — most of the men took jobs in clothing factories or restaurants. We were cooking, sewing ... There were a lot owned by Turks when I arrived. See that hotel there, across the street? It used to be a small factory where we sewed, it's where I had my first job. We had to take the jobs that were here because we couldn't speak the language well enough ... although people didn't like working for Turks. But more importantly, we took jobs, like sewing and cooking that men didn't do, that — in Kurdistan, this is done by women. So it was a big challenge to being a man. The men who came and did those jobs felt threatened, it even caused embarrassment at first. We had to change the way we think about being a man, you know? (Hasan).

For a society in which the traditional relationships between specific gender and productive domains are fairly clearly delimited, this was significant. I was struck by the multiple challenges to the integrity of Kurdish masculinity that were embedded within Hasan's description of Kurdish men's experience of job-seeking in their newly adopted country, and by the parallel drawn between material, social and symbolic forms of productivity — of 'male/female', Kurdish identity, the nation. I wanted to further explore how normative assumptions of gender within Kurdish society in Turkey were challenged by migratory experience, and what sorts of responses this generated in the local London discourses of 'Kurdish community' in exile. The interstices of ethnicity, gender, and politics as identity markers, and the relative social positioning enabled or conscribed by these in the context of a local 'ethnic' political economy dominated by Turkish entrepreneurs are thus the underlying themes of this chapter.

---

1   All names have been changed to protect the anonymity of participants.

Here I seek to recentre the construction of masculinity within these themes, which is not only an assumed but unknown quantity within Kurdish society as far as social science research goes, but which remains generally under-attended in prevailing Gender Studies — a field of enquiry in which 'gender' often continues to be synonymous with 'women'.[2] In addressing this theme within my own data and in studies of gender generally, and following from Hasan's observation that to 'change the way we think about being a man' involves a process of negotiation, we need to direct enquiry towards understanding the construction of both masculinities and femininities in relation to one another, and the 'different ways that masculinities are performed or enacted in specific settings' (Cornwall and Lindisfarne 1994, 38). From the point of view of the current volume, one of the fundamental shifts in setting which influences such performances is that of migration and the transformations in gender relations within this context. Therefore, although my discussion deals specifically with men's place within migration, it considers changing masculinity as shaped alongside changing (and re-embedded) ideas about femininity. That such labour roles were viewed by many as damaging social standing, and that engaging in female pursuits such as sewing added insult to injury, is implied by a comment from Anwar who told me:

> You should have seen the scandal when family at home found out my cousin was working in a factory, making women's clothing. Everyone thought we came to Europe for a better life, and Faoud had told them that he owned a shop. Wallahe, it caused so much gossip and he was really embarrassed, [laughs] all that time he had been sewing women's knickers. It was so terrible, people thought it brought a lot of shame to our family (Anwar).

London's Kurdish Community — Ethnic Unity and Internal Diversity

Kurdish populations in London are, like all diaspora groups, marked by a significant internal diversity (Werbner 2004) in religion, social class, language, region of origin, migratory experience and other factors. My reference to 'Kurdish diaspora' is based predominantly on self-ascription by interviewees, and includes those from all these diverse backgrounds and the four states which encompass Kurdistan (Turkey, Iran, Iraq and Syria), but within this chapter I am dealing specifically with groups from Turkey.[3] The north-east London borough of Hackney is home to a sizable Kurdish population originating mainly from rural, largely underdeveloped and conflict ridden south-eastern regions of the country. The enforced cultural and linguistic assimilation of Kurds by the Turkish state, and the concentration of both Turks and Kurds in the borough have created a particular complex of economic relations. Today

---

2   Ironically, this view, though often taken up by feminist scholars and those with a more explicit focus on women's studies, serves to perpetuate an epistemological system in which men and masculinity are 'unmarked categories' (Mooers 2003), the norm against which we measure 'pathologies' including that of women and femininity.

3   My use of terms such as 'Kurdish community' or 'Kurdish diaspora' are made with a full awareness of their potential to reify what are inherently fluid social categories, and thus gloss over the above differences as well as age and gender.

the Kurdish population in Hackney, where the traditional 'female' labour activities concerned are concentrated, is estimated to be approximately 10,000 (Hackney Council 1999a). Kurdish migrants began to arrive in Hackney from Turkey in large numbers during the early to mid 1990s, when tensions between the ethnically based PKK and the nationalist/Kemalist Turkish military led to armed conflict, and an eventual large scale refugee crisis. The fighting between PKK guerrillas and the Turkish army violently cleared thousands of villages in the south-east Kurdish region. The subsequent forced migration of many thousands of Kurds from these agricultural regions (Griffiths 2002) resulted in large numbers of semi-skilled refugee populations arriving in London with limited opportunities for insertion into the mainstream economic infrastructure. Many had previously been engaged in work as farm labourers (Hackney Council 1999b), and few had received opportunities for higher education, either because of their socioeconomic status, or because the conflict in the region disrupted the possibility for people to engage in such pursuits.

However London has long been home to other Kurdish minorities, many of whom arrived from Iraq and Iran in earlier decades, starting as early as the 1960s (Griffiths 2002). Unlike fellow-Kurds from Turkey, these individuals have often tended to be more urbanised, middle class and thus more highly educated. Their socioeconomic backgrounds and migratory experiences have generally enabled them to settle in more affluent neighbourhoods of west London, including Hammersmith, Fulham and Ealing where many became business owners and others entered professions. While many Kurds cite diasporic displacement as facilitating a wider consciousness about the depth and diversity of Kurdish culture and experience throughout the homeland (cf. Alinia 2004), this has not necessarily mitigated against the inevitable tensions of social class and political ideology which arise in such a complex diasporic landscape. Elsewhere in this volume, Herbert highlights the ways in which categorizations centring on ethnicity can overwrite tensions and divergences of class and migratory experience/aspirations (cf. Gardner 1995).

One of the key tropes within these contestations over defining an essential nature of Kurdish identity and experience has pivoted on the ascription of gender roles and behaviours. Kurds from middle-class backgrounds have been more active in defining bourgeois masculinities in which the emancipation of women is an aim if not always a reality of community life in the UK. Others from rural backgrounds have at times tended to maintain a system in which 'the family-as-microcosm of culture' (Appadurai 1996, 45) ensures a focus on fixed gender roles for both men and women. This seemingly dichotomised situation is complicated by the local mobilisation of nationalist discourses, specifically that of the PKK, whose ideological underpinnings advocate an egalitarian gender system based on Marxist-feminist theories. Thus the relationship between local economic realities and transnational political processes can make for exceedingly fluid and often contentious constructions of identity, gendered and otherwise. It is precisely this complexity, and its attendant uncertainties, that facilitate the imposition of fixed readings of masculine identity vis a vis feminine ideals of 'traditional' Kurdish culture, seen as under threat both from the conditions of conflict in the homeland of Kurdistan and from the uncertainties of belonging in a post-modern global city like London. That the men with whom I spoke are ambivalent even at an individual level with respect to their desires to maintain fixed gender roles on the one hand, while also wishing to embrace the changes wrought by migratory processes, is evident in their narratives.

Following from Allen, I observe that 'questions of sameness/difference and 'we/they' quickly evaporate in the face of personal, particular histories' (1994, 97); both the questions of difference and the particular histories are shaped partly by contingent questions of gender. Despite the particularities borne of the internal diversity of supposedly coherent ethnic or cultural 'groups' like the Kurds however, attempts to gloss this over with essentialist readings persist. The amorphous conditions within transnational migration, for example, can lead to reactive constructions of a monolithic identity in the face of situations which actively serve to destabilise absolutes (Hall 1996). Very often these essentialist constructions are propounded by social and political actors with a vested and privileged interest in maintaining the status quo; those political and economic elites, men, the state (Cornwall and Lindisfarne 1994). Thus, although the emergence of diaspora has generated substantial debates and internal conflicts over what constitutes 'Kurdishness' for this globally dispersed population, its flip side can be seen in attempts to stabilise a uniform 'Kurdish identity', which works largely for the claims of (Kurdish) nationalist interests (Keeler 2007). A key practice within this process involves the creation of essential Kurdish masculine and feminine ideals, and indeed we can observe here as in other cases the ways in which '(masculinised) power is consistently associated with those who have control over resources and who have an interest in naturalising and perpetuating that control' (Cornwall and Lindisfarne 1994, 21). I will return to the ways in which tangible representations of these gendered ideals play out in the local political economy of London's Kurdish diaspora, and how notions of 'masculine' and 'feminine' become complementary dimensions of an 'essential national character'. For example 35 year old Anwar, a restaurant manager who arrived in London at the age of 23 and is single, described his ideal partner as follows:

> To me, I would like a nice Kurdish girl. She should be educated, but ... sweet, I like a girl who is sweet and soft — a little bit happy to please the man, to make me feel like the man and I'm special. I would love to meet such a girl who could support me. And of course she would need to speak Kurdish. Some girls in Europe do not you know, but it is important, for me, if you want to have children (Anwar).

Anwar's narrative characterises an ideal of Kurdish femininity which, although challenged within increasingly competing discourses, remains pervasive as a way of representing the nation and as an aspiration for men like Anwar. Nationalist, ethnic and gendered ideals intersect in the course of contestations over power and identity, and within such ideologies women, whether in social or biological reproductive capacities, are often positioned as the sacrosanct embodiment of the nation, while men are cast as her protectors (Anthias and Yuval-Davis 1992; Allen 1994; Yuval-Davis 1997). Conditions of migration and diaspora may in fact serve to legitimise such representations as the heightened importance of identity, which stems from this dislocation from homeland, and symbolic forms of identity maintenance which underlie it, places an onus on migrants to uphold and protect a 'pure' notion of ethnicity, identity, and nation in gendered terms (Ignacio 2005). A material example of this can be observed in the prevalence of Kurdish women in traditional national dress within the popular iconography of Kurdish diasporic spaces in London, gracing everything from the paintings which adorn the walls of Kurdish community organisations, to the decorative rugs found in many Kurdish homes (also see Herbert, this volume).

Kurdish refugees from Turkey, unlike Sunni Kurds originating from Iran and Iraq, are predominantly adherents of Alevism (followers of Ali), and there is little consensus as to whether this group constitutes a Muslim sect in either beliefs or practices. Alevis, although sometimes seen as a sect of Shi'a Islam, also incorporate pre-Islamic dimensions into their religion, and engage in social behaviours and forms of worship that differ significantly from orthodox Sunni Islam which is present in religious communities in Turkey (Shankland 1993). Several of these, including joint worship between men and women — in a *cemevi* (or 'meeting house') rather than a mosque — and lack of prescription on the wearing of the headscarf or *hijab* for women, have important implications for gender relations. For these and other (often politically motivated) reasons, Alevis have often been vilified by the Turkish state as well as by Turkish Sunni populations in migrant receiving countries where large numbers of Alevi Kurds also reside (Mandel 1995). As such, Kurdish migrants and refugees in London are rarely more than culturally conscribed Muslims. Indeed their relations with other Muslim populations in the migratory context are occasionally fraught with tension and conflict, like their interactions with ethnic Turks in Hackney.

However, from an external viewpoint, especially given their placement within the sort of immigrant 'Little Istanbul' atmosphere of east London — filled with shops, cafes, and community services where Turkish is often an unofficial *lingua franca* — Kurds are viewed generically as 'Middle Easterners' and as Muslims. Here I want to provide a sense of the many layers and interstices which both inform and restrict the processes of identification for Kurds in London. Gender, religion, geography, ethnicity and class distinctions traverse, overlap, and contradict one another. Despite their relative attitudes of gender equality vis a vis some more orthodox Muslim populations, Kurdish society in the particular region of origin is still very often patriarchal in character (Mojab 2002), and marked by clear 'male/ female' divisions of labour. This is clearly indicated by Hasan's remarks, which opened the discussion, while another interviewee told me

> Sure, it was a big comedown when you leave home and — we thought we would be improving — then to end up sewing women's clothes or making bread all day [laughs]. These are the mum's jobs! (Hasan).

The reconfiguration of this gendered labour, and the subordination of particular ethnicised masculinities to dominant forms of masculine power (eg. Kurdish versus Turkish) draw on and interact with processes of gender construction located in regional, global and local political economies. In a social system in which inequalities are predicated largely on (internally and externally) constructed identity markers, and when those inequalities are tied up with latent or real conflicts, it is no great step to suggest that 'women are used in defining boundaries, and asserting the dominance of some men over other men through the protection of 'their' women' (Allen 1994, 98). In this context, women's bodies become the sites over which national, ethnic, religious and other struggles are literally and symbolically waged (Yuval-Davis 1997), but those who remind us of this gendered element in nationalist thinking tend to overlook their impact on men; they also experience culturally coercive imperatives to serve as the 'protectors' of this national/feminine ideal. In terms of everyday social interactions and activities, this includes the display of 'appropriate' characteristics and behaviours of 'our' masculine ideal. Murat, one of the first to arrive with the earliest of the refugee movements in 1993 and now a community leader, believes that:

> Unfortunately, the culture that we come from, well there is a lot of inequality … women are second-class citizens, for sure. This is accepted. But we know we need to change this and actually Kurds are doing a lot, they are the first to speak out against such things, like honour killing for example. Compared to other groups like Arabs in Iraq or others, the Kurds are the most critical (Murat).

Murat's statement indicates the ambivalence and competing loyalties for a multiply subordinated group — recognising the systematic domination of women within his cultural background, he is then quick to distance Kurdish cultural norms from those of contiguous cultural groups; implicit within this is an identification with liberal western ideals of human rights.[4]

Men's Labour, 'Women's Work' and Employment in Britain

East London has long been a point of settlement for labourers from diverse migrant backgrounds who quickly became embedded in the dense local manufacturing economy (Eade 2000; Ahmad, this volume). At the height of the Kurdish refugee influx in the early 1990s, Hackney was still home to a thriving economy of small industrial production, specifically in the textile industries. This relied on the substantial numbers of annual migrant arrivals who, for reasons of economic opportunity, social networks and language and infrastructural resources, chose the borough of Hackney as their home. Such populations have long formed an exploitable labour pool for the industrial economy in the area, only recently replaced by a service-based economy. The borough was also notable at the time for its considerable population of Turkish nationals, who, in the early 1980s, followed the settlement by Turkish Cypriots in the east London borough during the 1950s and 1960s. A typical chain migration pattern had by then been established, and local economic, social and cultural infrastructures had begun to develop accordingly. In this respect at least it is unsurprising that Kurdish migrants from Turkey, many of whom had a better grasp of Turkish than of their native Kurdish as a result of the assimilationist policies of the Turkish

---

4   These debates have become increasingly salient in recent months in Britain in the wake of several high profile cases of 'honour killings' (McViegh 2007) which have prompted Kurdish community leaders and women's right groups to call for reflection and action on the position of women and patriarchal power in Kurdish society.

state, also chose to locate in the area. Here, they could access legal, health, housing and educational services in a familiar language, and shop and socialise as well. However, in so doing, they had to further deny or suppress a distinct and hard fought ethnocultural identity which had been, through its often virulent repression by the Turkish military, a major impetus for their initial flight from the Kurdish homelands. As Hasan explains, many Kurds from Turkey carried a 'self esteem problem', both conscious of the deterministic demands of the market in the UK and also harbouring internalised and unresolved notions about cultural inequality in their homeland.

> They hid who they were because maybe they were ashamed or — they were — afraid for example they couldn't survive, wouldn't find a job. You needed to speak Turkish and anyway if you went to school in Turkey you were brainwashed (Hasan).

However, just as the refugees were arriving in growing numbers and in need of work, the domestic manufacturing sector began to dry up and increasingly move towards offshore manufacture The available work, as interviewees have pointed out, was generally in small textile factories, and increasingly towards the late 1990s, in cafes and kebab shops at the heart of the 'Turkish speaking community' in Hackney and throughout the east end. In such establishments, employees were subject to long hours, poor job security, often systemic denigration, and were left with virtually no chance to develop further skills or opportunities. Forty-one-year-old Karzan who arrived as a single asylum seeker in 1995 describes the labour conditions at the time both in terms of the physical demands and of the diminished social and political positioning of Kurds in this context:

> We worked in the — well yes, they were like a sweatshop. People couldn't speak a word of English, some had never been outside their villages. But you could get work in the factories because you spoke Turkish and so did the owners. It was not good work though, they made us work long hours and usually people didn't know their rights so they were sometimes paid illegally. And if you had political views [PKK support] ... well, you couldn't have political views! Later some people took jobs in cafes and kebab shops, when the factories started to leave. But for a man to be doing this ... it's not productive. What can it contribute to society? (Karzan).

Thus, unskilled and vulnerable to the changing contours of the British asylum system, such Kurdish arrivals in Hackney experienced multiple disadvantages; subject not only to a hegemonic political economy of white domination, but also to Turkish entrepreneurial elites who were happy to exploit their vulnerable social positioning. Many Kurds I spoke with saw Turks as demonstrating a greater racist bent than white Europeans. Kurdish migrants were daily confronted with the hegemonic conditions of their own oppression by the Turkish state, through its reproduction in social interactions with Turkish migrants in the UK. Further, the elision, through local procedures of categorisation, of distinct and in some respects mutually antagonistic ethnic identities — those of ethnic Turks and Kurds — into a single 'Turkish Speaking Community' (Ahmet 2005) was often seen to reproduce their subordination within the nationalist categorisations of who is and is not 'of the nation' in Turkey itself. As Karzan explained, local policies continue to assume

Turks and Kurds are culturally synonymous, as they 'do not understand the idea of a Kurd'. Thus the 'racialised capitalism' described by Ahmad (this volume) is dislodged from a simple black/white dichotomy, instead taking as its reference point the complexity of ethnic relations in the homeland. Displaced by the salience of antagonisms between Turks and Kurds in the local context, the dynamic of white oppression of ethnic minorities seems for the men I encountered to have been recast in gendered terms.

Nonetheless, this 'Turkish speaking' urban milieu also afforded opportunities for earning a livelihood in a context which was otherwise economically challenging for the arriving Kurdish refugees, many of whom came from semi-skilled village backgrounds. Often the earliest migrants found work (frequently illegal, and thus subject to considerable exploitation) in the small factories manufacturing garments and textiles for British retailers. By the time of the main refugee influx of Kurds in the 1990s, the Turkish population in Hackney were sufficiently established to be in positions of ownership and supervision within these industrial ventures. Despite the hegemonic system which this engendered with respect to culturally contiguous but often mutually antagonistic groups, it also brought about an informal process of integration and social change, as Kurds from small villages were exposed to the multiethnic city through the microcosmic spaces of their workplaces. Employed by Turks, they also came into contact with Vietnamese, Bangladeshi, Caribbean and other co-workers, and began to develop a greater sense of diversity and tolerance. This also meant, in practical terms, that English was the only shared language by which the various employees could communicate. For example, when Murat arrived, he worked in a textile factory run by Turks. He explained to me how interactions between various ethnic groups working alongside one another created both bridges and barriers, and helped in creating the 'ethnic' economy and multicultural environment of Hackney as we know it today:

> You see, when we first came … I didn't speak English and even though I didn't want to be working again (for Turks), having them tell me what to do, degrade my identity … I could get no job someplace else. So it was bad in one way because it means you can't establish yourself. I was — you're speaking Turkish all the time! But then, also we learned things from each other, there were many other people — Chinese, Vietnamese, and Bangladeshi people working in the factory. Can you imagine, if you come from a village in Kurdistan … I had never seen a black person before. So we had to all learn English then so we could speak to each other. And at lunch times … you learned about others' cultures, other kinds of food and things … so in this way we learned — we came to know multiculturalism (Murat).

Murat's experience speaks to the positive potential within destabilising processes wrought by transnational movement of people, ideas and goods. Although feeling exploited by Turkish factory owners who in Kurds' own essentialist discourses had played a part as coercive (and often demonised) oppressors, Kurdish labourers came to rethink their identities, in some ways replacing Kurdish ethnicity with a shared notion of an urban underclass of minority labourers. Murat's narrative suggests that this experience allowed for a partial liberation, and made possible identification with an 'other'. However, this partial identification with 'otherness', and the divesting of essentialist ethnic ideologies which it implied, did not carry over into gender in the same way. On the contrary, the challenges to masculinity, unlike those to ethnicity, did not bring about an identification with feminine otherness, but instead a reassertion of differential gender markers, and a distinction made between 'good Kurdish women' and amoral European women. The identification of employers as antagonists in the repressive homeland conversely may have led to an increased sense of identification with the host society and with other minorities, as Murat's comments demonstrate. Thus if the daily engagement with wage labour in a largely hostile host society reproduces hierarchies and inequalities entrenched in that global system (Mandel 1995; Sassen 1996), the reference points extend far beyond an obvious first/third world, black/white conception of things. Indeed, Kurdish men tend to narrate their experiences of discrimination in the UK in terms not of racism but of language, as their comments testify.

Ethnicity and Gender in the Symbolic Economy

The decline of manufacturing industry and the rise of a service-based economy has involved a transformation in the placement and significance of migrant labour within the global city (Sassen 1999). The aestheticisation of identity (be it ethnic, gendered or otherwise), and the place of the body — now product as much as producer — within that, has become commodified as a package-able (Zukin 1995) source of 'authenticity for sale'. When people come to dine in a Turkish or Kurdish restaurant, they do so not only to sample the lovingly reproduced traditional fare, but also to view and experience the process by which it is created and the atmospheric features which lend it cultural 'weight'. The cultural, social and economic encounters which take place in these spaces can serve as highly condensed moments of identification of or with particular 'others'. As demonstrated by Kurdish men's narratives of labour and migration in the multicultural context of the global city, these processes of encounter, identification, and 'othering' can be emancipatory or humiliating in equal measure (Lees 2004). The demeaning aspects of their experience are simultaneously expressed in ethnic and gendered terms; through their insertion into the local ethnic economy of Turkish speakers, the men experience an erasure of their Kurdish identity which recalls their disempowerment in the homeland. Further, the 'domestic' types of labour in which they engage destabilizes their relationship to notions of acceptable Kurdish masculinity. Ahmad (this volume) looks at the conceptual renegotiations which take place as the demands for patriarchal control among Pakistani men are confounded by the blurring of private and public spheres. For Kurdish men in Hackney this loss of control, though not expressed in terms of patriarchal power, may be experienced through being cast in female productive roles, or sometimes more directly, through harassing behaviour from white female customers which the men interpret as being inappropriately sexual.

Even for those Kurdish migrants who come to the UK with some skills and experience, there are challenges in acquiring livelihoods in London's economic infrastructure, due to a variety of factors including language barriers and what many feel to be the persistence of structurally embedded discriminatory practices. For example, 46-year-old Mustafa, who has been in London since 1999, trained as a teacher in Turkey. However, since he lacks language skills and his qualifications are not recognised in the UK, he now works in a café in east London. He told me of his experiences of job-seeking:

> I wanted to find work [in education] but it is difficult. If I spoke the language better it would be easier, but when you are trying to find work … I had to earn a living, it's not so easy to learn the language, there is no time, there is stress. I tried for two years to find a job with some teaching … but no one could help and finally I had to take this job. I don't like what I'm doing, sometimes I feel ashamed … but what could I do? I had to feed my family. Now I won't improve [English language]. There is no time, and the work — I am working twelve, sometimes fourteen hours … (Mustafa).

Although Mustafa thinks his employers are essentially fair and honest ('not like some bosses I heard of') sometimes, working late nights in the café, he describes being subject to uncomfortable situations and even racist abuse. Many men who work nights in kebab shops and cafes indicated that they find the work especially degrading because, as their establishments keep late hours when few other businesses are open, their workplaces are sites for illicit, potentially unsafe, and sometimes violent behaviour from customers leaving clubs and bars late at night under the influence of alcohol and drugs. It is evident from several of the men's narratives that they may at times feel that this exposure compromises their capacity for a 'correct' lifestyle that maintains their integrity as Kurds and as men.

Twenty-seven-year-old Ali, who came to the UK when he was only twelve in 1992, has grown up in London and worked in a kebab shop (often alongside his father) nearly all of that time. Speaking about the kinds of indirect sexual harassment he has experienced when serving customers, he said:

> In the past I saw … sometimes girls or women would come in — you know, if they had too much to drink or if they came from the club. They want to have a laugh or show off to their friends … they would be very rude, very sexual remarks sometimes … wearing very little clothes or acting in an inappropriate way — and also aggressive, being very suggestible! I think they thought "he doesn't understand what we're saying, we can say what we want" … You know, like thinking we're just Muslims or some stupid Turks and trying to take the piss, to embarrass me. But actually it was embarrassing, I usually didn't know what to do so I just did pretend not to understand … (Ali).

Ali's narrative indicates how, when his normative ideas about 'appropriate' female behaviour are confronted with new possibilities, he reasserts ethnic and gender stereotypes: those of wanton western women versus disciplined Kurdish men vulnerable to feminine 'corruption'. It also indicates how sexist and racist attitudes in the dominant culture make the multiple intersections of gender, ethnicity and class far from straightforward systems of dominance/oppression. Such complex realities call for an 'attempt to describe and analyse divisions of labour not as formal and static ideal types but in their actually occurring and contradictory cultural and historical manifestations' (Gutman 1997, 391).

In these social interactions 'there is a multiplicity of identities being formed and reproduced in these decentred spaces of the economy' (Sassen 1996, 184), and ethnicity and gender are continuously shifted, fore-grounded or subordinated relative to one another in a given context. Ali also indicated that for him, many Kurds actively participate in this system of marginalisation of 'decentred' productive spaces, further devaluing them; he spoke of his belief that Kurdish society in London is 'closed' and 'outdated', and that an emphasis on earning a living at the expense of self-improvement has prevented him and many peers from gaining educational qualifications which might lift them from these degraded and marginalised social positions.

> If I had gone to school more and spent time studying, instead of having to work with my father in the shop, I could have a proper job now, instead of stuck in this kitchen, waiting on people. This is no job for a grown man. I'd still like to go to university one day (Ali).

The productive roles that Kurds play in this context are given no place in the hegemonic gendered and ethnicised narratives of white British, Turkish or Kurdish society. Being valued by neither the British political economic mainstream nor the Turkish or Kurdish views of 'traditional' masculinity, Kurds are potentially subject to racist and sexist pejoratives and to the very real risks associated with work in late night establishments (Parker 1994). Like many migrant labourers who work on the margins, invisible within dominant economic, social and political narratives, these men experience feelings of exclusion and oppression in which they must 'regularly cross a perilous divide separating two different worlds', and where 'the characteristic economic relations between 'First' and 'Third' worlds are linguistically, socially, and culturally reproduced' (Mandel 1996, 151). The multiple experiences of devaluation and the impenetrability of spheres of privilege and disempowerment are vividly illustrated in Anwar's remark

> I have to tell people I am a Turk if I want to get a job, because still they or the Persians or Arabs control things … we just serve the kebabs. And also, British people, they don't know the difference. They come in and they just want a taste of Ali Baba, right? (Anwar).

The implied messages in these narratives about the hazards associated with work in the catering industry also serve to reveal the complex relations between local conditions of economic exploitation and more diffuse yet no less powerful Orientalist inscriptions of cultural otherness which facilitate these local inequalities. Research has shown how the commodification of 'ethnic' cuisine and the 'cultural-experience-for-sale' that comes alongside this can threaten the sense of cultural integrity many minority employees struggle to maintain in the context of cultural dislocations (Harbottle 2000). The subtle play of sexual politics and vestiges of colonial domination tied up in such seemingly innocuous relations as those between staff and customers in Asian take-away restaurants in Britain, as described by Parker (1994), further sheds light on Kurdish men's narratives, and the embarrassment they feel at the hands of female customers and in the eyes of their communities and society at large. Karwan too described situations in which he was

> … shocked by girls and the way they behave in public … everything sex. I wanted to tell them "aren't you ashamed?" but in the end I just smile, I don't want to lose my job

and they are not worth it. My daughters would not behave like this. I am not like some Kurdish men, looking for some quick fun on the side of [in addition to] my wife. We get this reputation, but then some of the [British] women — also they want to take advantage of this (Karwan).

He also expressed feelings of being 'ashamed for myself and for them'.

What Parker (1994) refers to as 'encounters across the counter' in catering work interrogate men's notions of gendered divisions of labour in potentially productive ways, but also reinforce culturally conscribed ideas about gender, particularly the acceptability of normative female behaviours in British or Kurdish society. When viewed through the prism of gender, the 'perilous divide' (Mandel 1996) between spaces of minority labour and exploitive European domination encompass transnational realities including these popular culture tropes, and all the 'loops that tie together fantasies about the Other, the conveniences and seductions of travel, the economics of global trade, and the brutal mobility fantasies that dominate gender politics' (Appadurai 1996, 39; cf. Bowman 1996) globally. As refugees with few practical resources allowing them to manoeuvre through exploitive systems in the UK, Kurdish men in this employment sector face a 'situation where impotence [is] structured into the social situation by political and economic forces' (Bowman 1996, 93), and which they often feel powerless to change if they want to maintain their tenuous place in London's global market and local ethnic economies.

Men who engage in such livelihoods are not only vulnerable to sometimes racist abuse from aggressive or drunken late night customers from the dominant white population in London (cf. Parker 1994), but also to a sense of being subordinated to racist/nationalist Turkish discourses recalling traumatic experiences in the homeland, which may involves a painful denial of their ethnicity. Kurds too, especially those from urban or middle-class backgrounds, also often view such labour as embodying all that is 'backward' and best left behind in their culture and its relative positioning within London's multicultural spaces (cf. Caglar 1998). Such ideas are embedded within the discourses of perceived differences of religion, class and gender within Kurdish migrant populations in London. For example, when opportunities arise for contact between the various 'sub-groups', and when discussions about the nature of Kurdish identity, social progress and the like arises (which is almost inevitably the case in such diasporic spaces), a frequently dismissive insult of others' opinions runs along the lines of 'go work in a kebab shop' or 'he should be selling doner someplace'. This equates such work with low educational levels and with the more traditional insults levelled at men who engage in 'women's work' (Morvaridi 1993). It also suggests the complexity of class differences and the significance of gender within this, as debates centring around women's rights set 'progressive' educated Kurds against 'peasants' from uneducated backgrounds. Nonetheless, while middle-class Kurds vocalise their belief in gender emancipation, such insults suggest the degraded spaces of 'female' productivity in their own estimations as well.

Thus, the types of physical labour, the geography, and the social relations which characterise this form of livelihood for Kurdish men regularly put them in situations where they feel ethnically, sexually and socially degraded. While dominant white British society valorises the labour activities of white, middle-class men at the expense of invisible, minority-dominated service industries within the capitalist economy (Sassen 1999), the 'ethnic economy' to which they are relegated further compromises the capacity for Kurdish men to express their sense of ethnic identity in the face of a continued perception of Turkish domination and cleavages within Kurdish disaporic space. In such cases, where 'understanding a situation and devising strategies of empowerment within it is often not a sufficient defence against the overwhelming powers of hostile states and exploitive international economies' (Bowman 1996), the men I interviewed tended to displace any sense of disempowered masculinity onto efforts to reassert notions of what constitutes 'good' or 'shameful' female behaviour, and cast this in primarily ethnic terms.

Conclusions — Gender, Ethnicity and Mobility

The role of Kurdish men from refugee backgrounds in local economies of difference has placed them at a tricky crossroads, tending to challenge ethnic essentialism but to reinforce gender essentialism. Their encounters with various cultural others in the urban milieu has been complicated by Kurdish political interests in local and transnational 'community' discourses (Keeler 2007). Within their nationalist discourses, the female remains an important marker of pure and recovered ethnic identity, upon whose bodies and images national identity is inscribed. This has the two-fold effect of making men both more empowered as brokers of political and discursive control, and conversely, as everyday social actors, less so by virtue of their invisibility within discursive structures. In seeking to remain loyal to what they see as a devalued ethnocultural identity, and to reclaim their collective if not individual ethnic integrity, Kurdish men frequently seem to fall back on archetypal notions of essential female characteristics in their narratives. This is evident in the ways they describe their encounters with non-Kurdish women in public spaces, as well as the ways in which they more broadly define their labour experiences (often vis à vis these western women), as 'embarrassing' or shameful' by virtue of their 'female' connotations. As Kurdish culture becomes more institutionalised in the migratory context of London, it resists invisibilisation and repression within state systems in the UK, and within a hegemonic 'Turkish' discourse which elides difference within a monolithic framework of Turkish nationalism. However, this process is paradoxical in its potential for liberation or continued oppression, for it also serves to reaffirm potentially coercive forms of identity discourse in gendered terms. Thus the notion of Kurdish femininity as rooted in and protected by 'tradition' has gained momentum in some quarters, which in many respects runs counter to the transformative notions of Kurdish masculinity hinted at by my interviewees.

Kurdish refugees face considerable challenges as they struggle to reclaim aspects of their culture which they see as having been degraded by British and Turkish hegemonies, and confront those aspects of their culture which they see as obsolete, all the while balancing loyalty to notions of ethnic 'purity', national struggle, fixed notions of gender, and integration into new homelands. Appadurai observes that

> ... deterritorialized communities and displaced populations, however much they may enjoy the fruits of new kinds of earning and new dispositions of capital and technology,

have to play out the desires and fantasies of these new ethnoscapes, while striving to reproduce the family-as-microcosm of culture (1996, 45).

To a certain extent, these ethnoscapes and the economic systems of which they are a part incorporate the sublimated sexual politics of the dominant western gaze in the context of commodified identities, alongside the characterisation of western and Kurdish women. Elsewhere the racialized nature of this political economy has revealed how white women and minority men, comparatively disadvantaged by virtue of their respective forms of otherness, are pitted against one another in a battle of 'have-nots' (hooks 1995). The tensions between accepting — even embracing — the implications of a post-modernity which both dissipates gender differences, and commodifies an essentialist version of ethnicity, and maintaining cultural integrity in the face of this are daily realities for Kurdish men whose participation in society serves to interrogate their notions of gender and labour. In the context of migration (often forced and traumatic as with the case of many Kurds arriving from Turkey), the characterisation of certain labour functions as 'women's work' — while also largely influenced by normative gender roles in Kurdistan — is a means for disenfranchised Kurdish men with limited opportunities in London's complex political economic landscape, to react to their exclusion and objectification.

For their part, the men I interviewed remain ambivalent about their newly acquired roles in British society. Although women emerge in these discursive spaces only rarely, and then in dichotomised terms as corrupt western aggressors or as idealised bearers of Kurdish identity (with little account of the dynamic realities that exist in the margins of such oppositional discourses), several of the men I interviewed pointed out the unforeseen advantages and new forms of social capital that emerged in these spaces of critical encounter in a global city. Hasan and Murat for example both discussed the transformations which resulted from their labour experiences, affecting both their thinking about being men and being Kurdish in positive terms. Ali, despite what he sees as negative aspects of his social positioning within Kurdish and wider society in London, aspires to a greater sense of achievement and integration. This suggests that although men in a wider context continue to be perpetrators and beneficiaries of women's subordination (see Ahmad, this volume), and despite their relative disempowerment vis à vis the dominant culture, the intersection of ethnicity, class and gender within the complexity of the global city can also serve to productively interrogate men's complicity in such systems.

References

Ahmet, P. (2005), 'Turkish Speaking Communities in Britain: A Rude Awakening', *Independent Race and Refugee News*, 8 March 2005, available at http://www.irr. org.uk/2005/march/ak000010.html.

Allen, S. (1994), 'Race, Ethnicity and Nationality: Some Questions of Identity', in Afshar, H. and Maynard, M. (eds), *The Dynamics of 'Race' and Gender: Some Feminist Interventions* (London: Routledge), 85-105.

Anthias, F. and Yuval-Davis, N. (1992), *Racialised Boundaries: Race, Nation, Gender, Class and the Anti-racist Struggle* (London: Routledge).

Bowman, G. (1996), 'Passion, Power and Politics in a Palestinian Tourist Market', in Selwyn, T. (ed.), *The Tourist Image: Myths and Myth Making in Tourism* (New York: John Wiley), 83-103.

Caglar, A. (1995), 'McDoner: Doner Kebab and the Social Positioning Struggle of German Turks', in Costa, J. and Bamoosy G. (eds), *Marketing in a Multicultural World: Ethnicity, Nationalism and Cultural Identity* (London: Sage), 73-97.

Chadya, J.M. (2003), 'Mother Politics: Anti-colonial Nationalism and the Woman Question in Africa', *Journal of Women's History* 15:3, 153-157.

Cornwall, A. and Lindisfarne, N. (1994), 'Dislocating Masculinity: Gender, Power and Anthropology', in Cornwall, A. and Lindisfarne, N. (eds), *Dislocating Masculinity: Comparative Ethnographies* (London: Routledge), 11-47.

Eade, J. (2000), *Placing London: From Imperial Capital to Global City* (New York: Berghan Books).

Griffiths, D. (2002), *Somali and Kurdish Refugees in London: New Identities in the Diaspora* (Aldershot: Ashgate).

Hackney Council Division of Planning (1999a), *Planning for the Turkish/Kurdish Community in Hackney: A Profile and Needs Study* (London Borough of Hackney).

—— (1999b), *Ethnic Diversity in the Making of Hackney: The Kurdish Population* (London Borough of Hackney).

Hall, S. (1996), 'Introduction: Who Needs Identity?', in Hall, S. and Du Gay, P. (eds), *Questions of Cultural Identity* (London: Sage), 1-17.

Harbottle, L. (2000), *Food for Health, Food for Wealth: Ethnic and Gender Identities in British Iranian Communities* (Oxford: Berghahn Books).

Ignacio, E.N. (2005), *Building Diaspora: Filipino Cultural Community Formation on the Internet* (New Brunswick: Rutgers University Press).

Keeler, S.J. (2007), *'There Has Been Enough Crying and Now I Want to Dance!': Belonging, Cosmopolitanism and Resistance in London's Kurdish Diasporic Spaces* (PhD thesis Canterbury: Department of Anthropology, University of Kent).

Knauer, L. (2005), 'Public Spheres and the Politics of Afrocuban Cultural Expression in Havana and New York City', paper presented at *IMISCOE Workshop on Ethnic, Cultural and Religious Diversity*, University of Amsterdam, May 2005.

Lees, L. (2004), 'The Emancipatory City: Urban (Re)Visions', in Lees, L. (ed.), *The Emancipatory City? Paradoxes and Possibilities* (London: Sage), 3-20.

Mandel, R. (1995), 'The Alevi-Bektashi Identity in a Foreign Context: The Example of Berlin', in Popovic, A. and Veinstein, G. (eds), *Bektachiyya: Etudes sur l'ordre mystique des Bektachis et les groupes relevant de Hadji Bektach* (Istanbul: Les Editions ISIS).

—— (1996), 'A Place of Their Own: Contesting Spaces and Defining Places in Berlin's Migrant Community', in Metcalf, B. (ed.), *Making Muslim Space in North America and Europe* (Berkley: University of California Press), 147-166.

McViegh, K. (2007), 'Father and Uncle Given Life for "Honour" Murder', *The Guardian*, 21 July 2007.

Mojab, S. (2002), '"Honour Killings": Culture, Politics and Theory', *Middle East Women's Studies Review* 32:1/2, 178-207.

Mooers, C. (2003), *Missing Bodies: Visibility and Invisibility in the Bourgeois Public Sphere* (Ryerson University Culture and Communication Working Paper Series, Toronto: Ryerson University), available online at http://www.cpsa-acsp.ca/paper-2003/mooers.pdf.

Morvaridi, B. (1993), 'Gender and Household Resource Management in Agriculture: Cash Crops in Kars', in Stirling, P. (ed.), *Culture and Economy: Changes in Turkish Villages* (Huntingdon: Eothen Press), 80-94.

Parker, D. (1994), 'Encounters Across the Counter: Young Chinese People in Britain', *New Community* 20:4, 621-634.

Sassen, S. (1996), 'Analytical Borderlands: Race, Gender and Representation in the New City', in King, A. (ed.), *Re-presenting the City: Ethnicity, Capital and Culture in the 21st Century* (Basingstoke: Macmillan), 183-202.

—— (1999), *Globalisation and its Discontents: Essays on the New Mobility of People and Money* (New York: New Press).

Shankland, D. (1993), 'Alevi and Sunni in Rural Anatolia', in Stirling, P. (ed.), *Culture and Economy: Changes in Turkish Villages* (Huntingdon: Eothen Press), 46-64.

Tastosglou, E. and Dobrowolsky, A. (2006), *Women, Migration and Citizenship: Making Local, National and Transnational Connections* (Aldershot: Ashgate).

Yuval-Davis, N. (1997), *Gender and Nation* (London: Sage).

Zukin, S. (1995), *The Cultures of Cities* (Oxford: Blackwell).

Chapter 11

Masculinity and Migration: Life Stories of East African Asian Men

Joanna Herbert

Since the 1990s there has been a proliferation of research on women in studies of migration and their experiences and role within the migration process (Morokvasic 1984; Pedraza 1991; Phizacklea 1999; Willis and Yeoh 2000; Ryan 2003), yet this has often led to the neglect and over-simplification of men's experiences. South Asian men, for example, have been cast in the role of aggressors and stereotyped as tyrannical patriarchs (Chopra, Osella and Osella 2004, 2-3). As a result, there has been a call for a more nuanced and complex understanding of how the changes that women experienced and the women's agency impacted on masculine privilege and how masculinities have intersected with other factors which threatened men's self esteem, such as racism and classism (Mahler and Pessar 2006; Connell and Messerschmidt 2005). There is a need to examine the experiences of men *in relation* to women and to examine masculinities by taking a more holistic account of the men's lives (Gutmann 1997).

This chapter seeks to explore these issues through the experiences of East African Asian men, by examining their narratives of work and the household. It argues that following their migration to Britain, the men's experiences in the workplace undermined their masculine identity and this was linked to their previous privileged status, economically, socially and racially, in East Africa. As women took paid employment outside the home the balance of power also shifted within the household and the men's relative authority within conjugal and intergenerational relations weakened. However, in the men's interviews, the act of retelling their life stories gave them the opportunity to recoup a masculine identity by emphasising their agency, pioneering spirit and constructing their role as the guardian of tradition or the heroic male.

East African Asians

To examine these issues, this chapter draws on life story oral history interviews, which were part of a larger project that explored the impact of South Asian migration to Leicester.[1] Leicester is home to a diversity of ethnic groups and is largely seen

---

1   The project included 59 interviews with South Asians and approximately half (52 per cent) were with East African Asians. Original interviews were conducted in 2002 and 2004 and interviews from existing archives were used, including the British Library National

as an 'Asian' city, yet from the mid 1960s, the city became an important haven for East African Asians and between 1968 and 1978 some 20,000 arrived from Kenya, Tanzania, Malawi and Uganda to make the city their home (Phillips 1981, 108). Their migration transformed Leicester's ethnic profile and East African Asians are the main South Asian group in the city. Their presence has distinguished Leicester from other British cities and they have often been credited as the vital ingredient in cultivating the city's international reputation for multicultural success (Singh 2003).

East African Asians embodied a collective history that was particularly distinctive compared to the experiences of earlier settlers who had migrated directly from the South Asian subcontinent. Many were 'twice migrants' having migrated from India to East Africa and then Britain, and there were mainly of urban, well educated, middle class and Gujarati speaking background, although they were also distinct form longer established middle classes in the subcontinent as their descendents were mainly from rural backgrounds. In East Africa they were the 'privileged minority' who formed a socially exclusive intermediate stratum between the African and the British elite and crucially they perceived themselves as an extension of the empire, rather then in opposition to it. They also tended to cluster residentially and social mixing with black Africans was minimal. They had prospered under colonial rule and secured jobs as teachers, managers, traders, and other professional and skilled positions, although there were variations of wealth and employment within East African Asians (Mattausch 2001).

In contrast to unskilled Pakistanis and Bangladeshis who came to Britain in the 1950s and 1960s, East African Asians brought with them a myriad of transferable skills; business acumen, language capabilities, expertise in urban and bureaucratic institutions and familiarity with English lifestyle. In addition, their migration was due to growing Africanisation programmes whereby governments sought to eradicate the economic dominance of South Asians that had developed under British rule. Consequently, East African Asians were more likely to come to Britain as forced migrants and complete family units, often encompassing three generations including elderly dependents, rather than male economic migrants. As a result they were less inclined to see eventual return as their main goal and instead made long term commitments in Britain by purchasing property and investing in businesses. East African Asians who had not transferred their savings to Britain tended to move to Leicester, rather than London, whilst those from Uganda were given an expulsion order in 1972 with only 90 days notice and typically lost their life savings (Banks 1994, 242). Their first priority was to rebuild their lives in Britain and purchase a house in contrast to direct South Asian migrants who were committed to remitting their earnings and making investments 'back home' (Ballard 2003).

Overall, the respondents were very keen to distinguish themselves from other South Asian groups in the interviews and the comments of Karim, who had migrated from Kenya, were typical:

Sound Archive (BLNSA), Millennium Memory Bank collection (MMB) and East Midlands Oral History Archive (EMOHA). For more details on the methodology see Herbert 2007 and on the project see Herbert 2008.

When I came here, I came straight to Leicester and there were a few Asians from East Africa in Leicester, but they were mainly from India and Pakistan you know, they were not with us. Our thinking, our education, our ideas were quite different from them and mainly those from Pakistan and India they used to work in factories, where as we were looking for good jobs. So there was a barrier there.[2]

Masculinity and Work

Whilst it is important to acknowledge that masculine identities are fragmented, multifaceted and negotiated and there are conflicting ways to be a man (Osella and Osella 2000), as Connell (1995; 2005) has argued one of these ways is always dominant. A primary manifestation of hegemonic masculinity, that is the 'most honoured way of being a man' that renders other forms of masculinities inferior (Connell 1995), is to be the main provider and breadwinner of the family. Men are expected to attain wealth and financial resources and to exert power and authority within the spheres of the workplace and the family. However, the men's experiences of employment in Britain compromised these masculine ideals and posed a threat to their status and self-esteem. Firstly, East African men emphasised their loss of occupational status as they attempted to rebuild their lives in the 1970s and 1980s. Prior to their migration the men envisaged Britain as a place where their professional standing would be enhanced, as Kapasi who was forced to flee Uganda in 1972 claimed, 'I thought everybody lived in palaces in England. I never thought (laughing) that there are houses here without inside bathroom and toilets (laughing) I never imagined that, but you see that's how it was. I thought I was going to land in a place of milk and honey'.[3] Despite these expectations the men typically found manual work in the factories and foundries as they soon realised that their previous experience, training and qualifications held limited value in their new country of settlement. Kapasi recalled, 'we came here, we took menial jobs because we didn't have anywhere to go, we didn't know what to do', 'we realised that we're not getting the right jobs and we're struggling there'.[4] The men's search for white collar jobs proved fruitless and they were compelled to take unskilled jobs that was characterised by low pay, job insecurity, unsociable hours and health risks.

Munisa's family migrated from Tanzania in 1964 and she recalled the vivid image of her father returning home from his new job with dirty 'black' hands and the distress this caused her mother. The memory clearly expressed the transition her father and the family grappled with as he was suddenly demoted from self-employed, managerial status to the stigma of taking an unskilled, physically demanding job in Britain.

My dad, poor dad he'd never worked in his life because he, you know he just ran a business you know at his desk. He had a chauffer who used to drive him to his shop and to his business and it was just virtually run by dad what he used to actually do is all the

---

2   Karim, 13 June 2002.
3   BL, NSA, C900/09135B J. Kapasi.
4   BL, NSA, C900/09135B J. Kapasi.

finance and the paperwork and now he suddenly had to end up working in a factory … in a mill where they used to grind materials … And he used to come home and the smell of chemicals and his hands used to be so black and his nails used to be so black and my mum just used to cry her eyes out and I remember "What a state are you in!"[5]

This experience of deskilling also affected her father's ability to fulfil the role of provider for the family. Munisa remembered sharing a one bedroomed house with her family of eight people and her two uncle's families, consisting of thirteen other people. She claimed 'we were all very, very depressed to come back to a sort of, to come back to a very small house'.[6] She also recalled the lack of adequate clothing, 'then it started to get cold and we didn't have enough clothes to wear and you know, not enough warm clothes and my mum used to go to jumble sales to get the uniform for us you know I can remember you know, I can remember wearing green tights with runs in there'.[7] Clothes have been identified by scholars as an important metaphor in stories of migration that have been used to articulate feelings and emotions that were difficult to communicate (Ryan 2002). The reference to clothes in Munisa's narrative clearly highlights the poverty and hardship her family endured and the difficulties adjusting to this, but the lack of clothes and the ruined tights also conveys her feelings of embarrassment associated with this.

As chapters by Keeler and Ahmad in this collection clearly show, this experience of deskilling and downward mobility was not unique to East African Asian men and applied to other South Asians such as men from Pakistan (see Charlsey 2005) and Bengal (see Gardner 2000). However, the former class status of East Africa Asian men had a paramount bearing on their experiences in Britain. The men typically discussed at great length their previous entrepreneurial success in East Africa. For instance, Ganatra claimed that when he migrated from India to Uganda he 'started in poverty', but progressed from the status of a clerk to managing three factories.[8] He emphasised the new company car he received each year and reflected 'I was working with that firm happily, nicely, we had very big respect'. His job clearly conferred recognition and self worth. Similarly, Mashru stressed his rise from lowly beginnings as he left school in Uganda to establishing his award winning business as a freelance photographer and photojournalist. His clients included a national newspaper in Uganda and the government. He claimed, 'we were quite well to do people and my business was growing more and stronger each year'.[9] These stories of their former success communicated the distinct message that the loss of the culmination of their achievements and hard earned professional status when they came to Britain was a powerful assault on their sense of self as successful men.

The men not only stressed their sharp decline in status within the workplace, but the consequent loss of their class position as they recalled the high standard of living they enjoyed in East Africa and particularly the servants they relied on. Mashru claimed that he had employed five household workers in Uganda and lamented

---

5   Munisa, 3 April 2004.
6   Munisa, 3 April 2004.
7   Munisa, 3 April 2004.
8   EMOHA, LOHAC, 836 LO/200/151 G. Ganatra.
9   EMOHA, LOHAC, 919 LO/274/225 M. Mashru.

'That's one of the luxuries which we miss in this country ... everything used to come to us on a plate'.[10] Considering the men's previous life in East Africa, their class transition was clearly deeply felt. As Karim explained,

[In Kenya] you don't have to worry because what you do mainly cooking there is someone there washing up, cooking, serving up, cleaning whole house mopping, brushing everything, cleaning windows, so as such the life was relaxed because there was helping hand there and why the life was good and relaxed because people must be earning good money in order to pay servants. So in that terms it was good, very relaxed. Over here yeah you got to cook yourself, DIY, everything, cooking at home, washing up, cleaning house, looking after children and at the same time you struggle for money ... they used to work in the industry, light industry, heavy industry, shoe industry whatever, all mechanical, people never did that before but they had to over here, they found it very hard.[11]

This class demotion was reinforced by racism which, as also discussed by Keeler and Ahmad in this volume, was experienced as a threat to regaining former occupational prestige. The men typically described the barrage of constraints they endured as they attempted to progress. Kapasi completed a degree in accountancy in Britain and first worked as an accountant in a knitting manufacturing firm. However, after seven years he claimed, 'I realised this is the glass ceiling'.[12] He left the post and sought work elsewhere, and obtained a job in a book-binding company, but stated 'again I soon reached the glass ceiling'.[13] Kapasi relayed his increasing awareness during the 1970s and 1980s of racist practices and as he attempted to overcome these difficulties and establish his own company, new patterns of exclusion surfaced. For instance, the bank refused to lend him money because in his words, they 'never trusted our people they always felt that if you lend money to these Asians they may one day run away from the country.' Saddled with this, British white businesses would not trade with his company, and as Kapasi stressed 'there were constraints everywhere.'[14] This experience was shared by other men. Mashru recalled his life story as punctured by similar predicaments, including barriers to promotion and the absence of financial aid from the bank when he attempted to start his own business. Their narratives created the impression that racism was experienced as all pervasive and ubiquitous within the workplace and wider society and this provoked strong feelings of injustice and frustration. As Mashru commented 'that's the vicious world we live in and we can't change this vicious world', reinforced later with the comment 'this is one of the vicious worlds we find and we are to accept it'.[15]

The importance of their former class status in shaping experiences is also illustrated by the findings from Ahmad (in this volume), which show how the Pakistani men working in East London in the 1970s highlighted the benefits of working at Ford and preferred to emphasize the rewards of their work, such as stable employment, rather

---

10 EMOHA, LOHAC, 919 LO/274/225 M. Mashru.
11 Karim, 13 June 2002.
12 BL, NSA, C900/09135B J. Kapasi.
13 BL, NSA, C900/09135B J. Kapasi.
14 BL, NSA, C900/09135B J. Kapasi.
15 EMOHA, LOHAC, 919 LO/274/225 M. Mashru.

than the struggles. Arguably, as economic migrants they had achieved success, whilst the East African Asians, coming from a more privileged and often entrepreneurial background, felt they had lost their accomplishments. Moreover, the racial hierarchy that had developed in East Africa with Europeans at the top, Africans at the bottom and South Asians in between, as the 'buffer community' also influenced their sense of demotion and feelings of resentment. That is, in Africa they shared the white British distrust of Africans yet following migration to Britain, they were both cast as 'coloured' migrants. Similarly, whilst black Africans had once worked for South Asians as servants and employees in their factories, in 1970s Britain they shared the same class position as migrant workers.

Clearly, the men's experiences of racism within employment and their declassed location diminished the status and recognition they had achieved and were accustomed to in East Africa and undermined their ability to perform the masculine roles of attaining material success and providing for their family. However, if the overall format and shape of the men's narratives is examined, rather than specific themes, it can be seen that by foregrounding certain facets of their life story; the difficulties they encountered finding a job, securing promotion or establishing their own business, the respondents were essentially presenting themselves as the heroic men who struggled and survived despite the harsh working conditions and restraints (see also Johnston and McIvor 2007). Whilst the women's interviews revealed their contribution and their children's role in helping to establish family businesses, this aspect was absent from the men's stories, who instead emphasised their individual responsibility and determinacy in overcoming problems. Mashru for instance, decided to set up a photography business in Leicester in 1974 and without financial aid from the bank, circumvented the high rates and rents in the city centre by establishing the business in the Belgrave area, to the north of the city. He claimed, 'I had the guts and I had the faith and I had the confidence that I might break it ... it was the determination which kept me going.'[16] Mashru described a process of gradually accumulating funds and expanding through the profits and he reflected, 'I had to be a carpenter on that there to build up the partitions. I'd never done it in my life but you know when you got determination nobody stops you.'[17] This emphasis on their agency, pioneering spirit, autonomy and personal resolve to succeed was a typical male narrative genre (Gardner 2002) and can be seen as a way of coping with and responding to the challenges to their masculinity (Guerrier and Adib 2004).

Masculinity and the Household

Did the men experience a similar loss of power and authority within the household? Ideals of South Asian masculinity were closely related to ideals of the household. Within the South Asian household, family members were guided by family duties and expectations of reciprocity and the principle of hierarchy was central (Khanum 2001). Individuals were situated within strict hierarchical relationships which were

16 EMOHA, LOHAC, 919 LO/274/225 M. Mashru.
17 EMOHA, LOHAC, 919 LO/274/225 M. Mashru.

expressed through rituals and codes of behaviour and demanded covert displays of subordination and deference to superiors. Within this system, a son was expected to show respect to his parents and provide for them in old age and wives were expected to be submissive to men, to alleviate family tensions and ensure the harmonious working of the family. Conformity to these ideal norms of behaviour was enforced through discourses of shame (sharam) and honour (izzat), which were vital mechanisms of social organisation. Yet the responsibility for family honour was not shared equally but confined to women and their conduct could either jeopardise or enhance family status. As a result, women's behaviour was effectively constrained. Moreover, men were not only expected to provide for his family, but also his honour ultimately rested on his ability to control women within the family. This can be seen as another aspect of hegemonic masculinity which does not necessarily match the reality of the men's lives, but provides models of relations with women and expresses the men's ideals and desires.

The male elders typically reinforced these ideal values in their narratives of household life. They invariably stated that they were the head of the family and were keen to stress their prestigious role within the family. Ganatra from Uganda emphasised his ability to implement decisions and traditions and boasted that he had arranged thirteen marriages and 'not a single person has got a problem, everybody is happy'.[18] The family was clearly a source of male pride and honour and offered him social status. These elders also consistently advocated the principles and functions of the family and emphasised elements which reinforced their dominance. For instance, throughout Ganatra's interview the core values of the extended family, arranged marriage and hierarchy within the family were expounded; hence for Ganatra the ideal situation was to 'be ruled by your family' as this avoids the problems which afflict the west, namely divorce.[19] Moreover, he presented his life story as a justification and proof that his beliefs were impeccable. This was echoed in other interviews which referred to the 'right' way of '*jointly* working for the family' and following 'set guidelines regarding talking to the people, regarding honouring the elderly people.'[20]

The emphasis on these principles suggests that the men demanded strict adherence to the ideal South Asian household and the prescribed gender roles this entailed. According to Gardner (2002) this type of narrative, in which the men presented themselves in essentialist terms, as the guardians of tradition, can be seen as a response to the ruptures of migration and an attempt to create a coherent identity. Yet scholars have also shown how minority ethnic men often assert a masculine identity in response to the powerlessness they feel in the wider society, invariably caused by racism (Archer 2001). Arguably the East African Asian men can be seen as attempting to reclaim and reconcile a masculine identity which they felt was threatened and undermined within the workplace. The household represented a sphere where they could restore a powerful dominant position.

---

18 EMOHA, LOHAC, 836, LO/200/151 G. Ganatra.
19 EMOHA, LOHAC, 836, LO/200/151 G. Ganatra.
20 BL, NSA, C900/12596 B. Vora. BL, NSA, C900/00066 T.V. Morjaria.

There was also ample evidence from the women's narratives, that on arrival to Leicester the men attempted to reassert control and effectively constrain their lives. Many women relayed examples of how they contended with their parents' gendered expectations which attempted to define appropriate behaviour and monitor their conduct. Examples included that they were prevented from attending sixth form college, due to 'fears of mixing with boys', and Munisa described a common experience in the interviews, whereby the women felt under immense pressure to marry. She recalled:

> My mum and dad called me in the front room and they said that "You are now getting old, you are nearly 17 and we're going to marry you off, and here is, you know, we would like you to marry him" and he showed me the photograph and do you know what? I just looked at the photograph and threw it on the floor. And then my dad said, "You do as you're told, you are my ..." in those days we sort of said "you are my izzat", a girl, a daughter is supposed to be an izzat, that means you can't, and you know you are my proud, pride.

> I know, yes.

> Yes. You know the word izzat? You are my pride you cannot do anything wrong because I have to live in the community, I have to face everybody. So just think how much pressure I had to live with.[21]

The reference to izzat (honour) demonstrates the pressures she felt, specifically as a 'girl' and as a 'daughter' because her actions were not only accountable to her family but to the wider 'community.' Versions of this experience were retold by many of the women who also typically described at great length the difficulties involved in meeting their proposed husband at the airport, their initial reactions and feelings towards him, their wedding day and their consequent new role as a daughter-in-law. The women also emphasised that these pressures had intensified following their migration and they contrasted their previous life in East Africa with the particular increasing demands they encountered in Britain in the 1970s. As Bhambra explained:

> [In Kenya] We knew that we could have boyfriends or the boys could have girlfriends we used to hang around the soda parlours we used to have soda parlours in Kenya and here it was different. We could not do that it was strange because I thought living in England westernised people would have westernised views but it was totally the opposite.[22]

She added later 'The life we had in Kenya was totally different from the life we had in England. In Kenya we could just go anywhere without asking anybody but in England we were sort of frowned upon, how we dressed up, where we went'.[23]

The women's suggestions that they possessed more freedom in Africa and more constraints in Leicester can be seen as a result of an attempt by the men to reassert their authority and power over the women due to their marginalisation within the

---

21 Munisa, 3 April 2004.
22 BL, NSA, C900/09149 M. Bhambra.
23 BL, NSA, C900/09149 M. Bhambra.

wider society. Yet it was also a way of reasserting their East African Asian identity which distinguished them from the white British and other South Asians. Bhachu's (1985) study of East African Asian Sikhs revealed that despite their westernised ways, East African Asians also become more culturally conservative in Britain and adhered more closely to traditions than direct migrants. This was manifested through rituals relating to the arrangement of marriages, gift exchanges and through the development of exclusive caste identities, through marriage, which also asserted their difference from other South Asians and enhanced their status within South Asian communities.

Nevertheless, the women's life stories reveal that these incidents, whereby their behaviour was monitored, were transient and were associated with the stage in their life cycle as daughters or daughter-in-laws. Moreover, whilst the narratives from the men and women suggest that many men attempted to reassert and intensify control over women during the initial years of settlement, they also reveal that over time the men had actually lost some of their authority within the household. In particular, the men articulated a distinct loss of power over the younger generation and this was discussed as a present day concern rather than a difficulty experienced in the 1970s or 1980s. Morjaria who moved from India to Uganda in 1938 and arrived in Britain in 1972, grappled with his anxieties:

> At times I'm really worried about our younger generation because they try to copy what the western people are doing. In the olden times when you are in East Africa the head of the family will work and the mother and the others the eldest will have the children and educate them, what is discipline what is the religion about which we have no time to do it.[24]

Morjaria's concerns were based on the premise that the dichotomy between the male public and female private sphere which assigned men to the role of providers and women as carers was undermined following migration. In particular, it broke with the precedent that women were the intergenerational transmitters of 'home' culture and as a result, left children exposed and vulnerable to the perceived moral vacuum in the west. Morjaria claimed the wider community sympathised with his position and served to substantiate his complaints: 'I've been talking to the community, to the people who feel I've done so much for my children but they're not doing anything for me.'[25] Accordingly, his children did not fulfil their kinship obligations which he had invested in. His views were further corroborated by his use of vocabulary which presented his opinions as part of an accumulated wisdom, entrenched within the group's history and culture. He proclaimed, 'There was a saying back in East Africa that when we came, we left East Africa, we lost our money and here after coming to this country, we will lose our generation, we will lose control over them, we will lose the family feeling which we had back in East Africa and India.'[26] The use of the term 'family feeling' denotes that some inherent essence of the family had been eradicated.

---

24 BL, NSA, C900/00066 T.V. Morjaria.
25 BL, NSA, C900/00066 T.V. Morjaria.
26 BL, NSA, C900/00066 T.V. Morjaria.

This notion of loss was conspicuous and was a recurrent feature of other narratives. Patel was born in India, lived in Nairobi and Mombassa for twenty two years and came to Britain aged forty with his wife and four children. He stated:

> The tradition that we find difficult to maintain here is because of the education firstly for our children, when they're educated in this country, they got a job in this country, so everyone has to work and when they go for work, the environment of the working places is different so the first thing, becomes clothing, what to wear and there the tradition starts dying away. They used to have saris for example, strictly, my wife still puts on saris 365 days she never tried anything else, but for my daughter and my daughter-in-laws, they're working in the offices, they put on skirts or frocks and that's how we accept that is going to change, traditionally we know it's not very comfortable, we're not used to that dressing but we have to accept that and we feel like we are loosing that you see.[27]

This reveals how men defined the parameters of 'appropriate behaviour', whilst the duty clearly lay with the women to be the paragons of virtue. More specifically, Patel's comments relate to women's ascribed role as symbolizing their nation or community. As Yuval-Davis (1997, 46) has contended the importance of this role was amplified in multicultural societies such as Britain, as women were expected to preserve minority identities. Thus women's 'traditional' clothes were a visible marker of the group's identity and difference. However this was threatened by women's entrance into paid employment as the public sphere represented a different cultural model to that of the home. Patel was unable to control these changes or impose his will; he could not monitor women at work and thus female employment had effectively curbed his leverage over other household members. Others also blamed employment as the main problem. According to Ganatra, 'When we were in Uganda, Kenya, East Africa or India, all men was an umbrella, all millions of rupees is there in one name', in contrast to 'here everybody has got their income, everybody has got a bank account', consequently, 'parents are not to interfere or help the child. They want to help but they can't. I have lot of problems here'.[28]

The loss of authority experienced by fathers as their children took paid employment was echoed in the interviews with the second generation. Suajani was born in Uganda and had migrated to India to study for her degree. Her father wrote to her asking her to join them in Leicester as they felt the strict immigration laws may prevent her from moving to Britain in the future. She recalled the difficulties experienced by her father: '[So] far in his life he was the sole head of the family but when children started earning money somehow the authority shifted and when children spoke English and were able to communicate to outsiders when he wasn't, his authority sort of lessened and I think he was finding it very very difficult'.[29] Here, the father's lack of knowledge of the English language was another factor which

---

27 EMOHA, CHC, 00524, CH/037/0154 M. Patel.

28 EMOHA, LOHAC, 836, LO/200/151 G. Ganatra.

29 BL, NSA, C900/00011 R. Saujani.

tipped the balance of power relations within the house and rendered him dependent on other family members.[30]

A further dimension that altered the power relations between men and women in the household was when the wives worked outside the home, although this was rarely discussed by the men. The relatively high number of South Asian women employed in work outside the home in Leicester, compared to other cities has been noted by other scholars and many women took whatever jobs were available to help make ends meet and raise the necessary funds to purchase a house (Byrne 1998, 718). Most women interviewed commenced paid work once their children had passed the stage of infancy and many commented that their wages effectively reduced their dependence on their husbands and enabled them to override male authority. As Kotecha remarked, 'in Africa for the lady they don't go to work so what husband you got to stay under husband.'[31] Others explained that when they started working, they were able to influence the men's decision. Naeema explained the change in the relationship with her husband, who had migrated from Malawi.

> He's a little bit more old fashioned than I am, there's some things that he's not been comfortable with. When my son was becoming, well he's always been extrovert at 16 he said to his dad "I'm going to go to a night club" and he said "oh you mustn't" and I said "whether we say yes or whether we say no he's still gonna do it. And I think it's best that we know where he's going and that he tells us where he's going and that he's honest with us". I said "let him go because even if he's gonna say no they'll still do it behind our backs", then my husband sat and listened. In fact recently before that when I started working I found that my husband was a lot more accepting and he started listening to me more I think that made a difference in our relationship and he's actually turned out to be more broadminded than I thought because he does all the housework (laughs).[32]

Others also claimed that the division of labour within the household was altered and men were accorded greater responsibility for household tasks. This was confirmed by Karim who noted, 'husband and wife, they have to share the work in the house and there are all sorts of opportunities for wife or woman. Okay, my husband's doing this, I'm going to do these things. In the evening he is going to look after my child so I can work part time in the evening.'[33] This is not to suggest that conjugal roles within the household were automatically transformed as the majority of the women still retained primary responsibility for the housework and childcare, however the women's stories reveal that as their relative authority gradually increased within the household, the men's position of authority correspondingly weakened.

---

30 For the decline in the power of fathers due to the lack of their language skills see also Husain and O'Brien 2000.

31 BL, NSA, C900/09083 B. Kotecha.

32 Naeema, 18 March 2004.

33 Karim, 13 June 2002.

Conclusion

The workplace and the household were vital to the construction of masculinities and were key sources of pride, honour and status. Following migration, changes within the household and workplace no longer enabled men to feel powerful and masterful within these domains and instead undermined these sources of male self-esteem. Research on other migrant groups has shown how masculinities were undermined by men taking on what is deemed to be feminised work such as cleaning (McIlwaine et al. 2006) or cooking (Keeler in this volume), however for the East African Asian men, the threat to their masculinity in the workplace was inextricably linked to wider social processes of racism and a decline in their class position and standard of living. The loss of power was particularly felt by those who had worked as entrepreneurs in East Africa and were accustomed to a position of authority and autonomy, in contrast to Britain where they were compelled to work alongside African Caribbeans in low status employment, where lack of respect was augmented by experiences of racism. Unlike direct South Asian migrants, East African Asians had more of a stake in the city and could not use the prospect of a return home to compensate for their experiences in the labour market.

Coupled with this, despite their attempts to reassert a dominant position within the household, in the long term, they also suffered a loss of their relative authority and this shows how masculinities need to be situated not only in relation to women, but in relation to their children. From this perspective, the men were not reducible to the role of tyrannical aggressors but rather the move to Britain had created intractable problems that threatened their masculine identity and were beyond their control. The men could not halt racism hence, Mashru's comments that we 'can't change this vicious world'.[34] Neither could they prevent the effects of women taking paid employment outside the home; consequently they emphasised the sense of loss they felt. These experiences help to explain the men's idealistic views of 'home' despite also their understanding any return was highly unlikely, since their wives and children were settled in Britain.

This is illustrated by the comments of Kapasi and his wife. Kapasi stressed the affinity he felt with Uganda and claimed 'personally if I had a choice I would prefer to live in Uganda.' He reflected 'There I have far better life because they've got much less stress, many less deadlines to meet and they really live a very carefree life, they've got nothing to worry about and there is a common saying in Swahili, *Kesho Mungu* which means tomorrow god is there'.[35] By contrast his wife missed her family in Kenya, but expressed a less idealistic view of her country of origin. When asked if Kenya was seen as her homeland she replied, 'Yes and no. When I go there I became very emotional because my family is there, my mother lives there still, my father lives there as well. I find it very emotional. But at the same time I feel now England is my hometown because I've lived here longer than I have lived in Kenya as well.'[36] Arguably, Kapasi's recollections of Uganda can be seen as a form

---

34 EMOHA, LOHAC, 919 LO/274/225 M. Mashru.

35 BL, NSA, C900/09135B J. Kapasi.

36 C900/09135A Y. Kapasi.

of nostalgia and a yearning for his carefree life, as a child and a student, when he had less responsibilities. Memories of the 'good old days' may also serve as a coping strategy to overcome the dislocation caused by migration, yet ultimately Kapasi's reflections on Uganda could not be disentangled from his experiences in Britain.[37]

Finally, a response to the men's experiences in the household and workplace can also be gleaned from their narratives. That is, the act of retelling their stories offered the men the central stage to reconstruct and reassert a masculinity identity. Despite their actual experiences, as narrators they were the 'heroic male' who survived despite the obstacles, the autonomous and pioneering businessman, or the unwavering head of the family and guardian of traditions. Taking a relational view of gender and analysing the men's narratives in the context of their life story enables us to go beyond a simplistic notion of the men as patriarchs, and helps to understand the difficulties and complexities that they experienced as they adapted to life in Britain.

References

Archer, L. (2001), 'Muslim Brothers, Black Lads, Traditional Asians: British Muslim Young Men's Constructions of Race, Religion and Masculinity', *Feminism Psychology* 11:1, 79-105.

Banks, M. (1994), 'Jain Ways of Being', in Ballard, R. (ed.), *Desh Pardesh: South Asian Experience in Britain* (London: University of British Columbia Press), 231-50.

Bhachu, P. (1985), *Twice Migrants: East African Sikh Settlers in Britain* (London: Tavistock).

Bhopal, K. (1997), *Gender 'Race' and Patriarchy: A Study of South Asian Women* (Aldershot: Ashgate).

Brah, A. (1996), *Cartographies of Diaspora* (London: Routledge).

Byrne, D. (1998), 'Class and Ethnicity in Complex Cities – The Cases of Leicester and Bradford', *Environment and Planning A* 30, 703-20.

Charsley, K. (2004), 'Unhappy Husbands: Masculinity and Migration in Transnational Pakistani Marriages', *Journal of Royal Anthropological Institute* 11:1, 85-105.

Chopra, R., Osella, F. and Osella, C. (eds) (2004), *South Asian Masculinities: Contexts of Change, Sites of Continuity* (New Delhi: Women Unlimited).

Cohen, D. (2006), 'From Peasant to Worker: Migration, Masculinity and the Making of Mexican Workers in the US', *International Labour and Working-Class History* 26, 89-103.

Connell, R.W. (1995), *Masculinities* (Cambridge: Polity Press).

Connell, R.W. and Messerschmidt, J. W. (2005), 'Hegemonic Masculinity: Rethinking the Concept', *Gender and Society* 19:6, 829-59.

Gardner, K. (2000), *Age, Narrative and Migration. The Life Course and Life Histories of Bengali Elders in London* (Oxford: Berg).

Gilmore, D. (1990), *Manhood in the Making: Cultural Conceptions of Masculinity* (London: Yale University Press).

---

37 For further discussion see Herbert 2006. For the role of nostalgia see Ryan 2006.

Guerrier, Y. and Adib, A. (2004), 'Gendered Identities in the Work of Overseas Tour Reps', *Gender, Work and Organization* 11:3, 334-50.

Gutmann, M. (1997), 'The Ethnographic (G)ambit: Women and the Negotiation of Masculinity in Mexico City', *American Ethnologist* 24:4, 833-55.

Herbert, J. (2006), 'Migration, Memory and Metaphor: Life Stories of South Asians in Leicester', in Burrell, K. and Panayi, P. (eds), *Histories and Memories: Migrants and their Histories in Britain* (London: I.B. Tauris), 133-48.

—— (2007), 'Negotiating Boundaries and the Cross-cultural Oral History Interview', in Rodger, R. and Herbert, J. (eds), *Testimonies of the City: Identity, Community and Change in a Contemporary Urban World* (Aldershot: Ashgate).

—— (2008), *Negotiating Boundaries in the City: Migration, Ethnicity and Gender in Britain* (Aldershot: Ashgate).

Hondagneu-Sotelo, P. (1999), 'Introduction; Gender and Contemporary US Immigration', *American Behavioural Scientist* 42:4, 565-576.

Husain, F. and O'Brien, M. (2000), 'Muslim Communities in Europe: Reconstruction and Transformation', *Current Sociology* 3, 1-13.

Johnston, R. and McIvor, A. (2007), 'Narratives from the Urban Workplace: Oral Testimonies and the Reconstruction of Men's Work in the Heavy Industries in Glasgow', in Rodger, R. and Herbert, J. (eds), *Testimonies of the City: Identity, Community and Change in a Contemporary Urban World* (Aldershot: Ashgate).

Khanum, S.M. (2001), 'The Household Patterns of a "Bangladeshi Village" in England', *Journal of Ethnic and Migration Studies* 27:3, 489-504.

MacAn Ghaill, M. (1994), *The Making of Men: Masculinities, Sexualities and Schooling* (Buckingham: Open University Press).

Mahler, S.J. and Pessar, P.R. (2006), Gender Matters: Ethnographers Bring Gender from the Periphery Toward the Core of Migration Studies, *International Migration Review* 40:1, 27-63.

Mattausch, J. (2001), 'After "Ethnicity": Migration, Identity and Political Economy', *Immigrants and Minorities* 20:3, 59-75.

McIlwaine, C.J., Datta, K., Evans, Y., Herbert, J., May J. and Wills, J. (2006), *Gender and Ethnic Identities among Low Paid Migrant Workers in London* (London: Department of Geography, Queen Mary, University of London).

Morokvasic, M. (1984), 'Birds of Passage are Also Women', *International Migration Review* 18:4, 886-907.

Osella, F. and Osella, C. (2000), 'Migration, Money and Masculinity in Kerala', *Journal of the Royal Anthropological Institute* 6:1, 117-33.

Pedraza, P. (1991), 'Women and Migration: The Social Consequences of Gender', *Annual Review of Sociology* 17, 303-25.

Phillips, D. (1981), 'The Social and Spatial Segregation of Asians in Leicester', in Jackson, P. and Smith, S. (eds), *Social Interaction and Ethnic Segregation* (London: Academic Press), 101-21.

Phizacklea, A. (1999), 'Gender and Transnational Labour Migration', in Barot, R., Bradley, H. and Fenton, S. (eds), *Ethnicity, Gender and Social Change* (London: Macmillan Press).

Ryan, L. (2002), '"I'm Going to England": Women's Narratives of Leaving Ireland in the 1930's', *Oral History* 30:1, 42-53.

—— (2003), 'Moving Spaces and Changing Places: Irish Women's Memories of Emigration to Britain in the 1930s', *Journal of Ethnic and Migration Studies* 29:1, 67-82.

—— (2006), 'Passing Time: Irish Women Remembering and Re-telling Stories of Migration to Britain', in Burrell, K. and Panayi, P. (eds), *Histories and Memories: Migrants and their Histories in Britain* (London: I.B. Tauris), 191-209.

Singh, G. (2003), 'Multiculturalism in Contemporary Britain: Reflections on the "Leicester Model"', *International Journal on Multicultural Societies* 5:1, 40-54.

Willis, K. and Yeoh, B. (eds) (2000), *Gender and Migration* (London: Edward Elgar).

Yuval-Davis, N. (1997), *Gender and Nation* (London: Sage), 29-44.

Index